12 50

Guns of the Frontier
The Story of How Law Came to the West

BOOKS BY WILLIAM MacLEOD RAINE

BORDER BREED

STEVE YEAGER

THE YUKON TRAIL

THE SHERIFF'S SON

A MAN FOUR-SQUARE

OH, YOU TEX!

THE BIG-TOWN ROUND-UP

GUNSIGHT PASS

TANGLED TRAILS

MAN-SIZE

THE FIGHTING EDGE

IRONHEART

BEYOND THE RIO GRANDE

THE BLACK TOLTS

UNDER NORTHERN STARS

THE BROAD ARROW

ROARING RIVER

THE TRAIL OF DANGER

SQUARE-SHOOTER

RUN OF THE BRUSH

TO RIDE THE RIVER WITH

BUCKY FOLLOWS A COLD TRAIL

KING OF THE BUSH

ON THE DODGE

SONS OF THE SADDLE

MORAN BEATS BACK

THE RIVER BEND FEUD

RIDERS OF BUCK RIVER

GUNS OF THE FRONTIER

THE HOLE-IN-THE-WALL GANG

Standing: Will Carver, Harvey Logan alias Kid Curry
Seated: Harry Longabaugh, Ben Kilpatrick, George Parker alias Butch Cassidy

Guns

OF THE

Frontier

THE STORY OF HOW LAW CAME TO THE WEST

BY WILLIAM MacLEOD RAINE

ILLUSTRATED

BOSTON

HOUGHTON MIFFLIN COMPANY

The Riverside Press Cambridge

1940

The Riverside Press

CAMBRIDGE · MASSACHUSETTS

PRINTED IN THE U.S.A.

'I drink alone in silence to the builders of the West...
Long life to the hearts still beating, and peace to the
hearts at rest.'

ROLLIN M. DAGGETT

Foreword

THE West was won by the pioneer. He blazed trails, gutted mountains, ran furrows, and planted corn on the prairies. His cattle roamed where the buffalo and the Indian had been. Small clearings in great forests marked his determination to wrest a living from the soil. Towns grew up to supply the needs of the settlers. The men who made the West were the farmers, the cattlemen, the merchants, the miners, the railroad builders, the carpenters, the stage-drivers. Every man and woman who snatched from the desert a little patch they called home contributed his or her share.

But the pioneer had pushed far ahead of the law. He had to be strong to hold his own against the Apache and the Sioux, to drag a living from a rough and barren land. Other difficulties confronted him. Nine out of ten of those who moved into the unknown West were good citizens and hard workers. Of the remaining ten per cent a large number were riffraff, scoundrels, and criminals. Professional gamblers, thugs, and parasites on society flocked to the frontier towns and mining camps, drawn by the rich pickings to be had in settlements where spending was free and

order not yet entrenched. More than four thousand homicides were committed in California during the five years
which followed the discovery of gold. The Texas Rangers
had a crime book which contained the names of thousands
wanted by the law. Many of them had gone to Texas to
escape punishment. In the early days the cattle industry
was a constant temptation to the rustler. Every big outfit
had on its outskirts bands of thieves who were stealing
calves and blotting brands.

The frontier tried a man. Conditions on the plains were
hard. It was easier to idle in a town and let others do the
hot and wearing work. It was safer to live by one's wits —
to gamble, drink, steal, ally oneself with the worse element
— than to plow the desert with the risk often present of
Indian attack.

The settlers wanted law. They drew together and for-
mulated codes. Strong fighting men were chosen to see
that order was enforced. All along the changing borderland which reached from Mexico to Canada, a line as
shifting and as broken as that of the tide along a rugged
coast, there was for years a struggle between honesty
and crime, decency and shame, order and disorder.

The sheriff, the marshal, the ranger, were the agents who
fought the battle for their communities. Sometimes they
were killers themselves, chosen because of their expertness
with weapons in the hope of discouraging lesser gunmen.
'Wild Bill' Hickok, Ben Thompson, and King Fisher were
of this class. Sometimes they were good citizens, hard and
resolute, who took their lives in their hands to bring order
out of chaotic turbulence. Such men were John Poe of
the Panhandle, Tom Smith of Abilene, W. H. Middaugh

of Denver, and William Tilghman of Oklahoma. There were occasions when crime had so trodden down the law that private citizens by sheer force of character organized movements, sometimes extra-legal, to stamp out evil by means of people's courts or an aroused public opinion. Among these were Colonel Sanders of Montana, William T. Coleman of California, and Judge H. Clay Pleasants of Texas.

Many a good citizen and many an officer gave his life in trying to bring wrongdoers to justice, but it is heartening to know that in the long run what they stood for prevailed. The good man was stronger, more enduring, than the bad one. Captain Bill McDonald of the Texas Rangers put the case in one of his salty sayings: 'No man in the wrong can stand up against a fellow that's in the right and keeps a-coming.' The sheriffs, the marshals, and the rangers knew they were in the right and kept a-coming. In the end they rubbed out the bad man.

Often the 'bad man' was not all bad. He might be a cowpuncher gone wrong, one with his thinking twisted, looking for an easy way and a short cut to make money. The Daltons were enemies to society, but they kept faith with one another even to death. Ben Thompson could do generous and friendly actions. King Fisher was a good husband and father. The Taylors and the Suttons were for the most part honest cattlemen living in a torn and distracted land, dragged into dreadful deeds by passion and anger and a mistaken loyalty to their living and dead kin. I have known more than one oldtimer who once followed crooked trails and cut loose from them to follow straight and honorable ones.

But a peace officer had to deal with facts and not explanations. He had to wipe out the lawbreaker to protect his community. There is a tendency to build up a maudlin sympathy for murderers like Jesse James and Billy the Kid, to give a Robin Hood slant to their atrocious careers. They have been turned into near-heroes by books and movies. The plain truth is that they were cold-blooded killers who had to be exterminated for the benefit of society. It is a travesty on justice to hold them up as Western heroes and to forget the millions of gallant souls who lived and died bravely as good and useful citizens.

In these true stories I have tried to show the conditions that made it possible for the bad man to flourish for a time. They lived by the sword and most of them perished by it. The killer had his day, then came to a swift and violent end. There were exceptions, but so few as to emphasize the rule. If the law did not get them another bad man did. They were out of step with civilization.

W. M. R.

Contents

FOREWORD   vii

I. IN THE ARIZONA CHAPARRAL   I

II. THE SLEEPY LITTLE TOWN OF EL PASO   26

III. THE VIGILANTES   44

IV. GOLD IN THEM THAR HILLS   70

V. 'GLORY, GLORY TO WASHOE'   93

VI. FOR AND AGAINST THE LAW IN THE NORTH-WEST   112

VII. ABILENE, WILD AND WOOLLY   134

VIII. A PLAGUE O' BOTH YOUR HOUSES   154

IX. 'STICK 'EM UP'   173

X. NATE CHAMPION FINISHES HIS DIARY   196

XI. BEN THOMPSON, GUN-FIGHTER EXTRAORDINARY   219

XII. BAT MASTERSON, PHILOSOPHIC GUNMAN   236

XIII. TOM SMITH, SOLDIER OF FORTUNE   258

BIBLIOGRAPHY   271

INDEX   275

Illustrations

THE HOLE-IN-THE-WALL GANG *   *Frontispiece*

HEATING BRANDING IRONS AT THE ROUNDUP   10

WATERING A TRAIL HERD   10

A VIGILANTE NOTICE   48

WAGON TRAIN IN CAMP FORMATION ON HOLLADAY
(NOW MARKET) STREET IN DENVER   74

J. H. (DOC) HOLLIDAY IN THE EARLY EIGHTIES *   142

TOM SMITH, MARSHAL OF ABILENE, 1870   142

JOHN SELMAN, 1878 *   142

JOHN KING FISHER, DEPUTY SHERIFF, UVALDE
COUNTY, TEXAS *   142

BEN THOMPSON *   220

BAT MASTERSON *   242

  * From the Rose Collection of Old-Time Photographs

I

In the Arizona Chaparral

IN PIONEER days one had to view Arizona with the eyes of faith to escape discouragement. The Apache chiefs Mangas Colorados, Cochise, and Geronimo plundered wagon trains, ran off stock, captured stages, and murdered settlers. Their smoke signals on far hills sent terror to the hearts of travelers and ranchmen. The toll of life taken by the Indians mounted into the thousands.

Moreover, the desert was grim, stark, and inhospitable. Everything within reach of its dry winds fought for existence. Vegetation was barbed and stinging, animal life savage and poisonous. Those who ventured there saw drought, starvation, fierce struggle, bleaching bones, intolerable heat. To survive they had to take on the attributes of the country — the toughness of the sahuaro and the lean vitality of the coyote. That some of the pioneers, the small minority of scalawags, picked up too the poison of the sidewinder and the pouncing lust to kill of the wolf, is not surprising. They had been driven from their homes on account of their worthlessness. In their new environment the evil in them might be expected to develop.

But if Arizona in those days had its Duffield, its Tewksburys, and its Clantons, it was the home also of Charles D. Poston, Judge Titus, John Slaughter, Don Estevan Ochoa, and Henry Garfias, strong and good men who helped to bring law and order to the desert settlements.

J. Ross Browne gives a description of Tucson in the early years: 'Scraggy bushes of mesquite, bunches of sage and greasewood ... a city of mud-boxes, dingy and dilapidated, cracked and baked into a composite of dust and filth ... littered about with broken corrals, sheds, bake-ovens, carcasses of dead animals, and broken pottery, sore-backed burros, coyote dogs and terra-cotta children ... barren of verdure, parched, and naked.' He adds that if the world were searched he does not think there could be found another set of villains so degraded as those forming the principal society of the town.

His judgment is less than fair, for there were good citizens in Tucson even then, as Captain John G. Bourke testifies in his book, *On the Border With Crook*. He found the little Mexican settlement the home of an unusual number of interesting men, individual and picturesque. Nor does the physical aspect of the town depress him, though he sees all that Browne did — the pigs staked out to wallow in mire, the unchained dogs running amuck, the burros browsing on tin cans. He notices too the fringe of emerald green in the 'bottom' of the cultivated land, the gently waving cottonwoods, the dark, waxy-green foliage of the pomegranates, and the crimson *rastras* of chile hanging like mediaeval banners along the house walls. And no doubt he saw too the porphyry mountain-peaks reaching up on every side of the town to the unmatched blue sky, the enchanted mesas blooming with color, the cañons of the Rincons and the Catalinas deepening at sunset into blue and purple lakes and the ridges edged with glittering flame. No man of imagination ever saw the Arizona Desert in its thousand changing aspects and forgot it.

Time in Tucson then was marked by notable events rather than by the calendar. 'The night afore Duffield drawed on Judge Titus' was a more easily remembered date-post than June 15 would be. There was no need of hurry or of specific accuracy. One sunny day followed another lazily. Editor Wasson of the *Citizen* tried to bring American efficiency into the sleepy Spanish village. Week after week his editorials hammered away about the dead burro on Main Street. Why did the authorities not remove it? The brown-faced Mexican alcalde shrugged his shoulders. 'What is the matter with the man?' he asked, perplexed at such impatience. 'Why is he in such a hurry? Only last week Ramon and I talked it over and decided it had better be taken away. But his team has been busy. One of these days he will get round to it. Of a certainty, yes.'

Though Tucson did not have street lights or sewers or sidewalks, life generally moved on very pleasantly in the little sunbaked Spanish town. It had its unwashed and its ruffians, but it had too its good citizens, both Mexican and American, some of them well educated and trained to courteous, friendly ways of life. The best of the thick-walled adobe houses held enclosed patios, with raised flowerbeds and ollas of spring water hanging from the roofs of shaded porches, the walks flagged and kept cool by fountains sprinkling on them.

At Levine's garden, at the foot of Congress Street, the people met for evening entertainment, as they did at *bailes* held at the Orndorff Hotel and elsewhere. A Mexican band played Sundays at the hotel. There were Japanese lanterns in the patio. Families promenaded up and down, coming in for dinner at the restaurant, where a specialty was made of wild game.

The orchestra at the *baile*, consisting very likely of a flute, Pan's pipes, a bull fiddle, and a bass drum, worked tirelessly all through the night. Officers and their wives came in from Fort Lowell to join the townspeople. They rode back to the fort under a desert sky flushed with the pink and mauve and violet lights of dawn. After the *baile* young men serenaded the pretty señoritas, singing to the windows above 'La Paloma' and other love songs.

All the men met in the gambling-houses, where Mexicans, Chinese, miners, merchant, muleskinners, and 'bummers' brushed shoulders round the wheel and at faro tables. They met too in the early days at the Shoo Fly Restaurant, run by Mrs. Wallen. It was domiciled in a long, low-ceiled adobe building, the floor of rammed earth, the walls washed in a yellow tint. The tables had lead casters with yellow glass bottles. The chairs were home-made, with rawhide bottoms. The waiters, in white suits with red sashes, carried fly-flappers which they wielded vigorously. But Mrs. Wallen gave her customers good food, including such luxuries as were obtainable. She served chicken, mutton, kid meat, jerked beef in stews, black frijoles, tomatoes, lettuce, and fine oranges from Mexico.

Also, there was always the famous Pete Kitchen bacon, made from pigs that very likely had known the sting of Apache arrows. (Pete had a standing order at the ranch for his employees to pull out all the arrows — if any — left during the night in his stock. Wags called his pigs Apache pincushions.)

Sentinel Mountain stands back of the town, and there a man was posted to keep watch for the Apaches. Usually the Indians were not bold enough to raid a town, but they might swoop down on the horses and the cattle in the outskirts. Travelers were sometimes cut off within a mile or two of Tucson's walls. Pete Kitchen's ranch near Nogales was raided and his son killed while at work in a field. A mail-carrier, trapped near the mission San Xavier, was filled with arrows. In 1871 the Prescott *Miner* published a list of over three hundred whites and Mexicans who had been murdered by Apaches in the preceding six years.

Pete Kitchen's ranch was a standing temptation to the Apaches. He had built his house on the top of a hill commanding a view of the valley below. A guard walked the flat roof of the adobe building constantly, and if there was any sign of a raid he fired his gun and brought the hands in the fields back to the forted house on the run. Many times the place was attacked, but Pete gave the painted braves as good as they sent. He killed so many of them that at last they gave his ranch a wide berth. Travelers all spent the night at his place, both because it was safe and because of its almost feudal hospitality. He had a thousand acres of good land on Potrero Creek, and on it he raised grains, vegetables, fruits, and melons. His special pride was his

herd of fine hogs. For hundreds of miles his hams and
bacon were famous.

Pete was a character. Like most men of the frontier, he
was an inveterate gambler. All the sporting houses of
Tucson knew him as one who played for high stakes. He
was a tough nut, and the man who got ahead of him had to
be good. On one occasion he followed three horse-thieves
across the border, shot two of them, and captured the
third. On the way back to the ranch Kitchen got sleepy
(so he afterward told the story) and took a nap at the foot
of a tree. Before doing so he tied a rope round the neck of
his prisoner, whose hands were bound behind him,
mounted him on a horse, and flung the rope over the limb
of the cottonwood under which the horse stood. The other
end of the rope he fastened to the trunk of the tree. 'And
do you know,' Pete always finished the story, 'that when I
woke up I found that damned horse had walked away and
left the rustler hanging there.' To emphasize the point,
Pete would always at this stage of the yarn nudge the lis-
tener in the ribs and burst into raucous laughter.

Toward the end of his life Pete sold his ranch for sixty
thousand dollars, went to Tucson, and gambled away the
money within three weeks.

When Arizona was organized as a territory, Milton B.
Duffield of California arrived as United States marshal.
Mr. Duffield stood six foot three, was broad of shoulder,
powerful, and quick on his feet. He was dark of complexion, had black hair, and very keen eyes. Every day Marshal Duffield drove a tenpenny nail into an adobe wall with
a bullet from a distance of twenty paces. Since he was dis-
putatious, in fact quarrelsome when he had a few under

his belt, it may be guessed that citizens walked warily when in his neighborhood. Only one man in Arizona at that time wore a high silk hat. This was not generally considered safe. But on top of the marshal's head the 'stovepipe' hat was no signal for merriment. For it was currently reported that he had eleven notches on his guns.

'Waco Bill' came to town and started on a tear. He announced that he would like to see Duffield, since it was his night to howl and the marshal was his meat. Milton B. arrived, all six feet three of him, lashed out with his fist, and sent the muleskinner spinning. Bill reached for a gun, but he was too late. A bullet ripped through the officer's coat-pocket and struck 'Waco Bill' in the groin. Duffield had not wasted time in drawing the weapon.

'I'm the gentleman you were seeking, sir, and I have just sent you my card,' the marshal mentioned, with a bow.

Captain Bourke tells that on one occasion, when friends were gathered around the wassail bowl, Duffield was induced to exhibit all the weapons he carried. He drew from his person eleven lethal instruments of war. From belt, holsters, pockets, boot legs, and other convenient places came bowie knives, derringers, daggers, and revolvers. Even this multiplicity of weapons failed in the end to save their owner. Mr. Duffield migrated to Tombstone and had a dispute with a young man named Holmes about an interest in a mine. Holmes was working the property when the ex-marshal went out there to run him off. Though covered by a double-barreled shotgun, Duffield would not stop at the order of the other. He continued steadily to advance and was filled with buckshot.

It is impossible to read the history of our Indian trou-

bles without realizing that the Apaches, the Sioux, and
the Cheyennes, as well as other tribes, were driven to warfare by unfair treatment on the part of whites and were
kept in the field much longer than was necessary by the
unwise negotiations of government representatives, both
military and civil. Mangas Colorados and Cochise were
originally friendly to Americans. Mangas is described by
Lieutenant Coutts as a stalwart man, six foot two in
height, with a fine, intelligent face. For years his name
spelled terror over New Mexico and Arizona. A great
leader to his people, he fought ferociously and without
mercy. No Indians were more cruel than the Apaches
under his direction. The record of the thousands slain by
him is a horrible one in the story of the winning of the
Southwest. Jack Swilling, one of the first settlers in the
Salt River Valley, persuaded him to surrender, and he was
treacherously murdered by soldiers that night. An account of this appears in Frank C. Lockwood's excellent
book, *Pioneer Days in Arizona*.

Like Mangas Colorados, Cochise was driven to put on
the war paint by the amazing folly of the whites. A band of
Apaches had plundered the home of a settler on the Sonoita
River and taken away the son of a Mexican woman, the
lad Mickey Free, who later became a great trailer but was
otherwise worthless. Cochise and his men were camped
near Apache Station. Lieutenant George N. Bascom was
sent to find out from him where the boy could be found.

There was a conference, during which Cochise denied
any complicity in the raid. Bascom arrested him and his
companions. Cochise escaped, though wounded. He tried
to exchange some of his prisoners for the Apaches detained

by Bascom, but the lieutenant refused. Bascom continued to reject peace overtures even when the prisoners of Cochise, brought near enough to be seen and heard, desperately begged the officer to save their lives. The men captured by the Apaches were put to the torture and executed. The American officer retaliated by hanging the Indians he had seized. For twelve years from this time Cochise harried the country, killing many hundred settlers and travelers. The blame for this stiff stupidity was later taken by another officer, who had been sent from Fort Buchanan to take charge.

A brave but cruel man, Cochise could recognize courage in others. Lockwood tells in *Pioneer Days in Arizona* the story of T. J. Jefford, known as 'Red Whiskers' by the Indians. He was superintendent of the mail service between Fort Bowie and Tucson. Within sixteen months he buried twenty-two of the men employed by him, all victims of Indian raids. Jefford decided to appeal directly to Cochise. He rode into the Graham Mountains and sent up a smoke signal to ask for a talk. Cochise was amazed at his courage. The two men became friends, and at last went through the rite of becoming blood brothers. Years later Jefford took General O. O. Howard alone to Cochise to arrange a peace. This was done, and a reservation was set aside for the Indians near the range where they had fought so long.

Like many Indian chiefs, Cochise was a man of great force of character. There was greatness in him, even though he was a savage, cruel, passionate, and unforgiving. On his deathbed he asked Jeffords if he thought they would meet again in another life. Jeffords said he did not know and asked his opinion. Cochise replied that he was not sure, but he thought they would somewhere.

The fear of the Apaches among those living on the Southwest frontier, built up by years of exposure to acute danger when at any time the dreadful whoop of savage warriors might ring in their ears, engendered a bitter and uncompromising hatred of the warlike tribes. I have never known an oldtimer who lived in a region subject to raids from Apaches, Kiowas, or Comanches hold any view other than the one that the only good Indian was a dead one. They had seen the bodies of tortured and scalped neighbors, with no regard to age or sex, and they could find no mitigating pity for the braves or their families. Emanuel Dubbs, a preacher of the Gospel and a gentle soul, justified the action of pioneers on the ground that to spare the Comanche children would be unsafe, 'lest in a few years they scalp yours.' As Hualpai Clark told me once, 'Nits make lice.' Clark was an old scout, jailor at Tucson when I knew him forty years ago. He was generally credited with having killed that worst of renegade Indians, the Apache Kid.

The Indian troubles died down toward the end of the seventies and the territory began to fill up. Irrigation projects developed and farmers settled the valleys. Up till this time Arizona had been a country where they chopped wood with a sledgehammer and cut hay with a hoe, but more normal methods came in as land was cleared for the plow.

Yet even today the state has more of the pioneer atmosphere than any other. If you visit Dodge or Abilene or Julesburg you find modern towns apparently untouched by their inheritance, but Tucson and Prescott are still dis-

WATERING A TRAIL HERD

HEATING BRANDING IRONS AT THE ROUNDUP

tinctively of the West in spite of skyscrapers and fine tourist hotels. When one motors through Tombstone along the Overland Trail he sees the old Bird Cage Theater where Lotta Crabtree played. A little farther down the street are the Crystal Palace and the Oriental gambling-houses, once bustling with a lusty, turbid life. The Crystal Palace is closed, but the building where the Oriental operated is now occupied by a drugstore. In front of it Luke Short killed Charley Storms. From a side door stepped Frank Leslie, informed that Billy Claybourn was waiting for him outside, and shot the cowboy before the latter could get into action.

Just west of town, at the summit of a hill, is the famous Boothill Cemetery. A large sign catches the eye of the motorist, for since writers have exploited the lurid past of the town it has done a little advertising on its own account.

WELCOME TO TOMBSTONE
AND BOOTHILL GRAVEYARD

Buried here are the Remains of Tom McLowry, Frank McLowry and Billie Clanton

Killed in Earp-Clanton Battle Sept. 26th, 1881.

Dan Dowd, Red Sample, Tex Howard, Bill DeLaney and Dan Kelly

Hanged legally by J. Ward, Sheriff, for the Bisbee Massacre, Mar. 8, 1884.

John Heath,
Lynched by Bisbee Mob,
Feb. 22, 1884.

M. R. Peel
Murdered at Charleston,
March, 1882

Billy Grounds, Dutch Annie, Indian Bill,
Pat Lynch, Billy Kinsman,
Black Jack, Brady Brothers, Mike Noonan,
China Mary, John Hicks.

One tombstone in the cemetery mentions that the McLowrys and young Clanton were 'murdered on the streets of Tombstone.' Two others record the fate of the six members of the Heath gang.

These men, most of them cowboys, rode into Bisbee one evening and held up the store of Goldwater and Castenada. Two men walked into the building and stood up those inside, while the others swept the street with bullets to terrorize the inhabitants. John Tapinier was shot dead while standing in the doorway of a saloon. Another bullet struck J. A. Nolly and crumpled him, a dying man, on the sidewalk. A restaurant-keeper, Mrs. Roberts, looked out of her window and was killed. Indian Joe went down, wounded. Meanwhile Jim Kriegbaum came out of a store shooting. One of the outlaws was wounded by him. Deputy Sheriff D. T. Smith ran from the Roberts Restaurant where he was eating and ordered the bandits to stop firing. He was hit twice, one of the wounds being fatal.

Five of the road agents galloped out of town carrying about twenty-five hundred dollars with them. The sixth member of the gang, John Heath, had taken no active part in the robbery. He was the leader of the outlaws and had come in advance of them to spy out the land. At once he became very active in the pursuit and led the posse on false trails into the Chiricahua Mountains. He was so urgent about the direction the posse should take that Deputy Sheriff Bill Daniels suspected him. A day later he was arrested. The other members of the gang separated but were picked up at various points in Mexico, New Mexico, and Arizona.

The bandits were tried and convicted. Five were sentenced to the gallows. Since Heath was not in the actual stick-up the jury gave him a life sentence. This did not please Bisbee. A mob drove over to Tombstone, stormed the jail, and hanged Heath on a telegraph pole. The other five were left to be executed legally.

John L. Sullivan came to Tombstone with his show and visited the jail. One of the outlaws jested with him. 'They say you can knock out a man with one blow,' the condemned road agent said, 'but there's a fellow here in town is going to knock out five of us at once.'

This was literally true. All five went through the trap at the same instant. They were hardy scoundrels. One of them told the priest who had come to give them spiritual consolation, grinning at the black-robed padre, to be careful not to let the sheriff hang him too by mistake. The hanging was an invitation function. Cards were sent out to leading citizens by Sheriff Ward. One of them I once saw. It said:

EXECUTION OF

DANIEL KELLY, OMER W. SEMPLE, JAS. HOWARD, DANIEL DOWD, AND WILLIAM DELANEY

At the Court House, Tombstone, Arizona,
March 22, 1884, at 1 o'clock, P.M.

Admit Mr. William M. Breakenridge

J. L. Ward
Sheriff

Not transferable

At Prescott, February 5, 1886, a cold-blooded murderer named Dilda was executed legally. The man had shot down Deputy Sheriff Murphy, who had been sent to arrest him for rustling. For some reason the sporting element of the town took a great interest in the man. Whiskey Row was on the west side of the courthouse square, and 'Take-It-Easy' Johnson held open house at his saloon for faro dealers, gamblers, and bummers. There was talk of rescuing the condemned man at the gallows. The Prescott Grays, under command of Lieutenant 'Bucky' O'Neill, lined up in military formation around the place of execution. Dilda walked firmly up the steps. He appeared entirely cool and unmoved, but as the trap was sprung Bucky keeled over in a faint. To see a man killed without being given a fighting chance for his life was more than the lieutenant could stand.

Today, more than fifty years later, there stands on the square an equestrian statue of Bucky O'Neill, Captain in the Rough Rider regiment which fought in Cuba. The statue, done by Solon Borglum, is dedicated to all the Arizona men who fought in that regiment, but the figure and face are those of Bucky. He died in the trenches in front of Santiago. Just before the bullet struck him in the throat he had been quoting a verse from Whitman's 'O Captain! My Captain!'

Richard Harding Davis could have found no more glamorous figure for the hero of a soldier-of-fortune novel than Bucky O'Neill. Born and brought up in the East, he was a graduate of Gonzales College and the National University Law School. Like many another young man, he went West to make his fortune. From the day of his arrival he loved Arizona and belonged to it. The freedom of the frontier, its excitements and dangers, its utter democracy and lack of conventions, suited him perfectly. Of the thousands who poured into the Territory during that decade, no other so impressed himself on the country as did this happy-go-lucky son of Erin. He was not Arizona's most useful citizen nor its most important, but he was the most picturesque. His reckless gallantry, his wildness and essential integrity, the zest for adventure that burned in him, combined to make him the beau-idéal of what a Westerner should be.

Nobody ever called him William. He was 'Bucky' to everybody. His plunging play at the wheel and the faro table won the cognomen for him. Though a lawyer by training, O'Neill was in turn editor, judge, sheriff, politician, and soldier. Always he was a knight-errant, ready to give his services to the weak and humble. In the early years when Whiskey Row was running full blast in Prescott, when chips rattled night and day at the Palace, the Legal Tender, and the Oriental (in Phoenix, Tucson, and Tombstone respectively), one heard scores of anecdotes about Bucky. Some were quixotic and some humorous, but all of them were characteristic of the qualities that endeared him to us all.

Neal the stage-driver, who ran for years the halfway house for the Tucson–Globe route at Oracle, told me that on one occasion Bucky was his sole passenger. O'Neill was scheduled to make a political speech at Mammoth. The Rillito was bank-full, the water plunging down with dangerous force.

The stage-driver was a strong, heavyset man with negro blood in his veins, a cool, determined fellow who had proved his nerve by standing off bandits when they tried to rob the coach.

'Do we go on?' he asked Bucky, pulling up on the edge of the churning stream.

'I can't speak at Mammoth if I'm not there,' Bucky answered.

Neal's whiplash snaked out close to the ears of the leaders. They splashed down into the river. It was a near thing, but they made it.

Will Barnes used to tell of another swollen river story in which O'Neill took a part. There were four passengers: Barnes, Bucky, and two Sisters of Charity. The men consulted about attempting the ford, but there were urgent reasons for getting to town. Bucky filled a bucket with small rocks and sat beside the driver. When they got into the deep water he pelted the horses with the stones to keep them moving. More than once the broncos faltered before the pressure of the pouring water, but at last they found a footing near the opposite bank. Bucky had emptied his bucket by that time.

There is the story of how Bucky drove a gang of hard-boiled railroad graders from a spring they had taken from the peaceful Navajos, and another of how he jounced a bristling bully up and down by the ears because he had called Bucky a liar. On one occasion he followed a bandit named Smith into New Mexico, shot him from his horse, gave him temporary medical attention, and carried him to the nearest town, where a mob of Smith's friends attempted to rescue him and were dissuaded only because Bucky made it clear that it could not be done without littering the street with several corpses, one of which would certainly be that of their friend Smith. The train robbery at Diablo Cañon gave Bucky another chance to show what

he had in him. With Tom Horn as trailer he followed the
bandits for weeks, harrying them from place to place. The
posse killed one of the robbers, but the others escaped.
Bucky got another with a long shot. The horses of the
pursuers gave out, except the one on which Bucky was
riding. He pushed on alone, surprised the band, and held
the desperadoes prisoners until Tom Horn and the others
arrived.

In spite of his jaunty gaiety Bucky was notoriously shy.
When his duties as judge forced him to marry young
couples he was always afraid he would have to kiss the
bride, according to the custom of the time and place. His
blushes matched those of the young lady.

A few minutes before he was killed Bucky was standing
on the trench looking through field glasses at the Spanish
entrenchments on the hill. Somebody told him he was
exposing himself unnecessarily. Captain O'Neill stepped
down, because he detested grandstanding, but he said
with a laugh, 'The Spanish bullet that will kill me hasn't
been molded yet.' Within five minutes he was dead. Perhaps he was fortunate in the manner of his exit. I think if
he had been given a choice, he would have asked to go out
in an hour of high excitement to the sound of drumming
guns.

The first white woman who settled in the Salt River
Valley was Adaline Gray. She was on her way with her
husband to California, and when they mule-wagoned into
the valley he suggested they stop and rest a few days while
their animals put on flesh for the last stretch. They rested
there sixty years. Adaline lived to drive an automobile, to
listen to a radio, to go up in a plane. 'All in all, I figure the

good and the bad of every generation just about balances,' she said after she was eighty.

'Punkin-eaters,' they called the first farmers in the valley, because in the early years they did not have much else in the way of vegetables to eat. Presently other settlers arrived and a town was started. Darrell Duppa named the village Phoenix, for the reason that there had once been an Indian settlement on the spot. He also chose the name of Tempe for another town, deriving it from the Vale of Tempe immortalized by Horace and Virgil. Duppa was an educated remittance man from England. He came of a good family, one listed in Burke's *Landed Gentry*, which could go back in an unbroken line to the time of Henry V. Bryan Philip Darrell Duppa had no claim to a title, but in Arizona to the end of his life he was Lord Duppa.

Though Phoenix was settled late and became the heart of a very rich agricultural section, it was still a small cow town when first I knew it. Cowboys six abreast used to gallop up Washington Street in a cloud of yellow dust and tie at the hitch racks in front of stores and saloons. They would go jingling into the Palace to buck the tiger, wearing big hats, bandannas, and shiny leather chaps, a gay and rollicking band of slim, sun-tanned youths.

Phoenix was never considered a bad town, but Colonel McClintock (a captain of the Rough Riders) mentions in one of his histories that six men were once killed there in a week. A Mexican armed with a saber went wild at a chicken-pulling, wounded several, and escaped. Henry Garfias dragged him back, and he was later shot down trying to escape. The Hardy gang came to town and started to shoot it up. They went down Washington Street firing right and left. Garfias was sheriff, one of the best Arizona has had. Citizens enlisted rapidly as deputies, among others Bucky O'Neill. The posse drove the cowboys out of town, but not until Bucky had shot one in the leg and dropped him from the saddle. Shortly after this two murderers were taken from the jail by a mob and hanged. After that Phoenix was as quiet as a Sunday School for years.

At Jack Keating's Tunnel Saloon in Florence, Arizona, occurred the duel between Pete Gabriel and Joe Phy, a typical frontier encounter of men who felt called upon to settle their own grievances in the manner of the border. The two men had been friends. When Gabriel had been sheriff of Pinal County he had appointed Phy one of his deputies. Both of them were brave men. Twice the sheriff had fought off mobs trying to take prisoners from him. In battles with bad men he had come out victor many times, and nearly always he had been in the right. Phy had a reputation as a gunman. He too was notably fearless, but was not always on the side of law and order.

While acting as deputy, Phy beat up a man he was arresting, injuring him so badly that the victim nearly died. The sheriff arrested Phy, disarming him and later discharging him from his position as assistant. This stirred in Phy a bitter animosity against his former chief. He had expected to succeed him as sheriff, but he had by his own folly thwarted his ambition.

Phy sent word to Gabriel that he intended to 'get' him some day. He missed no opportunity to abuse his former friend, both behind his back and in his presence. Gabriel paid no attention, beyond explaining to Phy that what he had done was in the line of duty and not personal.

More than once Phy buckled on a sixshooter with the intention of ending the matter, but was persuaded by bystanders not to carry through his purpose. Yet everybody in Florence knew that the crisis was only postponed.

Pete Gabriel came to the end of his term as sheriff and moved from town to operate a quartz gold mine in the hills. He went to Florence one day to buy supplies and settle some bills. Meeting old friends, he dropped into the Tunnel to have a drink. One led to another, and the hours slipped away. Strangely enough, Joe Phy did not either drink or smoke.

Phy decided to call for a showdown. He walked into the Tunnel, a sixshooter in one hand and a bowie knife in the other. Gabriel was at the bar, and looked up to see his enemy standing just inside the swing doors.

The first shot of Phy struck his foe in the breast. Though badly wounded, Gabriel sent a bullet crashing into the other's stomach. By chance the main light in the saloon was shot out, and the duel was continued in the dark. Another bullet struck Pete in the right side and splintered a rib. Twice more he was hit, in the wrist and in the body, but he moved toward Phy, lurching from the shock of his wounds but still firing.

Joe crashed through the swing doors to the sidewalk outside and pitched forward into the road. Gabriel stood looking at him, swaying on his feet. There were two bullets left in his revolver, but he had not the strength left to raise the weapon.

During the night Phy died. His last words were an in-

quiry as to whether his enemy would live. He was told
that Gabriel had no chance.

Yet Gabriel survived. He recovered his health measur-
ably and lived for years, though the wound in his side
always troubled him.

A battle of this sort was a savage, cruel business, but it
is difficult to see how a man like Pete Gabriel, a redoubt-
able frontiersman and an expert shot, could have avoided
the duel. The law of the West was that when a man had
been backed to the wall he had to fight or lose prestige
among all his associates.

From the first Cochise County had been inclined to
lawlessness. The proximity to Mexico made cattle rustling
easy. Even after John Slaughter had served notice to
stock thieves to 'get out or get killed' the southeast corner
of Arizona was infested with bands of outlaws preying on
settlers. There were many mountain ranges into the
gulches and pockets of which the banditti could withdraw
to hide after a raid. The Huachucas, the Dragoons, the
Santa Catalinas, the Gilas, and the Superstition Range
were all easy of access, with a hundred convenient gorges
that offered shelter for men on the dodge. Farther north
were the Apache and the White Mountains, and not far
from them the Tonto Basin, where law officers were not
welcome. No territory ever had a better average of com-
petent sheriffs than Arizona. Garcias, Slaughter, Breakenridge, Gabriel, Bucky O'Neill, Perry Owens, Jeff Milton [1]

---

[1] Only Jeff Milton of this group is still among the living. He has been in his
time a Texas Ranger, a deputy United States marshal, chief of police at El Paso,
a customs inspector, and a Wells-Fargo Express Company messenger. Jeff is
a living example of Captain Bill McDonald's apothegm that no man in the wrong
can stand up against a fellow that is in the right and 'keeps a-comin'.' Jeff is not

— the list of these officers reads like a roll of honor. But the county officer was always at the disadvantage that his authority stopped at the limits of his county, and even when he ventured beyond it into the high lands where the outlaws holed up, he did not know the terrain one tenth as well as the thieves. What Arizona needed was a body like the Texas Rangers which could operate wherever needed and follow the thieves week after week until a capture was made.

Under Colonel Alexander O. Brodie, appointed by President Roosevelt Governor of Arizona after the Spanish-American War, a force of twelve rangers took the field with Burton C. Mossman as captain. Each member was

a killer. He is the kind of peace officer who stands up to bad men, quietly and unafraid, and makes them back down without drawing a gun. At El Paso, before witnesses, he made John Wesley Hardin, the most notorious gunman Texas ever had, admit that he had lied when he said Milton had shot down for pay a desperado who had been rubbed out from ambush by parties unknown. Probably Jeff expected Hardin to kill him, but he felt he could not let a slander like that pass unnoticed. In Tucson he backed down Burt Alvord, a bravo and train-robber then rolling high in Arizona, though Jeff at the time had a shattered arm owing to an encounter with five bandits who tried to hold up a train on which he was the express messenger.

This holdup occurred at Fairbank, Arizona, in February, 1900. The leader of the outlaws was Jack Dunlap, usually called Three-Fingered-Jack. With him were Bravo Juan, the two Owens brothers, and Robert Brown.

Milton was busy unloading packages when a voice ordered him to throw up his hands and come out of the car. Jeff had a different idea. A bullet struck the bone of his arm. With a shotgun he put out of action one of the robbers, then slammed shut the door. A few moments later he became unconscious, but not until he had found time to throw the safe keys back of a trunk. Three-Fingered-Jack was mortally wounded, but his men looked for the keys, without result. The bandits suddenly grew panicky and rode away into the Chiricahuas.

Sheriff Scott White cut the trail of the robbers and found Three-Fingered-Jack abandoned in the mountains. Unable to travel farther, he had been left to die by his companions. The other four were run down shortly after this. Jeff was taken to California and operated upon, but he never recovered the easy use of his arm. No bad man ever complained that Milton did not shoot as straight with his left hand as his right. He was as cool and efficient an officer as he had been before the holdup.

hand-picked. He had to be expert with a gun, a first-class horseman, used to 'cutting' trail, and of tested nerve. The work done by the rangers was remarkable. They were a hard-bitten lot, and they went after outlaws in a businesslike way. Mossman was a cattleman, and after about a year retired in favor of Thomas H. Rynning, but just before quitting he crossed the line into Mexico and dragged back to justice Augustine Chacon, one of the most desperate murderers the border has known. The bandit had killed many times, often without any need to do so as a safety measure. At the risk of his life Mossman captured Chacon, who was shortly hanged at Solomonville.

Tom Rynning followed Mossman as captain of the rangers, and Tom had lived adventure all his life. The rangers were increased in number to twenty-five. Under Rynning and later under Harry Wheeler, another peace officer to whose memory Arizona takes off its hat, the rangers worked hard at the business of mopping up the outlaws. As Governor Campbell of Arizona has written, the rangers of that territory formed one of the best bodies of peace officers that ever sat a saddle or pulled a trigger. All three of the captains in those early years were first-class men, wise, self-reliant, game, and energetic. None of them ever asked the men to do anything he was not willing to do himself.

Rynning says that Harry Wheeler was probably the best shot in the world, and that he did not know what fear was. Several times he tossed five empty cartridge shells into the air, and before they came down he had hit them all with his Krag. Harry came from a family of soldiers. His father was a colonel in the United States Army. Unfortunately, Harry was a little too short for the West Point minimum. But he served as a scout, as a private in the Spanish-American War, as a Western peace officer, and as a captain, both of Arizona Rangers and in the World War.

Though he was a bad man to meet in a fight, Wheeler was never hard and callous. He was always generous and warm-hearted, even toward those whom he had to oppose. A wounded or beaten outlaw was to him just a poor fellow down on his luck. Dane Coolidge tells of the time the ranger heard shots in a Tucson saloon, barged in, and saw a dozen men with their hands in the air. The robber whirled on him, and in the exchange of shots was hit three times. Harry knelt down beside the dying man. 'Sorry I had to do this,' he said gently. ''S all right,' the holdup answered. 'You just beat me to it.'

The most famous of Wheeler's battles was the one with a desperado named Tracy who had killed a man in Nevada. This took place in Benson, Arizona, on the street between the Virginia Hotel and the station. Harry was eating lunch at a restaurant when a frightened man and woman rushed in to tell him that Tracy, the husband of the woman, was getting off the train and was going to kill them. Wheeler jumped up and went to meet the furious man. He told him he was under arrest.

Instantly Tracy whipped out a revolver and shot the ranger twice, in the thigh and in the foot. Wheeler fired four times, and in spite of his wounds scored four hits. The bad man went down, crying out that he was done for. Harry dropped his gun and ran to help him. The man fired at him twice. Snatching up a tin can from the ground, the ranger flung it at him. He too was down, unable to get to his feet or to crawl to the revolver he had tossed away.

He did not need it. Tracy was mortally wounded. Any one of the ranger's bullets would have been sufficient. Only the man's furious rage had kept him strong enough to keep shooting.

There was a reward for Tracy, dead or alive, of five hundred dollars. Harry sent it to the widow of the man the outlaw had killed in Nevada.

Wheeler died many years ago, but Rynning and Mossman are still going strong. When last I heard of him Rynning was retired and living in California. Mossman is a cattleman in New Mexico. Both of them have lived to see the result of their work in the mesquite flats and brushy gulches of Arizona. If there are any cow-thieves left there, they operate with trucks instead of with running-irons. Probably that state has fewer than Kansas, Nebraska, and Iowa. For Arizona long ago turned over a new leaf and is now rampant with righteousness.

II

The Sleepy Little Town
of El Paso

EVEN in those early days when El Paso was a sleepy little village a thousand miles from a railroad, the pioneers who had settled there were quite convinced that the town was marked by destiny for greatness. Across the river on the Mexican side was another small settlement, Paso del Norte, now known by the less euphonious name of Juarez. Most of the inhabitants of both places were Mexicans, and such business as there was consisted of exchanging supplies for ore with the mining companies of Chihuahua and of selling corn, beef, and flour to the chain of military posts in northwest Texas. None the less, El Paso was a transportation center. It had no less than four stage lines. The fine Concord coaches of the Overland Mail Company, operating between St. Louis and San Francisco, passed along its dusty main street. Three other lines, connecting with Santa Fe, San Antonio, and Chihuahua points, had here the terminus of their routes.

But though El Paso generally slept in a coma of sunshine, it had its eruptive moments. The pioneers were men of positive, self-assertive characters. Each felt that he had to right his own wrongs, and nearly all carried six-shooters at their belts. The center of life in the little town was at the post-office, managed by 'Uncle Ben' Dowell, who operated in the same room a saloon and several gaming-tables. Most of the shootings in the early days took place either inside the post-office or just outside on El Paso or San Antonio Street. W. W. Mills was Collector of Customs for six years following the Civil War. He mentions in his book, *Forty Years in El Paso*, that of the thirty young men employed by him during that time three were killed by Indians, one by robbers, one by a mob, two shot down on the streets, and one ambushed while on a journey. Texas offered its mild excitements.

There was a cottonwood tree growing on the bank of an *acequia* to which was nailed a bulletin board where men occasionally notified one another that they were liars and scoundrels. Here too the landlady of the boarding-house posted her patrons who did not pay their bills. Difficulties arose between hot-tempered men and were settled promptly. Sometimes those involved were buried after the meeting. The fierce political feuds of Reconstruction days led to impromptu duels among the most prominent citizens, most of whom were ranged for or against the carpetbag administration of Governor Davis. Several of these were shot to death on El Paso Street. But though there were homicides, no thieves or gangsters infested the town. These arrived with the railroads.

The 'Salt Lakes War' at San Elizario was more disturbing than most feuds because it involved racial antagonism.

This was brought about largely by the obstinacy of Judge Charles H. Howard, a hot-tempered man of impressive appearance who had served as an officer in the Confederate Army. The salt lakes had always been recognized as public property, and it was the custom of Mexicans to haul salt from them free of charge. After his election as judge of the El Paso district, Howard bought land certificates at Austin and located the site of the deposits.

This aroused intense indignation on the part of the Mexicans, who threatened to disregard the recently acquired rights of Howard. The judge had two of the more prominent Mexicans at San Elizario arrested for inciting riot, whereupon a group of their friends released them and seized Howard. It is likely that he would have been killed but for the efforts of Louis Cardis, an Italian who had gained the confidence of the Mexicans and become their political leader. Howard signed an agreement to give up his claim and leave the state, but as soon as he was out of danger repudiated this on the ground that it had been obtained by duress.

In justice to Howard it ought to be said that he was not the first who attempted to get private control of the salt lakes. Fountain, Mills, Cardis, and the native leader of the Mexicans, Antonio Barajo, had already tried to gain possession of them in one way or another. The judge was merely the boldest of those who saw in the lakes a means to fortune.

Because Cardis was an adviser of those opposing him, Howard became a bitter enemy of the Italian, claiming that the latter was conspiring to have him assassinated. He returned to El Paso, anger boiling in him. Cardis was a sub-contractor of the Texas and California Stage Company, which had its office at the store of Sam Schutz. He was in the store dictating a letter to Adolph Krakaner, sitting in a rocking-chair with his back to the door, when Judge Howard walked in, a double-barreled shotgun in his hands. Warned by Schutz, Cardis jumped up and found cover back of a high office desk. Howard fired at his legs, and when Cardis staggered out sent several buckshot through his heart.

Howard fled to New Mexico and demanded of the Texas Governor that rangers be sent to San Elizario to protect him in his rights. The Governor authorized Major Jones, head of the ranger force, to enlist a company of twenty at El Paso. This was done and Lieutenant John B. Tays was put in command. Relying on the rangers, Howard returned to San Elizario and put himself under their protection.

His arrival was a signal for instant insurrection. The excitement was intense. Hundreds of Mexicans armed and besieged the ranger headquarters, where Tays barricaded doors and windows and cut portholes in the walls. The lieutenant refused to give up Howard, and for four days a battle was fought intermittently. A sergeant was killed, as was an American merchant named Ellis. Tays dragged the sergeant back to cover under fire.

Gradually the lines of the Mexicans drew closer. Their leaders asked for a conference, to which the ranger lieutenant agreed. Bluntly Barajo told Tays that gunpowder had been placed during the night to blow up the building if Howard was not turned over to them.

Tays reported to Howard, who at once decided that he

must surrender to his enemies to save the others. He knew that he was going to his death when he and Tays walked out into the mob. There was a difference of testimony as to the surrender. Some blamed Tays, others John Atkinson, who was one of Howard's bondsmen. In any case the rangers came out and were disarmed. The rangers have always felt that this was the most disgraceful episode in the history of the force. They felt that a strong officer would never have given up as Tays did. One of the most astounding features of the affair was that Captain Blair of the United States Army reached the scene with fourteen men prior to the battle. During the siege he consulted with both parties but refused to take any part in the fight, though there were engaged in it more than a hundred Mexicans who lived on the other side of the Rio Grande. In his official report Blair said that there were about three hundred and fifty sober, determined Mexicans. They meant to get Howard and nothing less would satisfy them. Their anger flamed because Howard, who had killed their friend Cardis, was at liberty while two of their number had been arrested, fined, and imprisoned only because they *said* they would get salt, law or no law.

After long and stormy debate, during which the fire brands wanted to kill all the gringos and the conservatives only Howard, a compromise was effected. The judge, Atkinson, and Howard's agent McBride were condemned to death by the firing-squad. All of them met their fate bravely. Howard was the first. He gave the word to fire. When it came the turn of Atkinson he spoke to the mob in Spanish and reminded them that the party had surrendered under a promise of safety. He was shouted down.

Opening his shirt, he told them to fire at his heart. When the bullets struck too low he kept his feet and flung an insult at the rifle squad. '*Mas arriba, cabrones!*' [1] he cried. They continued to fire until they had finished him.

There were reprisals later. Five or six Mexicans were slain by the posse which went out to recover the bodies and to arrest the guilty, after which there was a congressional investigation that produced no results. The Salt War gradually faded out. Both sides were ready to stop.

It was not long after this that four trunk railroads began laying their tracks across the desert toward El Paso. Long before the first train arrived the sleepy little Mexican town was transformed into a hell-roaring American boom city consisting mostly of saloons, gambling-houses, dance halls, and variety theaters. The city marshal was George Campbell and his deputy William Johnson. Keeping the peace in El Paso had now become a sizable job, and the marshal resigned because he was not being paid enough. This left Johnson alone to take care of a town just popping with life. El Paso Street was filled nightly with hundreds of men, and hundreds more were crowding into the gaming establishments to play monte, faro bank, roulette, and chuck-a-luck.

On one especially wild night fusillades of shots were fired in the streets and many citizens alarmed. The mayor sent for the Texas Rangers, and for a week five of these long-legged, brown-faced gentlemen under the command of Jim Gillett paced the streets and no murmur of discord was heard. The gamblers and the gunmen had a tremen-

[1] 'Shoot higher, you ——.'

dous respect for this force of quiet but energetic young men. But the rangers were not enrolled to 'ride herd' on towns except during emergencies, and presently they departed. On the same day there arrived by coach a six-foot-two blond with a handlebar mustache and a ministerial air. He wore a black Prince Albert suit, a white shirt and collar, and a string tie. Dallas Stoudenmire had come to take on the job of marshal.

He called on William Johnson for the keys of the city jail. Most of the time William was drunk. He declined to give up the keys, whereupon Stoudenmire turned him upside down and shook them out of his pocket.

Almost before a week had passed the new marshal was given his test by fire. Not far from where some cowboys were running stock for the Manning Brothers two young Mexicans were found dead in the brush. The bodies were brought to El Paso by the rangers and an inquest was held. Johnny Hale, manager for the Mannings, was called as a witness before the coroner. The interpreter was a German named Gus Krempkau. Evidence seemed to point toward the cowboys as being implicated in the killings. When the trial adjourned at noon Krempkau was stopped by Hale and accused of twisting the testimony in his translation of it into English. Ex-marshal Campbell, known to be very friendly to the Mannings, who owned a large variety theater and gambling-hall, the Coliseum, ordered Krempkau to retract his interpretation of the evidence. The German refused. W. W. Mills was standing very near at the time and was surprised at 'the low, protesting, almost pleading tone of voice' in which the antagonists spoke to one another. The rangers had gone home for their noon meal, but Stoudenmire was standing near the entrance to the building.

Hale had been drinking and drew his gun, crying out at the same time, 'Cut her loose, Campbell!' He shot Krempkau through the head and killed him instantly. By this time Campbell had his sixshooter out. Stoudenmire came into action. His first shot missed Hale but killed a Mexican onlooker, his second sent Hale down, dead. Campbell backed away, his gun smoking. The new marshal dropped him to the sidewalk. He died next day. Within five seconds of the time of the first shot four men were dead or dying.

El Paso went around on tiptoe for a few days. It appeared that the town had a marshal who could be labeled dangerous. Bad men and thugs walked around him very carefully, eyeing him the way a dog does a large and bristly canine who has just arrived in the neighborhood. Nobody wanted to tread on Mr. Stoudenmire's toes. That did not mean the toughs accepted him gladly. They put up with him until they could find a convenient way of eliminating him.

Meanwhile the marshal went his even-handed way, disregarding the black looks and murmured threats. Some delinquents he arrested, others he beat up. He frequently had to use the keys emptied out of Mr. Johnson in order to toss prisoners into his calaboose. Better citizens on the whole were satisfied with Stoudenmire, though they admitted he was a trifle impulsive with a six-gun. What the West calls 'the sporting element' did not share this content. The chief objectors were the Manning brothers and their friends.

Bill Johnson, ex-deputy marshal, was selected as the cat's-paw. He was primed with liquor, flattered, and bribed until he consented to stand behind a pile of bricks and pour two loads of buckshot into Stoudenmire as he passed down San Antonio Street on his nightly round. Presently the marshal sauntered up from the Acme Saloon and Johnson unloaded both barrels at him. He scored two complete misses, but he did not live long to regret it. Stoudenmire also fired twice, and made two hits — both vital. The enemy contingent concealed across the road to see the show opened fire on the marshal and hit him in the ankle. He charged instantly, his revolver blazing, and the sporting 'gents' scurried away in the darkness like partridges.

A brother-in-law of the marshal, 'Doc' Cummings, was shot down in a saloon run by the Mannings, which did not increase the friendliness between them and Dallas Stoudenmire. Jim Manning was tried for the homicide and acquitted. Under the strain of walking daily with the likelihood of his own sudden death, Stoudenmire took to drink. When under the influence of liquor he became overbearing, even with his friends. He was asked to resign, and in his place was appointed James B. Gillett, an ex-sergeant of Company A, Frontier Battalion, Texas Rangers.

Gillett was one of the best of a splendid force. He was gentle of speech and mild of manner. His blue eyes were as friendly as a June sky, except when they took on the steely look that meant trouble was impending. Just prior to his resignation as a ranger he had distinguished himself by a piece of plucky insubordination entirely after the heart of Texas.

Two Baca brothers, Abran and Enofrio, had killed in cold blood the editor of a New Mexican newspaper and had fled to Texas. Gillett decided to get the murderers. He picked up Abran without much trouble, and later learned that a man who looked like Enofrio had been seen in the town of Saragosa, Mexico. The ranger sergeant knew that there was no chance of getting the man by diplomatic negotiations. Baca would hear of them and disappear. He decided to kidnap the killer, without the knowledge of his superiors in the service, who could not of course let him cross the line after his man. One of his men, George Lloyd, went with him. Both of them knew it was a forlorn hope, and that if anything went wrong they would both be shot 'into rag dolls,' as the Texas phrase was.

Through the bosques they rode to Saragosa. Lloyd held the horses while Gillett stepped into the store where Baca was working. The killer was measuring some goods for an old Mexican woman when Gillett covered him. The ranger backed his man out of the store and mounted him back of Lloyd. They left behind them an excited town. The church bell was ringing, vaqueros were swinging to the saddle, and guns were booming. A posse pursued them to the river ford, firing at them as they rode.

Gillett received a first-class lecture from his captain, George W. Baylor, for his imprudence and was sent to Socorro, New Mexico, with the prisoner. The sergeant delivered him, and within three hours a mob had broken into the jail and lynched the murderer. The anger of the Socorro citizens was too intense to keep unsatisfied through a trial. Baca had shot down the editor of the *Sun* in the presence of his wife because he had refused him admittance to a church festival while under the influence of liquor.

After Stoudenmire retired as marshal he was given an appointment as deputy United States marshal, with headquarters at El Paso. He was always friendly with his successor, and even when Gillett interfered in a gun fight and arrested him held no grudge. The cause of the trouble was too much liquor.

An ex-deputy marshal named Page had a difficulty with another man, and Stoudenmire patched up the trouble and took Page away with him. They did some drinking and later returned to the Acme Saloon to hoist a few more. Page and Stoudenmire quarreled. They drew their pistols. A shot or two rang out. Then Gillett walked into the front door with a sawed-off shotgun and stopped the fireworks by announcing that he would fill full of holes the first one that pulled a trigger again. Next morning the combatants were fined twenty-five dollars each.

But Gillett had already served six years as a ranger on the west frontier under such noted officers as Roberts, Coldwell, Reynolds, and Baylor. He had fought Indians and bad men as an almost daily diet. The brush country was getting cleared of its outlaws, and Comanches no longer rode on raids by the light of the moon. He and Captain Nevill, resigned from the ranger corps, were running a cattle brand of their own, and it was strongly in his mind to settle down to business on his own account. The Estado Land and Cattle Company asked him to be its manager, with the privilege of continuing his own herd in Marfa County. While he was hesitating he received a letter from Nevill mentioning that after a man had had more than a quart cup of bullets fired at him as ranger and marshal it was time to get into an occupation less hazardous. Nevill was taking his own advice, and Jim Gillett took it too. He resigned from the police force of El Paso and became a cowman.

When a man looked for trouble on the old frontier he usually found it. Some quiet citizen who seemed inoffensive generally accommodated him. Stoudenmire was becoming a nuisance when he drank. One day he suggested to some friends at the bar that he was going over to the Coliseum to fix things up with the Mannings or to shoot the fuss out.

There were four of the Manning brothers. They owned several saloons and gaming-houses. The oldest of them was a doctor, a small, well-dressed man, courteous of manner, with a cool, keen eye that overlooked no essentials in an emergency. He did the talking for the family when Stoudenmire arrived, and apparently arranged a peace with the marshal.

To show the town that all was now well between them, Doctor Manning and Stoudenmire strolled down El Paso Street and dropped into Ben Dowell's saloon. They were going to seal the compact with a drink. It is not known what Doctor Manning said to annoy his companion, but Stoudenmire whipped out a pistol and fired. As he did so, the doctor caught the revolver by the muzzle and pushed it out of line. The bullet went through Manning's hand, but he closed with his huge antagonist. Jim Manning heard the sound of the shot and burst through the swing doors. He sent a leaden slug through Stoudenmire's head that killed the marshal. Since it was clearly self-defense, both of the Mannings were acquitted.

The next eminent pistoleer employed by El Paso to maintain a reasonable but not too strict order, since the town was known as wide open, was a gentleman named John Selman with about a dozen metaphorical notches on his gun. Measured even by the standards of the South-west, John was 'as tough as they come.' It was known that he had spilled a lot of lead in Lincoln County, New Mex-ico, and more at Fort Griffin, which had once been the headquarters of the buffalo-hunters. There was a rumor that en route to the border town he had murdered two sheepherders to appropriate their flock. Very possibly his lethal record may have been exaggerated, since Mr. Sel-man had operated under more than one alias and his homicides were generally undercover jobs and not killings done in the light of day for all to see, like those of his more notorious brother assassin John Wesley Hardin. In any case the city fathers felt he was bad enough to make a good marshal.

Roughly speaking, they were right. He subdued his native impatience to the placid tolerance expected of a police officer, even while he saw that no lawbreaker 'put anything over' on him. None of the quiet citizens of the town had anything to fear from 'Uncle John,' as in course of time he came to be known, and no gambling-house or brothel was allowed to exceed what the marshal considered its proper and reasonable functions, which were of course to fleece the sucker efficiently and more or less lawfully.

When cowboys or outlaws came to town looking for grief, Uncle John saw they found it. One notable instance was the case of Bass Outlaw and some of his friends. Bass was by way of being a part-time law officer and a part-time law-breaker, but he had dropped into El Paso purely for entertainment purposes. He and the boys wanted to see the elephant.

During the evening they drifted into a honky-tonk and began to shoot up the furniture, whereupon Marshal Selman moved hurriedly in that direction. Bass Outlaw saw him coming and tallied first with a bullet in the leg. That was the total score for his side. John kept coming, though several guns blazed at him. When the smoke cleared away Bass Outlaw and two of his companions were ready for an undertaker and the others had vanished.

Meanwhile El Paso was growing into quite a city. It had a baseball team and a ladies' aid society and organizations for civic betterment. The reform element began to agitate against the open town, though those for and against public gambling and legal dance halls were all agreed that regardless of its outward morals El Paso was the finest town in the United States. Even the ministers who inveighed against its wickedness were ready to subscribe to that patriotic article of faith.

About this time Governor Hogg threw a monkey wrench into the peaceful existence of El Paso. He pardoned John Wesley Hardin from the penitentiary, where he had been locked up for one of twenty-seven or eight homicides he had committed. While in prison Mr. Hardin had seen the error of his ways. He had read his Bible, become converted, and taught Sunday School to the other less bad boys incarcerated. During his spare time — and he had plenty of it — he had studied law and was prepared to

take an examination to practice. However laudable his
intentions, John Wesley found the execution of them not
practical. The drag of the old life was on him, and by the
time he reached El Paso he was ready to admit he could
not reform. The economic life of Texas had no niche into
which he could fit.

Though Selman was the ranking 'gun-toter' in El Paso
prior to the arrival of Hardin, there were others held in
high esteem by their admirers. One of these was George
Scarborough, a deputy United States marshal. Another
was Manning Clements, a nephew of the one and only
John Wesley Hardin, and a plenty tough *hombre* in his own
right. Still another pistol artist with a reputation not to be
sneezed at was Jeff Milton, erstwhile of Arizona. With the
exception of Clements, who was not in town at the time,
all these gentlemen took a very personal interest in the
coming of Hardin. The pardoned convict had been out of
circulation a long time since the days when men mentioned him with lowered voices. Maybe he was reformed
and had come to hang out a law shingle and to teach a
Sunday-School class, but these sceptical souls were of
opinion that he would break loose again soon, and if he did
he was very likely to turn hostile eyes on them. None of
them relished the thought of an encounter with him, but
since they were realists they considered the possibility.

A criminal named McRose was living in Juarez. He was
wanted by the State of Texas enough to have had a price
put on his head, and one night was indiscreet enough to
cross the bridge into United States territory. There somebody pumped lead into him. While under the influence of
bad whiskey Hardin talked too much and accused Milton

and Scarborough of having killed the man for the reward.

Milton promptly 'called' this charge as soon as he met Hardin by demanding that he admit he had lied. To the surprise of all present, the notorious killer did not at once slay Milton. He said it had been the whiskey talking and that it was not the truth. As far as he knew, Mr. Milton was as innocent as Mary's little lamb.

The years in prison had done something to John Wesley. Apparently he had lost the desire to kill. But he was still not a model citizen. He held up a gambling-house and walked out with all the ready cash in sight. John Selman did not arrest him, and he appeared at his favorite resorts as usual.

The town watched him and Selman with intense interest. There would be trouble one of these days, unless Selman threw up his job and quit, which was an issue that nobody expected. Uncle John said nothing. Since Hardin was doing the drinking he talked. It is quite clear that he made light of Selman, for he did not take the ordinary precautions of all wary gunmen. Even after the marshal advised him to be ready Hardin showed no evidence of being aware of imminent battle.

Hardin was in the Acme Saloon shaking dice for the drinks when Selman walked into the place and without any warning shot Hardin in the back of the head. The marshal was tried for murder and was defended by A. B. Fall, later United States Senator from New Mexico and Secretary of the Interior. Fall got him off by stressing the fact that there was a tilted mirror above and behind the bar, and that Hardin made a motion of his arm that Selman thought was in the direction of a revolver. None the

less there was a strong feeling that Selman had committed
a cold-blooded murder. During the trial Fall made references to the relatives of Hardin to which Manning Clements took exception. He was prevented from killing the
lawyer later only by the chance entrance of two rangers
into the room where the men met. Shortly after this Clements was shot down in the Coney Island Saloon.

Trouble brewed between Selman and Scarborough. The
cause of quarrel is unimportant. Back of it lay the more
important reason that the men did not like each other.
Perhaps it was the old story of two notorious bad men,
each of whom wanted to be chief, though it should be said
for Scarborough that he always was known as a good officer
who served the public well. The grudge between them
simmered for a time, then broke into flame one night at
the Wigwam. In the alley outside the two men fought.
Selman went down after the second shot. There were con-
flicting stories about this duel, owing to the fact that after
the battle no revolver was found on Selman's body or near
it. Owen P. White inclines to accept the rumor that somebody had slipped the revolver from Selman's belt before
he left the Wigwam. This seems altogether unreasonable
to me. Professional gunmen were a cautious breed, and
Selman particularly so. Nobody could have 'lifted' his
gun from him without his knowledge any more than he
could have taken the collar from round his neck. And nothing can be more sure than that before he left the room he
knew the butt of a sixshooter was close to his hovering
fingers. He was not a callow amateur, to take chances on
such a vital matter.

In any case, he was buried, and in course of time became a legend. Scarborough walked the streets, observed of all. He was the man who had killed John Selman, a notable honor among pistoleers. A few years later two of the Hole-in-the-Wall gang of train robbers, Will Carver and Kid Curry, shot down Scarborough in New Mexico while trying to escape from a posse. *Sic transit gloria mundi.*

With the turn of the century El Paso shook off its wild and woolly ways. The newspapers and the Chamber of Commerce stressed the fact that the city was modern and progressive, and that it offered great attractions for home-seekers. Bad men became merely criminals and went to the penitentiary. Open gambling was frowned down upon. Guns went out of fashion and football came in. Citizens who had once garnished themselves with pistols carried golf bags instead. The good old days had gone forever.

III

The Vigilantes

ALL frontier communities have had to discover that law is not a lot of words written in a book. In such wild borderlands life and property became safe only when the will of strong men functioned to enforce order. At times this could be made effective solely by extra-legal methods. The early vigilante movements in the West came directly from the people, just as did the rulings of the Witenagemot from the Anglo-Saxon mass council. They stood for justice by direct vote rather than through an official machinery set up to represent the citizens. Such risings ought not in any way to be confounded with lynchings.

The situation in San Francisco after the gold discoveries is an illustration of this. In an incredibly short time a sleepy Mexican province was overrun by gold-hunters who crowded in from all over the world. Among these were many desperadoes, swindlers, and cut-throats. Former convicts poured across the Pacific from Australia. Gamblers and gunmen came by way of the Horn, the Panama, and the plains routes. During the first few years following Sutter's finding of gold there were more than four thousand homicides in California. At the diggings, and often at Los Angeles, Monterey, and San Francisco, one had only such safety as his bowie knife and pistol could guarantee.

The depraved and criminal classes ran wild. Among the worst of the offenders were the ex-convicts from the penal colonies of Great Britain. They became known as 'Sydney ducks.' Footpads and highwaymen infested the streets. In San Francisco there had been many murders and no punishment for the crimes. Honest men were too busy trying to make a fortune to bother with the enforcement of order. So the government had fallen into the hands of corrupt politicians rapidly growing rich by selling city contracts and by bribery from thugs.

Men of all nationalities brushed shoulders at the El Dorado and a dozen other gambling-houses. Life was wild and free. The names of the camps show the happy-go-lucky spirit of '49. Gospel Swamp, Hell's Delight, Whiskey Bar, Humpback Slide, Hit-Up-and-Git, Hangtown, and You Bet were some of the titles of the mushroom camps to which rushes were made. At first there was no robbery in the mining country. A sardine can of nuggets was exposed for a week at one camp where a hundred men could see it and the gold remained untouched. But this immunity did not last long. Thieves and bandits seeped into the back country from San Francisco.

For a decade bands of Mexican and half-breed outlaws preyed upon the country. These originated in the southern counties but after a time extended to the mining districts. The banditti were formidable in number. At one time and another there were many gangs of them. Andreas Armijo, Tomas Maria Carillo, Solomon Pico, and Tiburcio Vasquez were some of the leaders. The most notorious of all was Joaquin Murietta, who was finally run down and killed by Harry Love.

Life was cheap in California and the ownership of property uncertain. Violence was the order of the day. A hundred duels were fought, many with fatal results. California was moving toward a state where every man was a law unto himself. In very many men a shift in morals had developed, owing to the change from life in quiet, religious towns to an environment filled with temptation.

The convicts from Australia and Van Diemen's Land had their headquarters at the foot of Telegraph Hill. From their rendezvous they sallied out at night to rob and prey on decent citizens. They were known as 'the Hounds.' Among them were young men of previously good reputation who had succumbed to vice. Sam Whittaker was the leader. Transported from England for life in 1836, he had by grace of natural fitness become first among the convicts from New South Wales. The man was educated, good-looking, shrewd, and brave. His audacity knew no bounds. His followers more than once set fire to the city in order to make theft easy during the confusion. One of these conflagrations cost six lives and several millions in property.

A clear-cut issue had developed. Either honest men or corrupt scoundrels and murderous robbers must rule San Francisco. No relief could be expected through the regular channels of law, because the politicians in control were in alliance with those who made a business of crime. The worst of it was that there were good men who supported the state and city government which sanctioned the disorder.

Among these was the sheriff, Colonel Jack Hays, the most noted of the early Texas Rangers, a man famous for his blazing and headlong courage. He was a hero with all Texans. Not only had he fought the Indians, but during the Mexican War he had repeatedly distinguished himself. In the army of General Taylor he had been colonel of the First Texans, a regiment which showed the greatest dash at the storming of Fort Soldado and the Bishop's Palace. In thick mist, at three o'clock in the morning, September 22, 1846, Hays had led two hundred of his frontiersmen up the almost perpendicular cliffs of Cerro del Obispado and captured the stronghold. In '49 he had come to the Golden Gate and after a wonderful exhibition of horsemanship on the plaza had been elected sheriff with enthusiasm. He was a slightly built man, wiry, of medium height, temperate, soft-spoken, and modest. For years Hays had been a soldier. It was his business to obey orders. When Governor McDougal and the duly elected authorities opposed the vigilantes Hays lined up with them.

Yet law-abiding citizens realized the existing conditions could not continue. From free institutions flows a love of order that had to find expression in reform. Resolute men stepped forward to head the movement, very well aware that the price of failure would be death for themselves.

Sam Brannan, a Mormon, was one of the leaders of the revolt against the lawlessness. At his office a few intrepid men met to organize the forces of order. Among them were William T. Coleman, James Ward, Gerritt W. Ryck-

Vigilantes Around!!

No More Murders!!!

Behold the fate of this man. The same terrible end awaits all murderers. Life and the public security is too sacred not to be protected, even by a resort to the unpleasant means of Lynch Law.

Take Warning! Take Warning!!

Else, ye murderers, the fate that this brute Schramle has met with awaits you.

By order of Committee of Vigilantes

A Vigilante Notice

man, and William A. Howard. At the very time this group was meeting to extend its membership to other leading citizens, an ex-convict from Australia named John Jenkins robbed a warehouse and started to carry the safe away in a boat. He was caught and brought before the committee.

Jenkins was an old offender. A crowd gathered outside the building, many of those in it belonging to the criminal group. Armed vigilantes held them back from the door. Brannan spoke from an upstairs porch to the mob while the rest of the executive committee of the vigilantes deliberated inside. He was a good rough-and-ready speaker, bold, witty, a master of invective. He jeered at good citizens for their supineness and warned the desperadoes that their day of license was done.

There was some natural hesitation on the part of the committee to invoke the extreme penalty against Jenkins. There were few of them and many hundreds of the riff-raff. Each knew he was risking his life. At the decisive moment Howard put his gun down on the table, looked over his associates, and said, 'Gentlemen, as I understand it, we are here to hang somebody.' That blunt statement turned the tide against the prisoner. The fire bell tolled. Residents poured out to back the vigilantes, and Jenkins was hanged.

The coroner's jury, dominated by the corrupt city ring, found that the deceased had come to his death at the hands of an organization calling itself a vigilance committee. Some of the foremost members were named. The committee answered this attack by publishing at once the full list of one hundred and eighty leading citizens who had signed up as members.

Another 'Sydney duck,' James Stuart, was brought to judgment. He was a handsome, daring young fellow, also an ex-convict, and a leader of the thugs. He was moved from place to place before his execution to keep him out of the hands of the authorities, who were trying to rescue him from those they called 'the Stranglers.' Stuart was cooler than those trying him. 'Damned tiresome, this,' he yawned at one time. 'Can't we get on and finish the business?'

He was taken to the Market Street wharf and hanged from a derrick. Whittaker and a man known as McKenzie were the next two who suffered death at the hands of the vigilantes. Only the four were given capital punishment. Thirty were banished and scores departed, some on outbound boats, others to the mines.

The committee disbanded. It thought its work was done. San Francisco had been reclaimed from the ruffians who ruled it. All over the gold country miners' committees proceeded to clean house. Sluice robbers, murderers, and road agents were hanged. Crime in the back country became less frequent.

As time passed the politicians of San Francisco forgot the lesson of '51. Graft was unbridled, and the official group in control robbed the city right and left. They permitted robbery, in exchange for support from the vicious elements. Murder was again a common occurrence.

The situation was complicated by the growing bitterness between the North and the South on the subject of slavery. Already the line of cleavage in the Democratic Party was evident. There were many in San Francisco who had come from below the Mason and Dixon line, and many others, also Democrats, who hailed from New York and Boston. Senator-elect Broderick was the leader of this faction, but it had little in common with the group from the South. Most of them were hard-boiled roughneck politicians. Locally the two sections of the party were known as the Chivalry and the Shovelry.

The most valiant fighter against the corrupt ring was James King of William, the editor of the *Evening Bulletin*. He exposed the evil conditions and denounced the crooks fearlessly. No threats could deter him.

In November, 1855, United States Marshal Richardson was killed by Charles Cora, a notorious character. The

murderer was arrested and tried. The jury disagreed.
Eleven to one were for conviction. It was accepted by all
that the twelfth juror had been bribed.

King attacked the court officials who had permitted the
bribery. In the same issue of the paper he denounced the
ballot-box stuffers who were stealing elections, naming
particularly James P. Casey, who had been elected supervisor with the aid of the criminal element. The *Bulletin* of
May 14, 1856, published Casey's record as an ex-convict
in New York. The supervisor went to the office of the
paper and demanded of King the reason for the attack.
The editor answered in three words, 'It's the truth.' When
Casey threatened him he put the man out of the building.

Casey shot him in the breast as he was walking home.
Excitement was intense. Street speakers addressed meetings. 'Too many hung juries, not enough hung men,' one
of them cried.

William T. Coleman, who had been at the head of the
first vigilance committee, called some of its members into
conference. The committee was reorganized. Twenty-five
hundred armed men paraded before its headquarters on
Sacramento Street and cheered the organization. Those
opposed to the vigilantes met and called themselves the
Law and Order Party. Some of them were good citizens.
Governor Johnson appointed William Tecumseh Sherman,
at that time engaged in banking, to head the state militia
in opposition to the vigilantes. Sherman could do nothing,
for his troops melted away to join the enemy forces.
Though the vigilance committee had the support of the
public, it cannot be denied that it was an insurgent body.

The authority of the governor and of the courts was ignored. Arms belonging to the government were seized by it, barricades erected, and prisoners held until its purpose was achieved.

Its forces surrounded the jail, trained a cannon on it, and forced the authorities to surrender Casey and Cora. The two men were tried, convicted, and hanged in front of the committee headquarters. The fear instilled by the vigilantes was so great that eight hundred criminals fled from San Francisco.

The committee was active only a few months, and during that time the Law and Order Party opposed its work bitterly, though without success. While an arrest was being made by one of its policemen, David S. Terry, chief justice of the Supreme Court of California, stabbed the officer in the neck with a bowie knife. Terry was held a prisoner by the vigilantes for six weeks and released only when it was sure that his victim would recover.

The chief justice was a hot-blooded Southerner, a fine figure of a man endowed with a striking personality, but so turbulent that he was constantly engaged in physical brawls. United States Senator Broderick had stood his friend during the trouble with the vigilantes, yet some time later the men disagreed and Terry challenged the senator to a duel. Broderick had no wish to fight, and only did so because he was afraid to appear a coward. He was mortally wounded, dying from the effect of the bullet a few days later.

Indignation was so intense that Terry was obliged to resign his office and leave San Francisco. While practicing law he became embroiled with Stephen J. Field, a member of the United States Supreme Court, who sentenced him to six months in jail for contempt of court. It was known that Terry waited for a chance to revenge himself on Field, and the latter engaged Dave Nagle as a bodyguard to protect him.

The men met in the dining-room of a small station. As soon as Terry saw the man whom he considered his enemy he rose from his seat, walked round the counter, and slapped the face of the judge. Nagle drew his gun and shot Terry twice, killing him instantly. The guard was later arrested and put in the San Joaquin County jail charged with murder, and Field was also taken into custody as an accessory but was released on a writ of habeas corpus. Nagle was not convicted.

From California the idea of mass-meeting courts spread to the neighboring states and territories. During the early days in Denver five men were convicted and hanged by people's tribunals. A good many horse thieves were strung up and several criminals were taken from the authorities and lynched by mobs, but these latter may be put in a different category. A vigilance committee of Walla Walla, Washington, hanged six horse thieves. As late as 1882 such a group in Seattle attended the hearing of a murderer, and after the evidence had been heard took the prisoner from the sheriff and executed him. This should come under the head of lynching, since the guilty man was already in the hands of a court ready and willing to assess a proper punishment by the regular lawful means.

The most drastic vigilance committee that ever operated in the West, and one which was dominated throughout (with one possible exception) by first-class citizens exercising restraint and wisdom, functioned in the mining districts of Montana.[1] More than a score of ruffians were executed by the vigilantes of the Montana diggings, but it is known that these desperadoes had murdered not less than a hundred victims while on their way to or from the mines, and there is reason to believe that the number could be doubled and still be within the truth. All these murderers were given a fair trial, unless one counts out that of Joseph A. Slade, and were convicted on evidence which left no chance to doubt their guilt. The seventeenth man hanged by the committee, Alex Carter, made pertinent comment. 'Good work,' he told his judges. 'Not an innocent man hung yet.'

The early gold discoveries in Montana brought the usual motley rush to the diggings. Among those who poured in were miners, merchants, freighters, and workingmen, as well as scores of 'bummers,' prostitutes, gamblers, saloon-keepers, and criminals of all kinds already educated in the California gold fields to prey upon the public.

Lewiston was the capital of the new territory, which included roughly the present states of Idaho, Montana, and even a part of Wyoming. It was the nearest point by the river route to the placer mines of Oro Fino, Florence, and Elk City. As more remote gold fields were discovered the outfitting points shifted to other towns — to Florence, to Bannack, and to Virginia City, Montana.[2]

Each one of these towns was infested by bands of rob-

---

[1] The chief source book on the Montana vigilantes is Thomas J. Dimsdale's *The Vigilantes of Montana.*

[2] It must be kept in mind that there were two towns named Virginia City, one in Nevada and one in Montana. The former was situated at the Comstock Lode diggings, the latter near the Alder Gulch mines in Montana.

bers more or less organized. They had representatives at
all the mining camps who kept them informed of the movements of pack trains, gold shipments on stagecoaches, and
the departure of travelers carrying 'dust' from their
claims. Since dead men tell no tales, it was the custom of
the road agents to murder their victims if there was the
slightest chance that they might later be witnesses against
the plunderers. While not on the trail the outlaws frequented saloons, gambling-halls, and bagnios to fleece the
patrons of these places and to pick up information useful
for subsequent holdups. Conditions became so bad that
honest men dared not protest. Each of them stood alone,
and against him would be arrayed hundreds of the vicious
and the criminal element who would not hesitate to destroy anybody trying to establish law and order. Though
the good people were always numerically greater, lack of
organization made them quite unable to cope with the
villainous social scum preying upon the community. Here
were gathered not only California cut-throats but deserters
from the Union and Confederate Armies, and fugitives
from many states and several countries. Rude courts
were established, but the swaggering ruffians terrorized
witnesses and juries.

The fate of Pat Ford, a saloonkeeper at Lewiston,
deterred others from showing a bold front to the ruffians
who overawed them. Ford was both honest and fearless.
He urged the citizens of his town to stand up to the scoundrels who were running riot. The bandits marked him for
death.

Ford moved to Oro Fino, following the rush ensuant
on a gold strike. The roughs entered his saloon during

his absence, drank heavily, and proceeded to wreck the place. Ford arrived and drove them from the building. Gun in hand, he faced the desperadoes. The men were all old enemies of his at Lewiston. Three of them were Ridgely, Reeves, and Plummer. They opened fire on him. Wounded, he stood his ground and fired back. Twice he hit Ridgely. Plummer stood back of his horse, which was struck by a bullet. Ford emptied both revolvers before he fell dead. He paid with his life for having urged the enforcement of law against the vicious depredators.

To Bannack came, along with many others from Oro Fino, two men in company with each other. One of them was Jack Cleveland, known to be a bad man. Henry Plummer was the other, a person of good address and attractive personality, one destined to play a large part in the history of the Montana gold camps. Shortly after their arrival a young man named Evans was shot for his money while hunting horses that had strayed. Evidence that developed later tended to show that Cleveland was the murderer. The day before the killing he was known to have no money; the day after the crime he showed up in a saloon with plenty. The man was drinking heavily and became abusive.

'I'm chief in this town,' he announced, and said if anybody denied it he was ready to prove it.

He picked on Jeff Perkins, insisting that the latter owed him money. Perkins explained he had paid it months earlier. The drunken man accepted the correction, but kept coming back to his claim later. He waved a pistol, several times pointing it at Perkins. Among those present was Plummer. He told the desperado not to make a fool

of himself, that apparently the debt had been paid. Perkins slipped out of the room, and Cleveland turned his
attention to the others in the saloon, particularly to
Plummer. He was chief, he reiterated, and was afraid
of none of them. Glaring at his former fellow traveler, he
continued to threaten with his revolver.

Plummer jumped to his feet. 'I'm tired of this,' he
cried.

Drawing a revolver, he fired and missed, then fired again
and hit the bully. Cleveland went down, staggered to his
feet again, and received several more bullets. Attracted
by the firing, Hank Crawford and Harry Phleger came
into the saloon and took care of the dying ruffian.

Out of this incident a feud developed between Crawford
and Plummer. More than once the life of Crawford was
saved by his friends. He had been elected sheriff and was
therefore in the bad graces of Bill Hunter, George Ives,
Buck Stinson, Ned Ray, and other scoundrels who were
known to be road agents. No doubt these men fed Plummer's resentment against the new peace officer. On one
occasion Plummer challenged Crawford to draw his weapon
and settle the trouble once for all. The sheriff shook his
head. 'I'm no gunman,' he replied.

Furious at him, Plummer flung out an ultimatum.
'Get out your pistol, if you don't want to be shot down.'

Very steadily the sheriff looked at his foe. 'If that's
your game, you had better shoot me,' he said, and turning
on his heel, walked away.

Crawford could not understand Plummer's persistent
determination to kill him, though the reason was clear
enough later. But he knew he must defend himself or be

killed. He armed himself and walked warily. Usually
Phleger or some other trusted friend stayed close to him.
That there would be a shooting involving the sheriff and
his foe was the general opinion. Crawford ran a butcher
shop and Plummer, armed with a sawed-off shotgun, was
observed watching the place, apparently on the lookout
for a chance to shoot. When they did meet, the sheriff
got in the first blast. The bullet from his rifle struck
Plummer near the elbow and plowed down the arm to
the wrist. Much mortified, Plummer sent his opponent
word that he would be ready in fourteen days to settle
the matter finally.

It happened that Crawford had more pleasant business
on hand. He resigned as sheriff and set off for the East
to get married. Though Plummer was a professional
gambler and naturally was flung with hard characters,
he was well enough thought of to win the election for
sheriff. He chose as deputies Ned Ray and Buck Stinson.
It was not unusual to choose tough gunmen for such
positions, on the theory that when on the side of the law
they would make efficient officers. To these deputies he
added afterward Jack Gallagher and D. H. Dillingham.
Later Plummer served as sheriff at Virginia City also.

Shortly after this time Plummer married and gave up
his riotous habits. He voiced contrition for the wildness
of his youth. Next Thanksgiving Day Judge Edgerton
and his wife ate turkey at the house of the sheriff and his
young bride. Edgerton had been appointed Chief Justice
of the territory by President Lincoln. Colonel and Mrs.
Sanders were also guests on that occasion. The host was
a brilliant talker and held his own with the distinguished

company. He was a slender, lithe, graceful man, not given to boasting or to loud self-assertion.

Meanwhile conditions at the gold fields were growing swiftly worse. Stages were robbed frequently. Miners leaving the diggings to return home disappeared and were never seen again. Holdups were open and flagrant. There was no doubt that the bandits had a close-knit organization, with spies at all the camps. George Lane, known as 'Clubfoot George,' was one. He was a cobbler at Virginia City. Word of any shipment of gold or any departure of successful miners reached the road agents in time for them to station themselves in some gulch where an attack could be safely made. The gang had 'shebangs,' as they were called, rendezvous in out-of-the-way hill pockets, where they could hide out and equip themselves with fresh mounts when they were needed.

But these shebangs were for only occasional use. Many of the miscreants lived in the towns that had grown up around the diggings. They mingled with other citizens on the street and in saloons. Most of them were 'bummers,' men without any visible means of support, but others had occupations they used to camouflage their real business. Observant watchers suspected Bill Hunter, Boone Helm, George Ives, and Buck Stinson long before the evidence against them was conclusive, but other members were considered decent pioneers. Granville Stuart tells a story about Bill Bunton, who was in charge of the ranch used by the stage line as a station. The weather was cold, and Bunton was very hospitable to the passengers who stamped in half-frozen from the coach. He was especially generous with his liquor, and next morning just before the start he appeared with a bottle and a glass to offer a last nip to those going out into the frosty air. Bill himself was going on the stage. From the performance he gave one might guess he had been a ham actor earlier in life. When the road agents galloped up with their order to throw up hands Bill stole the show.

'For God's sake, don't shoot!' he begged. 'Take what I have, but don't kill me. Spare my life, for heaven's sake!' He made far less fuss when the vigilantes strung him up a year or two later.

It became apparent to good citizens that there would be no order or safety in Montana until people's courts were not only organized but backed by strong men willing to risk their lives for the good of the community. Nathaniel P. Langford, Samuel T. Hauser, J. X. Beidler, James Williams, and Colonel Wilbur F. Sanders were already moving under cover toward such a mass government.

A crime occurred at this time which pointed the need of a vigilante committee to back the verdict of a people's court. Among Plummer's deputies was one honest man, Dillingham. He learned that Hayes Lyons, Buck Stinson, and Charles Forbes were going to rob some travelers to Virginia City, and warned one of them. The bandits learned of this and determined to get rid of Dillingham.

All those named were present at a miners' court which was trying a civil case in the open air on the outskirts of Virginia City. Charley Forbes was clerk of the court. He was a handsome, well-educated young fellow, cool, gay, and altogether charming in manner. No more dashing villain could be found in the pages of fiction.

Dillingham had come from Bannack to look for stolen

horses. Stinson and Lyons, who had been lounging in the crowd, came up to the table where Forbes sat and whispered with him. He nodded agreement with what they said. The three men beckoned Dillingham and drew him aside.

Forbes cried, 'Don't shoot!' as though afraid Dillingham were about to fire at him, and at the same time sent a bullet into his chest. The other two murderers pumped slugs into the body of their victim.

The guilty men were arrested and tried. Forbes was given a separate hearing because of what he had cried out and of the fact that his pistol was found to be loaded, owing to the kindness of Jack Gallagher who had reloaded it secretly. Prior to the trials Haze Lyons asked that his companions be released as he alone was guilty. He no doubt hoped that they would arrange a rescue for him.

During the trial of Lyons and Stinson carpenters were busy building a scaffold. The two men were convicted and sentenced to be hanged. Forbes was an eloquent speaker. He made the most of the points in his favor — his cry, 'Don't shoot,' and the still loaded pistol. His references to his mother drew tears from the women present. So potent was his appeal that he won an acquittal.

The other two were put into a wagon and taken to the scaffold. Lyons begged for mercy, while Stinson jeered at him. Women joined in the tears of the condemned man. Somebody read aloud a letter Lyons had written in farewell to his mother. His friends called for another vote. This was decided upon, and by some hocus-pocus the count was in favor of the criminals.

'That frees them!' Jack Gallagher cried. 'Let 'em go, boys.'

There were shouts for and against this, and in the confusion the guilty men mounted horses that were conveniently near and galloped away.

The result of this miscarriage of justice, the second of its kind in the Montana gold fields, strengthened the determination of the friends of order to put teeth in the decisions of the people's courts.

George Ives was of the very stuff of which desperadoes are made. The man was strong, fearless, implacably cruel. He was so reckless that he boasted of his crimes. Shortly after the fiasco at the trial of the Dillingham murderers Ives, assisted by Bob Zachery and 'Whiskey Bill' Graves, robbed the Salt Lake stage at a point beyond Stone's ranch. Next day Ives was bragging in a honky-tonk that he had made Tom Caldwell, the stage-driver, throw up his hands. A little later he killed in cold blood a man suspected of having betrayed the names of the road agents. Before his victim had been buried he shot down Nicholas Tiebalt, to rob him of the money obtained from the sale of a span of mules. A posse arrested Ives at one of the shebangs of the outlaws. With him at the time were Bob Zachery, John Cooper, Bill Graves, and Alexander Carter, all of whom were later picked up, tried, and executed by the vigilantes for their crimes. Ives was taken to Nevada City and locked up.

The outlaws sent 'Clubfoot George' to Bannack with a message urging Plummer to come and demand that Ives be turned over to him for trial by the civil authorities. Thousands of miners gathered from Virginia City and other mining camps to take part in the proceedings. The hearing was conducted in a fair and orderly manner.

Colonel Sanders was chief counsel for the prosecution. Hitherto it had been the custom for the lawyer representing the people to press the case tepidly for fear of vengeance from the outlaws, but Sanders showed no fear. He knew that many of those present were friends of the accused, but he knew too that the time had come for honest men to show their colors boldly. After presenting the evidence concisely, he urged forcibly that justice be done on this man who was proved to be guilty of both robbery and murder.

From first to last there was not a break in the cool bravado of the road agent. During the ride to Nevada he had taken advantage of carelessness on the part of his captors to make a dash for liberty. After a long chase he was run down and forced to come out from the rocks among which he had hidden.

'Almost got away that time, boys,' he said, grinning cheerfully. 'You'll have to keep better guard than that.'

As the trial progressed he must have seen that those who had it in charge meant business, but he showed far less concern than any of the hundreds present who waited tensely to see the issue.

The verdict was guilty.

'The Stranglers won't dare hang him,' a voice shouted.

Sanders was already on a box, his hand lifted for silence. He moved that without any delay the sentence be executed and the prisoner hanged by the neck. Inspired by the inflexible boldness of the prosecutor, the miners voted 'Aye!' with a shout. But even as Ives was being led to an improvised scaffold scores were shouting protests. Some wanted to banish him. Others yelled threats of vengeance. The guard pushed the condemned man steadily forward.

After the bandit had declared his innocence Sanders cried with a clear, ringing voice, 'Men, do your duty.'

Ives paid the penalty for his crimes.

The criminal element was stunned at this swift justice. Carter, Bill Bunton, and several others left at once and were pursued. The party would have been captured if Erastus Yager had not carried to them a message of warning written by George Brown at Virginia City. Yager and Brown were arrested and tried. Proof that they were members of the gang was given and a conviction followed. Before his execution Yager gave the vigilantes a list of the cut-throats, who had slaughtered more than a hundred citizens, together with a description of his place in the organization.

Chief of the cut-throats was Henry Plummer, his lieutenant Bill Bunton. Cyrus Skinner was a fence and spy, as was also 'Clubfoot George.' Bill Hunter and Hayes Lyons were lookout men, whose job was to keep informed of gold shipments and the movements of travelers. The secretary of the gang was George Brown. John Wagner and Carter kept the shebangs and looked after the horses needed on raids. Ives had been one of the leaders. Jack Gallagher, Boone Helm, Steve Marshland, Whiskey Bill Graves, Bob Zachery, Gad Moore, John Cooper, Bill Terwiliger, and Buck Stinson were used for road work, though the others also could be called upon for holdups. The password was 'Innocent,' and they wore neckties fastened in sailor's knots to recognize one another.

Some of the leading vigilantes were not surprised to

learn that Plummer was at the head of the bandits. He had been under suspicion for some time, and it had been discovered that he had killed and robbed in other camps prior to his arrival at Bannack. Looking back on his early days in Montana, it was easy to see now that he had killed Cleveland because the latter knew of his record and had been threatening to talk. His bitter animosity against Crawford had been due to the fear that Cleveland might have divulged to the sheriff before his death information connecting Plummer with these earlier crimes.

He was arrested, together with Ray and Stinson, while preparing to leave the territory. Plummer was at first very cool and composed. The claim that he was a bandit appeared to amuse him. He was a leading citizen of the community, a law officer sworn to run down crime. His protestations did not help him. He was hanged on a gallows he had himself built. Ned Ray and Buck Stinson were executed before their chief. Plummer took off his necktie and tossed it to a boy who boarded at the same house with him. 'A souvenir of the occasion,' he said.

On the next day a posse went to the cabin of Joe Pizanthia to arrest him for investigation. He shot two of the party, killing one. Immediately afterward he was eliminated by the posseman he had wounded. Within the next three weeks fifteen more of the desperadoes had been arrested, tried, and hanged. The places of punishment included Bannack, Virginia City, Deer Lodge, Frenchtown, Fort Owens, and Hell Gate. Those sent to the gallows included nearly all the members of the Plummer gang.

Many examples of individual courage were shown by citizens during this trying time. Neil Howie arrested at

great personal risk 'Dutch John' Wagner, a desperate and
ferocious character, after twenty men in a wagon train
declined to help him. Hill Beachy followed the murderers
of Lloyd Magruder from Montana to San Francisco,
tracing them step by step. He dragged them back to
Lewiston and saw them executed after due process of law.

Five of the murderers were hanged side by side at Virginia City. George Lane was the first. He caught sight
of somebody he knew, called 'Good-bye, old fellow,' and
jumped from the box on which he was standing.

'One gone to hell,' Boone Helm said. Of all the abandoned ruffians in the gang Helm was probably the worst.
He watched Gallagher's jerking body. 'Kick away,' he
jeered. 'Be with you in hell in a minute.' A moment later
he shouted: 'Every man for his principles. Hurrah for
Jeff Davis!'

The ruffians met their fate in various ways. 'Red'
Yager died bravely, admitting that he deserved the punishment. Others were quiet and composed. Some cursed and
swore and pleaded. Perhaps the one who showed the
most callous indifference was George Shears. As he stood
with the rope around his neck, on an upper rung of a
ladder, he said, 'Do I jump or slide off?' and added, in
explanation, 'I've never been hung before, you know.'

The last victim of the Montana vigilantes was Joseph
A. Slade. The case stands by itself. Slade was in no way
connected with the Plummer outfit. He was an honest
man and a vigilante. In earlier years he had performed
an excellent service in managing several hundred miles
of stage line through a country infested by hostile Indians
and wild horse thieves. But he had let himself become a

victim of drink, and while under the influence of it was dangerous to all who came near him. His carousals put too many residents of the mining camps in fear of his drunken explosions. After a particularly violent one, during which he had defied the authority of the miners' court set up by the vigilantes, he ended his life on the gallows. The best men in the community would have preferred banishment, but the miners who had poured in from the smaller towns to Virginia City would have none of that. Though Slade had killed nobody since coming to Montana, his record as a bad man was against him. It was safer to make sure he could not exact vengeance from individuals later.

Mining camps had no facilities for keeping prisoners. An offender could be whipped, banished, or executed, but he could not be held for any length of time under guard. Nor was it feasible to take him back to 'the States' for punishment. If the verdicts of frontier people's courts sometimes seemed drastic, the difficulties of the time and place should be considered. Law and order had to be fought for, in order to save the free institutions that came to these pioneers from their fathers.

The leaders of the vigilantes of Montana were representative citizens driven reluctantly to punitive action in order to save the young settlements from complete degeneration. Some of those they brought to judgment were 'good fellows' in a superficial way, men whom they met daily and brushed shoulders against on the street as they passed with a pleasant greeting. It is on record that scores of men walked away from these open-air tribunals white-faced and shaken in spirit because young fellows they knew had brought themselves to such an end. Yet those who supported the people's courts had no doubt whatever that they had done their duty.

Many of the foremost men of Montana during the succeeding decades were prominent in the vigilante movement. Samuel T. Hauser was appointed governor of the Territory by President Grover Cleveland. One of the state's first senators at Washington was Colonel Wilbur F. Sanders. The author of *Vigilante Days and Ways*, Nathaniel P. Langford, was for many years a national-bank examiner for the Pacific Coast country. Neil Howie, John X. Beidler, and John Fetherstun, though never prominent in a financial or a political way, could always be depended upon to contribute to better ways of life for their towns. At Helena, in the state capital, is a tablet to the memory of James Williams, who acted as a fearless executive officer of the vigilante committee. It reads:

> The sluice was left unguarded
> When Williams' work was done,
> And trails were safe for honest men
> Through victories he had won.

A curious fact in connection with the members of the Plummer gang is that more than one half of them came from good families and had received excellent early training. Some were well educated. Plummer and Forbes were men who might have made their mark in any community if their energies had been turned in the right direction. The freedom of life in the early West had a disastrous effect on many. Under the temptation of saloons, gambling-houses, and brothels the weakness in their moral fiber showed itself. The glitter of gold dust dazzled their eyes. Looking for an easier way of winning it than hard work, they began fleecing the patrons of these resorts and stepped outside the law. Graduating into footpads and road agents, they were forced to murder to protect the secret of their method of livelihood. Human nature has not changed since Virgil many centuries ago wrote the pregnant line, '*Facilis descensus Averni.*'

IV

Gold in Them Thar Hills

GOLD was the magic word that laid the foundations of Denver. In the spring of '59 there was a grand stampede for the Rockies from 'the River,' which in those days always meant the Missouri. Four trails led to the 'Pike's Peak country.' The northern one followed the South Platte, the southern the old Santa Fe route. Between these were the Smoky Hill River road and the one along the Republican.

The stage from Leavenworth to Denver took this last path. On the Concord coach arrived Horace Greeley and Albert D. Richardson, a first-class progenitor of the Ernie Pyle type of journalist. In his book, *Beyond the Mississippi*, Richardson records that the stage passed ten thousand travelers on the way. The dusty road was dotted with the white covered wagons. At night hundreds of campfires flung up their smoke. If necessary one could have traced the trail by the cook stoves, picks, shovels, and bedsteads tossed away to lighten the load, by broken-down wagons, by the skeletons of worn-out horses and oxen, by the graves of emigrants who never reached the Promised Land.

All kinds of conveyances brought the fortune-seekers. They came in wagons and carts and broughams, on horseback, in wheeled ships rigged up with sails to catch the wind. They pushed and pulled handcarts. They packed supplies on their own backs. Nothing like this had been seen since the great California excitement ten years earlier.

To Greeley, Denver must have seemed a dreary spot for the stage terminal. It was a town of shacks. There were no women except the squaws of the Arapahoes, who hovered on the edge of town in tepees surrounded by horses, dogs, and children. The emigrants wore tattered buckskin breeches, slouch hats, and woollen shirts from which the pattern had long since vanished. A good many of them were in moccasins. Nearly all carried knives and revolvers. They were a queer conglomerate of humanity, and a considerable percentage of them sloughed rapidly the refinements of the civilization they had left. The dust was six inches deep on the streets and the wind blew a good deal. It was impossible to stay immaculately clean, and some of the inhabitants decided to go Indian and not try.

Even those who held to their self-respect adopted the jargon of the locale. Bayard Taylor, one of Colorado's earliest tourists, noticed that a house was always called a shebang. A man did not shout; he 'let a yell out of him.' One who made a blunder 'cut open a dog.' If one wanted pie in a restaurant and there was none left, the waiter announced, 'The pie's played out.'

Few of the early residents ran to fat. The nature of the country set a premium on leanness. Most of the settlers at one time or another scraped the bottom of the barrel.

An advertisement in newspapers for mail-carriers to ride the Indian country stressed this point.

> *Wanted.* — Young, skinny, wiry fellows not over 18. Must be expert riders, willing to face death daily. Orphans preferred. Wages, $25 per week. Apply, Central Overland Pony Express.

The office was crowded with applicants to enter this suicide club.

Greeley was the best friend the West had in the East. He was invited to speak in the great gaming-hall of the Denver House. The bartenders served no whiskey and the faro dealers shuffled no cards while Horace gave a blunt talk on the evils of drink and gambling, to which good-humored attention was paid. When he had finished, the rattling of chips and the pouring of liquor began again immediately. Oldtimers say that ninety per cent of the early population gamed. Men who had been church deacons at home succumbed to the wild freedom of the West. The sheriff pawned his guns for money with which to play.

The real-estate dealers had been very active. Already four town sites had been laid out in the district that now lies within the city limits. Their names were Montana, St. Charles, Auraria, and Denver. Presently there was to be another on the other side of the Platte, the town of Highlands. Bitter rivalries sprang up, with occasional bloodshed. For the Pike's Peakers had large ideas. Each bit of platted ground was to be the center of a great metropolis that would spring up around it. Before the infant town on Cherry Creek was a year old its citizens had drawn up a constitution and were knocking on the doors of Congress to be admitted as the Territory of Jefferson.

In Auraria on the west side of Cherry Creek and Denver on the east there were perhaps a thousand inhabitants. The population was a strange mixture of half-breeds, Mexicans, Indians, and whites. Among the latter were trappers, speculators, gamblers, bad men, crooks, politicians, miners, and business men. As nearly always in a frontier country, the law did not function effectively. The Pike's Peak district was an appanage of Kansas, and between the two stretched four hundred miles of desert.

Life was of the simplest. The floors were of dirt and there were no glass windows in the cabins. Stools and tables were rudely fashioned by the owner. Boxes served for cupboards. Pole bedsteads were usual. Most cabins had adobe fireplaces and sod roofs. Food was expensive, since it had to be brought across the plains. There were few luxuries. From New Mexico came Dick Wootten, old scout and trail-builder, with a wagonload of 'Taos lightning' to burn out the stomachs of the reckless drinkers in Auraria. He erected the finest store there, with a hall above for town meetings. It had the first glass window in the settlement. Jim Beckwourth spent much of his time lounging there. Jim was a famous old trapper who wrote a book filled with his mythical exploits. He did not stay in Denver long after he killed a negro prizefighter for paying too much court to his wife. After his acquittal he returned to the mountains which had long been his habitat.

Already Denver had a good newspaper, the *Rocky Mountain News*, which appeared first April 23, 1859, and after eighty years still serves the people faithfully. William N. Byers was its editor and owner. David Moffat, who later built the railroad which bears his name, ran a small bookstore where one could buy the latest novel of Charles Dickens. A school had been established by C. J. Goldrick. Father Machebeuf was raising money for a church. The private mint of Clark, Gruber & Co. turned out ten- and twenty-dollar gold pieces. The town was busy as an ant hill on a warm spring day. Ox and mule teams flung up clouds of dust as they moved along the streets. The sound of the bull whip, heard frequently, was like the crack of a revolver.

Odd specimens of humanity always appear at mining stampedes. Into the Elephant Corral, after having driven some hundred miles in an outfit pulled by oxen, stepped 'Professor' Goldrick attired in silk hat, 'boiled' shirt, kid gloves, and Prince Albert coat, a bullwhacker's whip in his hand and a degree from Trinity College, Dublin, in his pocket. Could one obtain refreshment for the outer and inner man, he inquired? The corral wrangler scratched his head at that one and passed.

After a term at school-teaching Goldrick graduated to the *Rocky Mountain News* as reporter and city editor. His pomposity reached its apogee in an account of the Cherry Creek flood which deluged Denver and caused the loss of several lives:

> About the midnight hour of Thursday the nineteenth instant, when almost all in town were knotted in the peace of sleep, deaf to all noise and blind to all danger, snoring in calm security, and seeing visions of remoteness radiant in the rainbow hues of past associations, or roseate with the gilded hopes of the fanciful future — while the full-faced

Denver Public Library Western Collection

WAGON TRAIN IN CAMP FORMATION ON HOLLADAY
(NOW MARKET) STREET IN DENVER
1866

queen of night shed showers of silver from the starry throne
down o'er the fields of freshness and fertility, garnishing
and suffusing sleeping Nature with her balmy brightness,
fringing the feathery cottonwoods with luster, enameling
the housetops with coats of pearl, bridging the erst placid
Platte with beams of radiance, and bathing the arid sands
of Cherry Creek with dewy beauty — a frightful phenom-
enon sounded in the distance, and a shocking calamity
presently charged upon us. The few who had not retired to
bed broke from their buildings to see what was coming.
Hark, what and where is this? A torrent or a tornado? And
where can it be coming from or whither going? These were
the questions soliloquized and spoken, one to the other.
Has Creation's God forsaken us, and has Chaos come again?
Our ears might bewilder and our eyes deceive, but our
hearts, all trembling, and our sacred souls soon whispered
what it was — the thunder of omnipotence warning us
'there's danger on the wing,' with death himself seeming
to prompt our preparation for the terrible alternative of
destruction or defense; presently the great noise of mighty
waters, like the roaring of Niagara or the rumbling of an
enraged Etna, bursts upon us distinctly and regularly, in its
sounding steps, as the approach of a tremendous train of
locomotives.

That was only the lead to the story. Goldrick's account
poured on, paragraph after paragraph, as overwhelming as
the flood itself, to a sonorous and alliterative finale.

Denver was to the gold-seekers merely a stopping-point
to and from the diggings at Gregory Gulch or Buckskin
Joe or Tarryall. It was filled with hard characters and
thugs. Stabbings and shootings, robberies and murders
were of everyday occurrence. Every fourth or fifth building along the business streets housed a gambling-den or a
drinking-place. The largest was the Elephant Corral: one

of the worst the Criterion, owned and run by Charley Harrison, a notorious gunman and killer possessed of engaging qualities. Ed Chase started one on Blake Street and at the grand opening had it blest with prayer by the Reverend William Chivington, presiding elder of the Methodist Church in the district. Chivington's chief claim to fame came a little later. He was commander of the Colorado regiment engaged in the Sand Creek massacre, afterward bitterly denounced as a murderous outrage by a joint Special Committee of Congress.

In his book, *Here They Dug the Gold*, George F. Williston quotes Greeley's opinion that there were more brawls, fights, and pistol shots with criminal intent in this log town of one hundred and fifty dwellings than in any community of equal numbers on earth. A gang known as 'the bummers' banded together to rob and steal openly and insolently. When they helped themselves to the Christmas turkeys brought to town by a rancher, good citizens grew irate and hurried to a public meeting called by Sheriff W. H. Middaugh. Resolutions were passed ordering half a dozen of the worst thugs to leave town under penalty of death if they remained. Among them was 'Buckskin Bill' Karl, who had recently killed a negro slave who did not belong to him. The desperadoes congregated openly at the Criterion and derided the friends of law and order. Twice that evening Middaugh was shot at by gunmen. Rangers were called out to patrol the town. Harrison decided not to force the issue and advised the ruffians named to leave.

The crisis brought out strong men on both sides. Sheriff Middaugh and Editor Byers were the leaders of the party

opposed to the desperadoes. Charles Harrison ruled and
supported the riffraff element.

Harrison was a handsome man with dark hair and fine
silky beard. His clothes were the best obtainable, his cus-
tom-made boots always perfectly polished. From the
South, he had the courteous manner and the soft voice of
his section. A friendly indolence marked his demeanor.
Men called him an honest fighter because he did not kill
without warning. Bat Masterson wrote of him, in the
magazine *Human Life*, that he was the most brilliant pistol shot he had ever seen and far more deadly than most of
the great gun-fighters. While in Denver he shot three men
and hanged one. An escaping murderer was galloping
wildly down the street and the gambler nonchalantly
dropped him from his horse with a bullet from his
pistol.

Shortly after this Harrison killed a patron in the Criterion who was annoying him. The man was well known,
and there were loud threats of vengeance. Middaugh hurried to the saloon and found it closed. He was admitted
when he knocked. Present were several score of cut-
throats garnished with weapons. They surged about the
sheriff threateningly. The two coolest men present were
Middaugh and Harrison. The gambler quieted his followers and agreed to surrender if guaranteed protection. At
the subsequent trial the jury disagreed. Harrison had arranged that beforehand.

To show that he had no prejudice against informal
courts, Harrison hanged a scamp who had shot one of his
friends. He did not trouble to call a people's meeting. The
Criterion crowd served as judge, jury, and executioners.

Harrison's next victim was a negro bullwhacker, also a patron of the Criterion.

The entire summer of '60 was given to violence. At all hours the crack of the sixshooter could be heard. To meet the emergency a people's tribunal was formed. William Young deliberately assassinated Moses West by means of a load of buckshot. He was tried publicly, convicted, and executed next day. A young engineer, James A. Gordon, well-educated, and pleasant and agreeable when sober, ran amuck with drink and started a personal reign of terror. He killed a bartender, Frank O'Neil, in Auraria, shot twice at another ruffian and killed a dog. In Denver he shot up the Elephant Corral, wandered here and there, still drinking and shooting, and finished his jamboree by killing another bartender named John Gantz. Middaugh had been out of town, and came back in time to hear the bad news.

The *Rocky Mountain News* came out with a blast against the wave of murders, naming especially the crimes of Gordon and the killing of the negro Stark by Harrison. Three desperadoes abducted Byers from the *News* office and hurried him down to the Criterion. Two of them were guilty of murders in Denver. The third was George Steele, who had already been ordered several times to leave the country. Harrison had an instinct which told him when his men were going too far. He slipped the editor out of a side door and saw that he got back safely to his office. Steele was not satisfied. On horseback he returned to the *News* office and fired several shots at those inside. Byers and his men returned the fire and wounded the bad man. As Steele rode away two citizens jumped their ponies and pursued. One of them, Tom Pollock, caught up with him and filled the outlaw full of buckshot.

Middaugh set off in pursuit of Gordon. After a chase of several hundred miles he arrested his man in the Indian Territory and dragged him back to Leavenworth. An infuriated mob of Germans attempted to take the prisoner from Middaugh and another officer named Armstrong. The crowd surged around them, trying to drag Gordon from the two who had him in charge. Middaugh and Armstrong fought with their fists, with the barrels of their revolvers, and with their feet to save the murderer. The clothes were torn from all three of them. More than once a rope was flung around the neck of the killer, only to be tossed off by Middaugh. Bruised and bleeding, the sheriff and his assistant at last got their man to safety.

The authorities refused to let Middaugh take Gordon to Denver because he had not brought with him sufficient evidence of the man's guilt. Back to Denver went Middaugh alone to get the evidence. A few days later he stepped from the stage again at Leavenworth. Gordon was turned over to him and he returned with the fellow to the gold camp town.

There was a good deal of talk among the bummers of rescuing Gordon. Among the noisiest of these was Tom Warren. He challenged Dick Whitsett to a duel, and received the answer that Whitsett was in favor of hanging him too but did not consider him worth a duel. He then challenged William N. Byers for reflecting on his character in the *News*. The answer of the editor was that the desperadoes could murder him if they chose, but he did not intend to help them do it by standing up to be shot at by one of the ruffians.

The people's court was presided over by A. C. Hunt, later a governor of Colorado Territory. Attorneys for the prosecution and the defense were appointed, and the trial was held in the open air in front of the Tremont House. Gordon was found guilty. He requested that Middaugh take charge of the hanging. Jim Gordon was a strikingly handsome young man with flaxen hair, blue eyes, splendid physique, and pleasant manners. Many in the town felt sorry for him, but he had to pay the penalty of his crimes.

Two years later Middaugh was shot near Julesburg, Colorado, from ambush while on his way east. His assassin was never known, but the general opinion was that the deed was done by some one of the cut-throats the sheriff had run out of Denver.

Altogether the people's court of Denver hanged five men in '59 and '60. In addition to these a good many horse-thieves were lynched. One rustler confessed and implicated a member of the city council and one of the territorial legislative assembly. All three of them were suspended from cottonwoods. On one occasion six horse-thieves were hanged on Plum Creek, a few miles from town.

There was much less lawlessness at the mining camps than there was in Denver. A few killings took place. If the fatality occurred after a fair fight nothing was done about it. In the case of a cold-blooded murder a miners' court tried the guilty party and executed judgment. A thief convicted of stealing anything valuable was given thirty lashes and run out of camp. If there were mitigating circumstances he might be let off with having one side of his head shaven. The thugs and desperadoes never ran the mining camps as they did Denver.

Since they were used to local government in the states
from which they came, the residents of the Pike's Peak
country were determined to have it in their new home.
They tried to cut through legal knots by the vote of a convention held at Auraria, in April, 1859. It was resolved
that henceforth this should no longer be a part of Kansas
Territory but the State of Jefferson. A constitution was
drawn up for the new state. Those were rough-and-ready
days. One of the delegates wrote an account of the proceedings, which appeared in the Nebraska City *News* of
November 12, 1859.

'If old Jimmy Buchanan does not like it he can whistle,'
the writer commented. 'We ask no odds of him or of his
Congress for the present.... Thus far the general govern-
ment have done exactly nothing for us. We have no mail.
... We have no Indian agent ... no troops to defend us.
... We are not even given a government.'

When at last Congress did act the new territory was
named Colorado and not Jefferson. The parties were in
too bitter conflict to honor a Democrat.

As in the rest of the country, Denver and the diggings
were greatly agitated by the growing war clouds. A large
minority of the Pike's Peak residents were Southerners,
and quarrels about secession were frequent. There were
several formal duels. Five hundred spectators lined up on
the east bank of Cherry Creek to see Richard Ed Whitsett
and W. P. McClure shoot at each other with Colt's army
revolvers at ten paces. The latter was severely wounded in
the hip. Both men were prominent in the community.
McClure was postmaster, an appointee of President
Buchanan. He was a partisan of the South, and very much

a firebrand. His name appears in the paper a little later because he took two pot shots at Goldrick, who in hurried flight won a world's record for covering a hundred yards in a silk hat and double-breasted coat. The current account in the *News* did not mention whether it was the professor's literary style that offended the postmaster. Later McClure had trouble with E. W. Wynkoop [1] about delivering mail to the latter until his box rent was paid. Wynkoop promptly challenged him, and a duel was arranged. It is said that McClure had a friend drop in on Wynkoop to mention to him casually that the postmaster could hit larks on the wing, whereupon Wynkoop said grimly, 'Larks don't have guns.' He gave a little demonstration of his own by tossing a silver dollar in the air and hitting it with a bullet while in motion. The friend duly reported to McClure, who decided to send an apology. After the war started most of the secession element departed to enlist with the Confederacy. Though it is not certain, there is evidence to show that both McClure and Harrison were killed by Indians in Kansas while returning to the gold fields to attempt to arouse the Rocky Mountain region in behalf of the South.

At the Broadwell House a dinner was given by a man named Conklin to a dozen friends. Champagne was drunk and politics were discussed. In the course of a toast Lucien W. Bliss, secretary of state for the new territory, made reflections on Doctor J. S. Stone, a member of the legislature. Immediately Stone left the room and sent a challenge to the man whom he felt had wronged him. Bliss accepted the challenge and named double-barreled shot-

[1] A business street in Denver still bears the name of Wynkoop.

guns at forty paces as the weapons. They met on the banks of the Platte. The secretary of state was a stout man of medium height, his opponent a slim, tall man of soldierly bearing. Both were young, both bachelors. While the seconds were arranging positions Bliss twice raised his weapon and coolly sighted his adversary. At the first fire Stone fell, desperately wounded. He lingered in great pain for some weeks and then died.

Lynn Perrico, in a thesis for a Ph.D. degree at the University of Colorado, showed a photostat of a challenge to a duel printed at Central City, Colorado, four years later by an irate lawyer. The offending party was a judge who had refused the client of the lawyer bail.

> Knowing his conduct to be Infamously tyrannical, and in violation of all law [so the poster read] I determined on Sunday morning that the Scoundrel's Fear should grant what justice demanded. . . . I addressed to him the following note, to which up to this date he has made no reply.
>
> *Sir:* I demand from you an apology by the hands of the bearers of this note, Joseph A. Thatcher and Thomas R. Sanders, or by some other friend whom you may select, for the ungentlemanly manner with which you treated me yesterday, and I also demand from you assurances of professional and gentlemanly conduct for the future.
>
> I am, etc.,
>
> To Hon. Charles Lee Armour.   James M. Cavanaugh
> Believing myself to be entirely justified in my course, I do hereby Pronounce and POST Charles Lee Armour, judge of the Third Judicial District of Colorado Territory,

A LIAR AND A COWARD

> Dated at Central City, Sept. 22, 1863.
> James M. Cavanaugh

The mountains swarmed with prospectors who scraped away with pick and shovel at thousands of hillsides and washed pans of dirt in every creek. The discovery of each new camp started a stampede to locate a claim there. Towns sprang up like mushrooms. There were four in South Park — Tarryall, Hamilton, Jefferson City, and Fairplay. Each grew to sizable places containing several thousand inhabitants. All of them except the last named have completely vanished. Not a brick or a tin can remains to identify the site of a dozen vanished camps in Colorado where were buried the hopes of so many eager miners. Marysville, in Chaffee County, once was a city of ten thousand. It is now a vacant spot in the wilderness. Buckskin Joe flourished greatly. Nothing is left of it now but the crumbling foundations of Tabor's store.

The Rockies are full of cities of the dead. Ghost towns, they are called. Montgomery, Gothic, Nevadaville, Oro City, California Gulch, Sugar City were a few of those which had their day and ceased to be. Years ago I looked through the dusty windows of a drugstore in a deserted town. A stock of drugs in glass bottles still stood on the shelves. Dust and decay were everywhere. Old newspapers of an earlier decade littered the floor. Ashes of the last fire were still in the stove. What had become of the owner? Why had he left the store, the stock of goods, the furnishings? Nobody knew. Perhaps he had joined a rush to a new camp and found better luck on a hazard of new fortune. Perhaps Death had locked the door.

Most of these ghost cities had for many years one or two oldtimers who hung on buoyed by the hope that the days of glory would some day return. They could not be-

lieve the mines were played out. A few more feet of drilling
would bring another bonanza. At Gothic, Colorado, the
ghost city of the Elk Mountains, one old bearded man remained for forty years. His name was Judd. He spent his
time dreaming of the days in the early eighties when six
thousand feet tramped the now deserted streets. As late
as '29 Leonard Nichols lived alone in Nevadaville. The
widow of Tabor, the one-time multimillionaire, remained
for years in a cabin close to the shaft of the once-great
Matchless Mine. She was poor and desolate but indomitable. From others she wanted no help. The Matchless was
coming back. It had produced millions and if rightly operated would do so again. There she was found dead not
many years ago by a neighbor who had climbed Fryer Hill
to take her supplies.

Yet there had been a time when everything that
H. A. W. Tabor touched turned to gold. He was running
a country store when the Little Pittsburg brought him millions. The New Discovery added another fortune. So did
the Matchless. He had an interest in a score of other
mines. Tabor became Colorado's most prominent citizen.
He was mayor of Leadville, lieutenant governor, United
States senator. He built an opera house at Leadville and
one in Denver. The one in Denver was the finest theater
in the country west of Chicago. It was suggested that
Shakespeare's picture be hung above the curtain. Tabor
vetoed this. 'Who is Shakespeare?' he wanted to know.
'What did he ever do for Colorado? Put my picture
there.'

His money went almost as fast as it came. He was generous and recklessly extravagant. Foolish investments

undermined his capital. His vanity would not let him re-
trench. When Eugene Field was a newspaper man on the
old *Tribune* in Denver he delighted in poking fun at Tabor's follies. One day he had the cartoonist do a picture of
Tabor, shivering in bare shanks in front of a large safe
while he tried to remember the combination so that he
could get out of it one of the hundred-dollar nightgowns he
had put there for safekeeping. I can remember him as an
old man, even then almost forgotten by the new generation, walking feebly along the streets of Denver supported
by Baby Doe, his wife.

The sight of him, a weak and broken man, brought to
mind forcibly the verses of Charles Kingsley stamped on
the curtain of his own Tabor Grand theater curtain:

> So fleet the works of man
> Back to the earth again,
> Ancient and holy things
> Fade like a dream,
> And the hand of the master is dust.[1]

For many years the leading industry in Colorado was
mining. At one time Central City had a larger population
than Denver. That was true also of Leadville at a later
date. A decade ago Central City was almost a ghost town.
One or two mines operated feebly. There were a boarding-
house and a store. The partial revival of the place has been
due to the sentimental interest of oldtimers who have
established a play festival of national interest that oper-
ates two or three weeks each summer. Leadville is now
about one-tenth the size it was in its heyday.

[1] The last verse of the stanza is omitted from the Tabor Grand curtain.

The first little villages in the Pike's Peak region had scarcely started before pioneer farmers were beginning to cultivate the river valleys. On the Huerfano and the Arkansas Rivers, on the Platte and the Cache la Poudre, crops of wheat, corn, barley, potatoes, beans, and small vegetables were being raised as early as 1860. W. M. Pierson was milking over a hundred cows to supply butter and cheese for the mines and small settlements. A year later John W. Iliff, later to become known as the 'Cattle King of Colorado,' bought his first herd and ranged it on the native grasses. He built up his holdings until he controlled about 650,000 acres of land, upon which ran vast herds of Texas longhorns. After the death of Iliff a large British corporation, called the Prairie Cattle Company, was organized. Its property comprised three vast ranches. The Colorado division covered 2,240,000 acres, about 3500 square miles. Nearly 60,000 cattle fed on this domain. The Oklahoma ranch of the company was even larger. The headquarters of the Texas branch was at Tascosa, a wild town in its day.

The early mining camps were more orderly than the end-of-the-railroad villages and the trail-end towns on the plains. Not until the bonanza days attracted thugs, desperadoes, gunmen, and professional gamblers did Creede and Leadville get reputations for lawlessness. Central City and Aspen and Breckenridge never were bad towns.

But the high plains settlements along the railroads were wild from the start. Kit Carson, Julesburg, and Trail City (a vanished settlement on the site where Holly now stands) were all outposts of vice. Julesburg in particular rivaled the famous Kansas cattle-shipping towns. It had been a tough spot in the days of the pony express, and it grew no tamer when the longhorn herds came from Texas.

In pony-express times Julesburg, situated on the South Platte, was a raw village of sod houses and shacks. Here the trail forked. The gold-hunters continued up the Platte toward the diggings, and the Oregon Trail outfits struck through Fort Laramie for the Northwest.

Jules Reni had founded the town and was its most prominent citizen. Naturally he was made division agent for the company. The choice was not a happy one, for though influential in the community Jules was lazy, domineering, and quarrelsome. Gangs of horse-thieves were numerous, and he had too many friends among them. During his régime thefts of stock were very numerous. Because of poor management the stage was usually late.

The stage company removed Reni and put Joseph A. Slade in his place. Slade was a remarkable man. Fearless, energetic, rigidly honest, and very faithful to the interests of his employers, he was in some respects an ideal man for such a place. His defects were discovered later.

The appointment of Slade was taken in very bad part by Jules. It diminished both his income and his importance. When the new agent forced him to return some company stock which he had appropriated to his own use, he made a good many threats. Warned not to set foot on company property, Jules lay in ambush and pumped buckshot into his rival. Slade was taken to St. Louis, and to the surprise of all recovered from his wounds.

Jules had fled the country, but he now returned. He gave it out that he had come back to gather his cattle and to kill Slade. The agent took up the challenge at once. He sent out his men to arrest the French Canadian. They brought Jules to Chansau's ranch, a station on the line, and Slade at once took the stage for that point. He found his enemy, under guard, in the corral. Jules was permitted to make his will, after which Slade killed him with a pistol. The agent at once rode to Fort Laramie and surrendered to the officer in command of the troops there. After an investigation, he was discharged. Jules had been the aggressor and brought his fate on himself, the authorities decided.

Slade made an efficient division agent. He hunted down horse-thieves remorselessly. The man was indefatigable, and he became a terror to outlaws. In *The Pony Express*, Arthur Chapman tells of the time when Slade rode to a hideout occupied by four men, a 'shebang' as it was then called, kicked the door open, and began smoking. In the battle three of the bandits were killed. The fourth bolted. It took courage to attack such desperadoes, but Slade had plenty of that.

Unfortunately, Slade was given to wild debauches during which he was a menace to all with whom he came into contact. He wrecked saloons and put innocent men in fear of their lives. When the spree was over he always made the rounds and settled the bills for the damage he had done. None the less, he was becoming a nuisance the company could not tolerate as agent.

When sober he was a courteous, obliging man of pleasant manners. Drunk, he was a fiend. Mark Twain in *Roughing It* speaks of Slade as particularly quiet, gentle, and affable.

He was so friendly and gentle-spoken that I warmed to
him in spite of his awful history. [So Twain wrote.] It was
hardly possible to realize that this pleasant person was the
pitiless scourge of the outlaws.... And to this day I can
remember nothing remarkable about Slade except that his
face was rather broad across the cheekbones, and that the
cheekbones were low and the lips peculiarly thin and
straight.

The company balanced the assets and debits. On one
side was the man's efficiency, his honesty, his care for the
company's property, and in addition a friendly kindness
that was often remarkable. On the other, the times when
he was a reckless and irresponsible demon. The decision
tipped against him, and he was discharged.

Slade rode his last mile in Montana. He went to Virginia City in 1863 and started a freighting business. There
was money to be made in hauling supplies to the rich
mines at Alder Gulch, and he did well at it. But he could
not let drink alone. His conduct became unbearable. He
and his friends would ride into stores and shoot out windows. They would go whooping into bars and drive customers away. No warnings deterred him.

It was the time of Plummer's road-agent band. His
gang killed scores of men, held up stages, robbed freight
outfits. No more desperate and murderous outfit has ever
infested the West. They elected their leader sheriff and
defied the law. In self-defense honest men organized as
vigilantes. Slade was one of these law-enforcers. A great
many road agents were caught, tried, and executed. The
committee felt that its work was finished. Slade chose this
time to go on another spree. He had a great many friends,

and he was in no way connected with the Plummer gang. Perhaps he felt that his reputation as an honest man would protect him. Several times he had been arrested and paid fines. But that did not satisfy storekeepers forced to close their places of business when he was intoxicated nor citizens those lives had been threatened by him.

All night Slade roared around the town, drinking heavily at first one place and then another. Sheriff Fox arrested him in the morning and took him before a judge of the miners' court set up by the vigilantes. The sheriff started to read the warrant for his arrest. Slade snatched it from him, tore it in pieces, and stamped on it. He flouted the judge and strode out of the place, followed by his companions.

A leading member of the vigilance committee met Slade and earnestly advised him to go home to his ranch at once.

Slade stared at him. 'Why?' he demanded.

'Don't ask me questions. Get your horse and leave town at once.'

Drunk though he was, Slade was impressed. He started to leave, stayed for one more drink, and under its influence grew pot-valiant. Meeting Judge Alexander Davis, he covered him with a pistol and said he would hold him hostage for his own safety.

Meanwhile the committee had met and sent a call out for the miners to gather. A friend carried the news to Slade, who was instantly sobered. He hurried to Davis and apologized humbly.

His contrition was too late. After arresting him the miners were afraid to let him go on account of his reputation as a killer. They felt he would be a danger as long as he lived. Slade was marched to a corral adjoining a store. A beam was fastened to the gateposts and from it Slade was hanged. Before sentence was executed several good citizens, including Judge Davis, spoke for his life. When they saw this was of no use they hurried from the scene. Slade had brought his punishment on himself. There was nothing to be done about it.

With the coming of the railroad Julesburg lost its importance as a division point. The town site was moved a few miles, and in course of time it became a wild and woolly trail-end town filled with the dust of herds and the bawling of cattle. With the rise of Cheyenne Julesburg began to decline. There came a day when the sporting men loaded their gaming-tables, bars, and liquor on flatcars, and with the women of the demimonde set out for the new Wyoming town. A sardonic observer, watching the departure of that loaded train, dubbed it 'Hell on wheels.' He did not know he was seeing the end of an era for Colorado. Henceforth its cow towns were to be only a memory.

V

'Glory, Glory to Washoe'

BUSY as a hive of bees on a warm summer afternoon was Placerville. Men poured in and out of saloons. Every table was crowded at the gambling-halls. Customers waited in line to get into restaurants. Grocery and hardware stores were filled to the doors with customers buying flour, pork, nails, shovels, gunpowder, and whatever other supplies they needed for a long camping trip. Along the crooked streets booted and bearded men jostled through the mud. Miners, speculators, gamblers, merchants, and bummers had one common destination. They were bound for the new El Dorado, for the land of Washoe.

Everywhere freight outfits were on the move. Pack-animals were waiting to start, loaded with all manner of supplies, from patent medicines to whiskey. Ox teams swung along the streets on the way to Virginia City. The little town of Placerville, sometimes called Hangtown because of a recent orgy of lynching, was a picture of orderly confusion caused by many cross-currents of humanity animated by a single purpose, the urgent desire to reach the foot of Mount Davidson while there were still fortunes waiting to be picked from the ground.

The name Washoe was on every tongue. It dominated every mind. All the old prospectors who had come round the Horn, who had followed the Kern River, the Fraser, and the Gold Bluff stampedes, were on their way to the new diggings. The stampede was grime and filth and hardship, but it was also a rainbow hope, romance, the stuff of which songs are made. From a saloon came a raucous voice, putting the dream into words.

> Exciting times all round the town,
>   Glory, glory to Washoe!
> Stocks are up and stocks are down,
>   Glory, glory to Washoe!
> Washoe! Washoe!
>   Bound for the land of Washoe,
> And I own three feet
> In the 'Old Dead Beat,'
> And I'm bound for the land of Washoe.

To give point to the enthusiasm a train of sixteen-horse ore wagons, painted red, the beds filled with ore that might assay thousands of dollars to the ton, the harness of the horses jingling with little bells that could be heard a mile, rumbled down the mountain-slope into town on their way to the California mills.

Never in the history of the world had there been another camp like this at Virginia City. A man might strike a pick into the ground and find a fortune. A washwoman could buy ten feet in the Ophir and retire to Nob Hill and her own carriage. So the rumors ran in San Francisco, and the truth was so amazing that it beggared imagination.

From the miners who trod the streets which ran along the steep slopes of Mount Davidson came as multimillionaires Flood, Fair, Mackay, Stanford, Hearst, Sharon, and a score of others. On the newspapers of the town served the most talented writers of the West. There were Mark Twain, Dan De Quille, Joe Goodman, and Rollin Daggett. San Francisco sent her most famous lawyers, including William M. Stewart, long the leading citizen of Nevada, and his gallant young partner, Henry Meredith, who died leading a company against the Paiutes. Among these was David S. Terry, formerly a justice of the Supreme Court in California, the fiery rebel who killed Senator Broderick in a duel and was himself later shot down by Nagle, the bodyguard of Stephen J. Field, associate justice of the United States Supreme Court.

No frontier mining camp ever had as high a level of intellect and culture among its residents or as great a percentage of murderous lawlessness. At Maguire's Opera House Adelina Patti sang and Artemus Ward lectured. Here Helena Modjeska played Lady Macbeth, and Edwin Booth, Hamlet. For less critical tastes there were Lotta Crabtree and Adah Isaacs Menken. There was enormous vitality in the place. Many of the inhabitants had lived in tents and now lived in dirt-floor cabins, even among those of them who were on the way to great wealth. This was nothing, for all men stood on their own feet.

Nevada absorbed the best and the worst of California's seasoned veterans. Gay, reckless, debonair, the gold-seekers took the arduous trail. Every man was a law to himself, carried in his holster the redress of wrongs. The wildest excesses prevailed. The most brutal crimes went

unpunished. For years there was no night at Virginia, at
Austin, or at Eureka. The flare from dancehalls, hurdy-
gurdies, and gambling-houses flung splashes of light on
masses of roughly dressed men engaged in continuous
revelry.

But it would be unfair to condemn Washoe because it
did not measure up to the standards of Boston. At its
worst no good woman was ever more protected than here,
no child's innocence more guarded. And, as time proved,
the strength of the bad man lacked the endurance of the
one who was good. Law came slowly to Washoe, because
Nevada was under the jurisdiction of Utah, so far away
that its civil authority was only a shadow.

At Wimmer's Bar a strange company stood up to the
rail shoulder to shoulder. There was a lank Missourian
named Samuel Clemens who under the name Mark Twain
was to turn out one of the country's greatest writers. Next
to him, his broad shoulders pushing the reporter roughly
aside, was a swaggering, brutal ruffian, florid of face, with
red hair and whiskers of the same color tied in a knot
beneath his chin. He was Sam Brown, killer extraordinary,
'Chief' of the camp by reason of his long list of cowardly
murders. On the other side of this villainous scoundrel
stood graceful Charley Fairfax, scion of an old Virginia
family and legally a peer of the House of Lords in England,
a man notably courteous and gentle and brave. Talking
with him was Hank Monk, a stage-driver whose fame has
come down through the years, a superb reinsman and a wit
whose humor exactly suited the Comstock camp. After he
had cracked a whip for years over the backs of six racing-
horses he overturned a stage at last on the mountain grade

leading down the gulch to Carson City. He was deeply
humiliated but did not show it. Asked by the manager if
there had been any injuries, he brightened at once. 'Nary
a one. Not a horse hurt. No damage a-tall, except to one
tenderfoot who got a busted laig.'

Day and night the ledge streets were crowded. A dozen
gambling-halls and honky-tonks were going full blast.
Freight outfits jammed the roads, merry little bells tink-
ling as the horses moved. Adventurers passed back and
forth in cross-currents that flowed steadily twenty-four
hours of every day. Along the mountain-side screamed
furious winds that played impish tricks on exasperated
citizens. Tents were snatched from their moorings and
sent flying into the cleft cañon below. Carts were picked
up and hurled down the slope upon the roofs of cabins. A
dog on B Street went sailing through the air and dropped
yelping down the chimney of a shack on A Street. There
was a stereotyped reply to the tenderfoot who naturally
inquired in the course of time whether the wind always
blew this way. The answer was, 'No, sometimes it blows
the other way.'

In Virginia City they called these blasts from Mount
Davidson Washoe zephyrs. While these gentle breezes
lasted all sorts of possessions rolled down the hill like tum-
bleweeds. They ranged in size from a thimble to the roof
of a house. The shrieking wind, violent as a tornado at
times, never interfered for a moment with the thumping
of pianos, the squeaking of fiddles, the stamping of feet on
the floors of the dance halls. Life in Washoe was turbulent
and incessant.

There was much claim-jumping at first. Unscrupulous

men hired gangs of roughs to drive away locators. With six thousand miners on Sun Mountain, conflicts as to claims were inevitable. For years there was plenty of litigation for the big lawyers from San Francisco to straighten out. Often the claim-jumpers solved all legal knots by killing the rightful owner and relocating his claim.

In all the frontier outposts of the West there were more homicides than in the settled communities of Iowa, Ohio, and New England. The reckless Esaus made up a considerable proportion of the men who had gone West. They had cut loose from the ties that bound them to decency and morality. In saloons, gambling-houses, and bagnios they met, all wearing deadly weapons. They drank, wagered their money, bantered one another, disputed, fought. Myron Angel in his history of Nevada lists categorically four hundred and two killings during those wild early years, more than one half of them for entirely trivial reasons. A good many he missed. The hundreds massacred by Indians he does not mention.

Men quarreled over liquor, over a throw of dice, over women in whom they were not really at all interested. They shot one another down over a word spoken in jest. They killed or were killed resisting arrest for offenses the punishment of which was only a small fine. Only twelve of these homicides were done for money.

Judge Colt was the law. Each man knew that if danger confronted him on account of a quarrel, the only chance of safety lay in the revolver hanging at his hip. When one killed another in fair fight the authorities asked no questions. If the crime was cold-blooded murder and the victim had friends, there was no appeal to the courts. The vigilantes organized, captured the guilty man, tried him, and shut off his breath with a rope round the neck. In those first years the vigilantes hanged thirteen. Thirty-nine were acquitted on the ground of provocation or self-defense. Most of the offenders were never tried. Only eight were legally executed by a sheriff, and these only after the communities had settled down to accept the law.

Sam Brown reached the camp early and at once put in a claim to be 'Chief.' He was a heavy-set ape man of little intelligence. Vicious and cruel and cowardly, he came to the diggings with fifteen notches on his guns. (He was one of the rare boastful fools who actually did file a notch on the weapon after each of his murders.) Beneath his dirty Prince Albert coat he wore a belt with holsters. In the leg of his right boot the handle of a long knife could be seen. At his heels hung heavy, clanking Spanish spurs. He roared like an ogre in a fairy tale. Men sidestepped him as if he had the plague. Yet there is no record of this ruffian's having killed even one man in fair fight. It was his habit to pick on some inoffensive tenderfoot without friends, drive him to puny resentment, and cut him down without allowing the poor stranger a chance for his life. He did it once too often, and himself knew the ghastly fear of waiting for the blow to fall while he pleaded to be forgiven.

Brown's first victim at Washoe was poor William Bilboa. The killer looked around the saloon at Carson City into which he had dropped, deliberately selected the little Easterner for death, and slashed the man a dozen times with the great knife he had dragged from his boot. This was in February, 1859. Less than a year later he chose Homer Woodruff for his private cemetery. A man named

McKenzie was shot and killed by him. So sure of his reputation was the murderer that he fell asleep on a billiard table half an hour later, confident that nobody would molest him. In his *Saga of the Comstock Lode* Lyman speaks of four other murders after that of McKenzie, but I find no record of them in Angel's list.

There was one man on the Comstock Lode not afraid of the bully. That man was Bill Stewart, later perpetual United States Senator from Nevada. William M. Stewart stood well over six feet and weighed more than two hundred pounds. The man had a leonine head. His hair and great beard were sandy-colored and his eyes gray. He was broad-shouldered, long-legged, and quick as a panther. And he had undaunted courage.

He was helping the district attorney prosecute a murderer when Sam Brown came into the picture. The case was being tried at Genoa, and 'Fighting Sam' rode down into the Carson Valley to take a hand, for the fellow on trial was one of his protégés. The appearance of the dangerous scoundrel in the courtroom had something of the same effect as if a tiger had jumped in the window. The prisoner gave a whoop of delight. The jury started to duck for cover.

Bill Stewart took charge. His pistol came out swiftly. 'Reach for the roof,' he ordered Brown.

The hulking desperado stared at him dumfounded. 'M-me?' he stuttered.

'You heard me. Be damn quick about it.'

The great hairy arms went up. Brown was disarmed. He explained lamely that he had come to give testimony and not to terrorize the court. He was put on the stand

and examined by Stewart, who bullied him, hectored him, drove him from pillar to post in his testimony.

The great Sam Brown, 'Chief' of Washoe, walked out of the courthouse crestfallen, his prestige shaken. Something must be done about it. If the word spread that he was not cock of the walk somebody would pick up heart and fill him full of lead. To save face he would have to 'get him a man for breakfast' at once.

He slouched into a bar at Genoa and picked a quarrel with its owner, a smiling, round-faced man named Webster. But the saloonkeeper had already heard the courtroom story and he promptly reached for a gun. The killer made swift apology and departed. He picked on Bob Lockridge next, and Bob showed fight. Again he explained his words away. His third attempt was more disastrous.

Henry Van Sickle, a stolid German, kept a roadhouse three miles above Genoa. Brown arrived as the bell was ringing for supper. Van Sickle came out to relieve him of his horse. The bully drew a pistol and said he had come to kill the hotelkeeper. The threatened man rushed into the crowded dining-room, followed by the ruffian. Those at table jumped to their feet in fright, and Van Sickle slipped through the door into the kitchen and from their to the safety of a haystack.

Brown could not find him. He stamped around, threatened, boasted, and at last departed. Van Sickle was very much afraid the fellow would return and keep his word. He was so thoroughly frightened that he decided to turn man-hunter. His double-barreled fowling-piece was loaded with bird shot. He rammed some buckshot home on top of that, pulled himself into a saddle, and gave pursuit. The farther he rode the more angry and more worried he got.

He caught up with the killer. They exchanged shots and Brown was wounded, whereupon the 'Chief' of Washoe dug in his heels and galloped away. Van Sickle followed, his gun empty. At a ranch-house the hotel-keeper reloaded. Half an hour later he overtook Brown again, this time at Mottsville. They wasted more ammunition. While Van Sickle was loading a second time he lost sight of his man. Somebody told him at Old's Station Brown had not yet passed. He lay in wait for Sam by the roadside.

Brown came up, spurs jingling. As he dismounted, Van Sickle confronted him. In abject terror Brown knelt and begged for his life. Van Sickle gave him both barrels. The verdict of the coroner's jury was informal but explicit. The words were, 'It served him right.'

Candidates in plenty offered themselves as successor of Brown for the title of 'Chief.' Langford Peel seemed the most likely one. He did not reach Washoe until after the demise of Brown. A slender, quiet, mild-mannered youth, he did not look like the stuff of which a bad man is made. But he had plenty of courage, was a good shot, and was cold-blooded enough to kill without remorse. He brought a record of homicides to Virginia City with him, and he added to it while there.

Peel was no such bully as Brown. He did not seek quarrels or run away from them. Liquor made no appeal to him. As he stood in a gambling-house stroking his sandy beard, a man never boisterous or overbearing, his looks belied the reputation he had brought with him. Only the keen blue eyes gave warning of danger. Dick Paddock decided to try him out.

'You don't look like a chief to me,' he said bluntly.

Peel said quietly that he wasn't making any claims. Paddock laughed and said something about a false alarm.

'You wouldn't want to take that up, would you?' he asked.

'Farmer' Peel mentioned that he thought he would.

'What's your game?' demanded Paddock, meaning with what weapon did he fight.

'Your game is mine,' Peel told him.

'Then come outside.'

In an exchange of shots Peel hit his man twice, once in the breast and once in the right hand. Paddock recovered.

An oldtimer was asked recently to tell the story of the gamest exploit he had ever seen during his long residence on the frontier.

'I have to give it to "Farmer" Peel,' he decided. 'While he was in the Bitter Root country a rival gunman threatened to shoot him on sight. Peel found the man standing in front of a bar, and he took the place next to him.

'"So you're looking for me," Peel said gently. "I'm plumb scared so I'm shaking like a jelly. See my hand." He reached across to the glass of the other man and picked it up, letting the liquor slop over on the top of the bar. "I reckon you'd better drink it before I waste it all." With a flip of the wrist he tossed the whiskey in the face of his foe.

'The rival bad man put his hand on the butt of his revolver. Peel laughed scornfully. "You haven't nerve

enough to kill me," he jeered. "Tell you what I'll do.
I'm going to turn my back on you and walk to the end of
the room. Then I'll wheel round and kill you."

'While his enemy was brushing the liquor from his face
Peel started up the room. The other bad man dragged out
his sixshooter and fired three times before Peel whirled.
Farmer (so he was usually called) shot only once. The
bullet went through his foe's forehead, just above and
exactly halfway between the eyes.'

In Virginia City was a young man named John Dennis,
familiarly known as El Dorado Johnny. He was a pink-
faced boy with a well-developed streak of vanity in him.
He was not getting ahead very fast in Washoe, so he
decided he would like to be 'Chief.' History does not
record whether he was drunk or sober when he announced
that he was going to 'get' Farmer Peel.

Probably he regretted it later, but Johnny was no
coward. Having made a public boast, he decided to carry
through. But he did not intend to be an untidy corpse.
He walked into the best barber shop in town and said
that he wanted 'the whole works — shave, shine, haircut,
and whisker trim,' because he was going out to get him a
bad man.

El Dorado Johnny was certainly a fool and just as
certainly a brave one. He found Peel in a saloon on C
Street and said he had come to settle the 'Chief' business.
Very likely he knew he had no chance, but he did not
have long to worry about that. Washoe made a gala event
of the funeral. The body lay in state on a billiard table of
the saloon where he was killed. Farmer Peel paid for the
coffin, the best available, and almost everybody in town

went to the funeral. It was felt that Johnny had done himself proud. Peel, it may be mentioned, was killed a few years later at Helena, Montana, by John Bull.

Washoe was not all fighting, wrangling, and mucking in the dirt underground. Up at Virginia it was a country bare of trees and grass. The land was bleak and unproductive and the winds howled all through the long white winters. But boys and girls walked down the Geiger Grade and looked at one another shyly. Lovers met with rapturous kisses. Babies were born. Schools and churches were built. On that mountain-slope a city grew, and underground was another city of shafts and tunnels and stopes from which poured millions to help finance a great war that was to save the Union.

Fanned by the winds, fires swept the camp. Water was scarce, and the danger was great. Fire companies were organized and manned by volunteers. The friendly rivalry was great. The finest young men in the city belonged, and the social life of the camp centered in these organizations. Their political influence was also important. Tom Peasley was chief, and he was a strong influence for law and order among the turbulent and the wild.

No more glamorous figure than Tom Peasley ever walked across the stage of a frontier drama. He was a leader in a community which harbored a thousand strong individualists who would brook no leader. An amazing athlete, tall, strong, handsome, he ruled by reason of the force in him. He was reckless and gentle, gay and brave, and a fine and gallant spirit animated his tremendous energy. Tom impressed both the good and the bad. Mark Twain pictured him for posterity in his character

Buck Fanshaw. Farmer Peel submitted to have his head slammed against the wall by him, according to Lyman.

Of the many theatrical attractions that came to the camp, none so fired the imagination as Menken in 'Mazeppa.' Mark Twain went to the play intending to scourge it with a caustic criticism in the *Enterprise*. He fell under the spell of Menken's voice and never forgot the magic of it. She rivaled Lola Montez as a siren. Men of all types were drawn to the flame. Isaac Menken, a Jew, had married her. So had John C. Heenan, the great heavyweight champion who had fought Tom Sayers. Men had shot themselves because of her. She was fire and ice, a passionate lover of life who could be cold as a marble statue, one who drained it to its dregs. She fell in love with the wild Nevada camp, as it did with her. Its exuberances matched her own reckless spirit.

She was to go from Virginia City to the great world and play before kings. The great Victorian writers she swept from their feet. Dickens wrote the introduction to her book of poems. Rossetti included several of them in an anthology he published. Burne-Jones pictured her. Alexandre Dumas and Swinburne were her lovers, and the latter wrote to her a bitter, stinging lyric, 'Dolores,' that has taken its place among the world's remarkable poems.

> Fierce midnights and famishing morrows,
>   And the loves that complete and control,
> All the joys of the flesh, all the sorrows
>   That wear out the soul.

O garment not golden but gilded,
   O garden where all men may dwell,
O tower not of ivory, but builded
   By hands that reach heaven from hell.

It was a far cry from this raw mining camp to Swinburne's wail that 'love is more cruel than lust,' but Menken, born Dolores McCord, took to the salons of London
and Paris as she did to the gambling-houses of Virginia
City. The favorite among her cavaliers in the West was
Tom Peasley, who walked beside her as lightly as if he
were treading on eggs. She danced and played faro and
dined with him. His was as untamed a soul as hers. But
presently she was gone, and Tom was left with his mem-
ories.

In the end his own recklessness trapped him. It was
written of him that he would rather break down a door
than unlock it. Playfully, while in liquor, he slapped
'Sugarfoot Jack' on the back too hard. Challenged to
fight a duel, his false pride made him accept regretfully.
His opponent was killed, and for the rest of his life he felt
himself a criminal. He could not escape his record. Now
a 'killer,' bad men singled him out for attack. At the
Ormsby House, in Carson City, he was shot down by a
ruffian unexpectedly. He dragged himself to his feet,
followed the escaping man, and sent a bullet crashing
through a screen door. The murderer died before Peasley.

Characteristic of the Comstock were Sandy and Eilley
Bowers. He had been a hard-rock miner and she the
keeper of the boarding-house where he lived. When they
struck it rich the prospect dazzled them. They built a
home that had in it everything expensive money could

buy. Europe made contributions of mirrors and chandeliers and marble statues. The Comstock provided silver for door hinges and gold for handles. The Bowers mansion was a monument of folly. The cost of it furnished was over four hundred thousand dollars. Perhaps it was Eilley who yearned for other worlds to conquer. The Bowerses decided to take in Europe.

Virginia City gave them a farewell banquet at which champagne flowed like the brackish water of the town. Sandy made a reply to a toast that is still remembered.

'I've got money to throw at the birds,' he said. 'There ain't no chance for a gentleman to spend his money in this here country and there ain't nothing much to see, so me an' Mrs. Bowers is going to Europe to take in the sights. One of the great men in this country was in this region a while back. That was Horace Greeley. He didn't look no great shakes to me. Outside of him the only great men I've seen in this country is Governor Nye and Old Winnemucca. Now me and Mrs. Bowers aim to see the Queen of England.... I hope you'll all jine in an' drink Mrs. Bowers' health. I have plenty of champagne, and money ain't no object.'

So they went to London and met Queen Victoria, who was perhaps more 'amused' than she was on another famous occasion. The Bowers spent a quarter of a million on the trip, but they always felt they got their money's worth.

It may be that Sandy Bowers could hardly write his own name, but the level of culture and intelligence at Virginia was far above that of most mining camps. Side by side with the roughest makeshifts, the most primitive of cave dwellings, there existed a civilization which would be satisfied with nothing less than the best. If one lucky miner expressed himself with champagne and door stops of gold, another perhaps as lucky lifted his eyes to the stars and wrote his soul out with fire-tipped pen. No town of greater contrasts ever existed.

Mark Twain wrote his mother:

> The country is fabulously rich in gold, silver, copper, lead, coal, quicksilver . . . murderers, desperadoes, gamblers, sharpers, coyotes, poets, preachers, and jackass rabbits. I overheard a gentleman say the other day that it is the d——dest country under the sun — and that comprehensive description I fully subscribe to. It never rains here, and no dew falls. No flowers grow here, and no green thing gladdens the eye.

Preachers found it hard to convert those living in a country so lawless. Life was so unconventional, reckless, robust, and colorful. The Reverend J. H. Byers was burying a man at Elko. During the services the 'Lightning Express' from New York arrived for the first time. The congregation deserted to a man. The funeral had to be postponed until the train had gone.

Some of the ministers were, however, rugged souls fully a match for their fellow-citizens. The Reverend T. H. McGrath was chaplain of the legislature, and one of the solons complained that his prayer was too long. If the prayer would bring practical results, he would not mind. For instance, if it would make the rock in his tunnel any softer or increase the needed flow of water. The parson finished his invocation next morning with a personal appeal to the Almighty. 'Oh, Lord, we pray Thee to remember Brother Brown. Make the rock in his tunnel as soft as his head, and the water in his ditch as abundant as the whiskey he daily drinks. Amen.'

Those were the days of personal journalism. An editor had to know how to fight as well as how to write. George W. Derickson was killed by an irate reader at Washoe City. Dan De Quille had a run-in with the notorious Langford Peel. Joe Goodman, editor of the *Enterprise*, fought a duel with Tom Fitch of the *Union* and lamed him for life. When Jim Laird labeled Mark Twain 'a liar, a poltroon, and a puppy,' the *Enterprise* reporter retorted in kind and sent a challenge to the editor. A duel on the Comstock meant business. Colt's revolvers at ten or fifteen paces were generally used, and a coffin had to be ordered for somebody. Neither Mark Twain nor Jim Laird wanted to fight. They had maneuvered themselves into a position from which they could not gracefully retreat. At the last minute Laird declined to appear. On account of a recent law prohibiting dueling Clemens and his opponent both had to leave the country.

Yet those were great days in the Comstock for newspaper men. It was more thrilling to run a line 'By Pony Express' than one Associated Press. Perhaps 'Pony Bob' Haslam had brought the story at breakneck speed through a hundred miles of dangerous Pai-Ute country, risking his life every mile of the way. The journalists were living in an amazingly vital community filled with forceful and energetic pioneers. The note of the writing was a gay extravagance. Young editors and reporters were 'Josh' and 'Joe' and 'Dan' to one another. They led a rollicking life filled with high lights. The world was young and full of wonders, and they were in on the making of it.

It was no wonder that Rollin M. Daggett, nearly twenty years after the glories of Washoe had faded, wrote a long poem informed with nostalgia and sadness. The brave companions of his youth were gone. Either they had passed from the world or had shrunk from their Homeric size to tired old men. He called it 'My New Year's Guests.'

The winds come cold from the southward, with incense of fir and
    pine,
And the flying clouds grow darker as they halt and fall in line.
.   .   .   .

As I sit alone in my chamber this last of the dying year,
Dim shapes of the past surround me, and faint through the storm
    I hear
Old tales of castles builded, under shelving rock and pine,
Of the bearded men and stalwart I greeted in forty-nine.

The giants with hopes audacious; the giants of iron limb;
The giants who journeyed westward when the trails were new
    and dim;
The giants who felled the forests, made pathway o'er the snows,
And planted the vine and fig tree where the manzanita grows;

Who swept the mountain gorges, and painted their endless night,
With their cabins rudely fashioned and their campfires' ruddy
    light;
Who builded great towns and cities, who swung the Golden Gate,
And hewed from the mighty ashlar the form of a sovereign state.

All gone, even then, as the hot rampant life of Virginia City too was gone. Daggett concluded his verses with the only solace left him:

I drink alone in silence to the builders of the West —
Long life to the hearts still beating, and peace to the hearts at
    rest.

VI

For and Against the Law in the Northwest

DURING the first years of the gold stampede into the Black Hills the Cheyenne–Deadwood trail was a bonanza for road agents.[1] There was a daily stage service to and from the mines, and sometimes there were as many as two holdups a week. Also, the Sioux Indians frequently raided the station corrals at Running Water, Rawhide Buttes, or Red Cañon, driving away the fine horses bought by Gilmer and Saulsbury to draw the Concord stages.

A famous western character known as 'Stuttering Brown' was superintendent of transportation. Since he could not be all places at once, horses were rustled at one post while he was inspecting another. The thieves were well known to the stock-tenders, but their audacity was so great that while planning a robbery they would often spend a night at one of the company roadhouses.

Brown reached the Hager's Ranch Station one night and heard that a fine team had just been stolen. A notori-

[1] The term 'road agent' was the one generally used for a stage-robber.

ous horse-thief called Persimmon Bill sat toasting his boots at the fire. He turned to the superintendent and asked with cheerful malice, 'How's everything going?'

This effrontery was too much for Brown. He snatched out a gun and stuttered curses at the outlaw. 'Y-you're going, you s-s-scoundrel,' he cried. 'G-get out of here, or I'll b-blow your head off.'

Persimmon Bill departed, with a cryptic warning. 'Be seeing you later, Stuttering,' he said.

Impetuous and fearless, Brown paid no attention to the threat. He ordered his four-mule hitch and with two employees took the road for Hat Creek. Near the Alkali Springs a shot came from the brush and the mules bolted. When they were at last stopped Brown gave orders.

'Each of you cut loose a mule and light out for Indian Creek.'

'And you?' one of the men asked.

'I'm through,' the superintendent said quietly. 'He got me in the stomach. Burn the wind, boys.'

The others rode away to get help. On their return they came on Brown lying on the road four miles from the scene of the attack. The indomitable man had unhitched a mule, dragged himself to its back, and stuck there until he fainted from loss of blood. A few days later he died.

During the early years of Deadwood half a dozen gangs of stage-robbers operated on the road. A story is told of two drivers who pulled up en route to exchange news.

'Got held up three miles this side of Custer,' one announced.

'That makes it fifty-fifty,' the other added. 'The boys stopped me in the gulch a quarter of a mile back. They're waiting for you, and told me to ask you to hurry so's they wouldn't be late for supper.'

One of the most notorious of these gangs included Sam Bass, the bandit who has become a legend on account of the song which details his exploits. With Joel Collins and Jim Berry he had come north from Texas as a cowboy employed to prod a trail herd a thousand miles. Collins had been a substantial cattleman but had gone wild. At Deadwood he spent in gambling-halls the money received for the herd, part of which belonged to other Texas ranchmen.

Under his leadership two or three stages were robbed. Very little money was obtained from the passengers and the treasure box. Neither Collins nor Bass were of the killer type, but on March 25, 1877, they held up a stage on Whitewood Creek and the driver, John Slaughter, was shot by a cowboy of the Collins trail outfit, Jack Davis. The bandits had been drinking, and when the startled horses plunged and ran a load of buckshot tore through Slaughter and killed him. A passenger kept the six horses going, and the road agents lost their booty.

Collins and Bass had had enough of stage holdups. They drifted south to Ogallala, Nebraska, and pulled off the boldest train robbery that had yet occurred in the West. There were six of the outlaws. In addition to Collins, Bass, and Berry, three cowboys took part in the robbing of the Union Pacific train at Big Springs. Their names were Jack Davis, Bill Heffridge, and 'Old Dad' Underwood.

Collins spent several days looking over the ground before making the attempt. Ogallala was at that time one of the trail-end towns, and hundreds of Texas cowhands came and went during the season. The presence of these six men aroused no interest. At a store kept by a man named Leach some of the bandits bought a few supplies. Jim Berry needed a pair of boots but had no money. Collins paid for them, and had Leach cut from a bolt two yards of calico.

The engineer of the train had no sooner stopped the engine at Big Springs than two masked men jumped into the cab. Other train officials were covered at the same time. All these were guarded by Berry while the other robbers searched the passengers and the express car. The safe had a Yale time lock and the messenger, Miller, was unable to open it. Davis started to beat him up, but Collins stopped this. It appeared that the only booty the outlaws were going to get was what they took from the passengers, but before they left Collins noticed four small boxes in a corner. They were very heavy. The lid of one was broken, and in it was found nothing but newly minted gold pieces. The boxes had more than sixty thousand dollars in them.

Before the holdup Collins had cut the telegraph wires. He made the engineer and fireman draw the fire from the locomotive, after which the masked men rode into the night. Next morning the Collins gang were lounging around the Ogallala saloons as usual. They joined in the talk about the holdup. Nobody suspected them. The money had been hidden. It had been a perfect robbery, Collins felt. Nobody hurt, no clew to suggest the identity of the guilty.

Half the men in Ogallala rode out to Big Springs to have

a look at the scene of the holdup, among others the merchant Leach. In the hollow where the horses had been stationed Leach picked up a small piece of calico. It had been trimmed from another piece that he guessed had been used as a mask. That scrap of calico he recognized as a remnant of the yardage he had sold Collins. Leach knew he had a clew to the identity of the robbers held by no other man. The finding of that fragment of cloth resulted in the death of three men. A newspaper of Mexico, Missouri, made the caustic comment a month later that of course other men had lost their lives fooling with a piece of calico, but not with so small a bit.

Greatly excited, the merchant rode back to town. On a placard in town he read this notice:

> Ten thousand dollars reward will be paid for the capture of the parties who robbed the U.P.R.R. Express at Big Springs, Nebraska, on the 18th inst., and the return of the money, which consists mostly of gold coin. Pro-rate of the above reward will be paid for any portion of the money so returned and for the capture of any of the robbers.

Collins thought it wise not to hurry their departure. He mentioned in the store that he certainly could use that ten thousand, but of course somebody else would get it since he never had been a lucky guy. Leach watched him and Berry, noted the others with whom they chiefly associated.

The six Texans bought supplies for the return trail trip to Texas. They said '*Adios!*' and departed. Leach was a remarkable man. He did not mention his suspicions to any of the sheriffs, special agents, and United States marshals who were combing the country. He hired a horse and took a trip.

He struck the trail of the robbers and stuck to it closer than a calf to its mother. Several times he crawled through the brush at night until he was near the camp. He watched the Texans sitting round their big fire. But it was not until they had traveled a hundred and fifty miles that he obtained proof of their guilt. While watching their night camp he actually saw Collins divide the loot, ten thousand dollars in gold to each man. He heard them decide to separate for the rest of the journey. It would be better to travel in pairs, since they had entirely escaped suspicion. Collins and Heffridge were to make for San Antonio, Berry and Underwood for the home of the former in Audrain County, Missouri, and Bass and Davis for Denton, Texas.

The storekeeper had seen enough. He hurried away and notified the authorities. Descriptions of the bandits were sent out. Sheriffs were informed of the route. The Texas Rangers waited for the arrival of the robbers.

Collins and Heffridge rode into Buffalo Station, Kansas, and were startled to see a description of themselves and Sam Bass tacked to a wooden wall. They departed hurriedly, the packhorse at their heels. A lounger in the dusty street at once notified a United States army officer who with ten men was camped on the edge of town. The troop followed the outlaws and the lieutenant questioned them. Collins, very cool and jaunty, laughed at the suggestion that they were train-robbers. Certainly they would ride back to town and clear themselves. Yet Joel Collins knew the game was up. He murmured a word to his companion. Their sixshooters flashed out, but the soldiers were watching. Both men fell riddled with bullets. On the packhorse was more than twenty thousand dollars in gold.

At his home in Mexico, Missouri, Berry was surrounded by a posse. He refused to surrender and was killed. A wife and a houseful of children mourned for Jim Berry. Old Dad had left him somewhere farther up the road. He disappeared and was never caught. Davis and Bass reached Denton County, the pursuit hot on their heels. The former slipped down to the Gulf and took a boat for South America. Bass stayed in Texas and organized another band of outlaws. They held up several trains. Gillett, an officer of the Frontier Battalion of Texas Rangers, says in his book that probably a hundred officers were continuously on the watch for Bass, yet he visited Fort Worth and Dallas at night frequently. His gang was partially broken up, and he was driven out of his usual range.

One of the gang, Jim Murphy, betrayed the others. He sent word to Major Jones of the rangers that they were going to rob the bank at Round Rock, Texas. Jones made preparations to receive them. He notified the sheriff. Two deputies made the mistake of trying to arrest the bandits in a store. Both of them were killed.

The bandits had arrived sooner than was expected. A ranger, Dick Ware, jumped up from a barber's chair and ran into the street. He met the bank robbers and engaged them. Rangers Connor and Harold joined him. Major Jones hurried up. The outlaws made for their horses. Barnes was killed, Bass very badly wounded. Frank

Jackson, a boy, stood up to the heavy fire of the rangers and helped Bass mount. He then vaulted to his own saddle and followed his friend out of town, bullets splashing all around him.

Bass knew he could not live. Jackson assisted him to the ground and wanted to stay with him, but Bass would not have it.

'I'm done for,' he said. 'Get out while you can.'

Reluctantly the boy left him. Jackson hid in the Denton County swamps for a time and then vanished. No ranger or law officer ever saw him again, as far as is known. There have been a hundred rumors in the past fifty years about his whereabouts, none of them ever verified.

For some reason Sam Bass has become a Texas hero. He is regarded as a modern Robin Hood. One can name hundreds of fine men who have done their share toward the upbuilding of Texas, from Travis and Fannin down to Gillett and Goodnight but an outlaw whose life was a menace to the good of the state has captured its imagination.

Last year I stood in the cemetery at Round Rock and read an inscription on the stone above the outlaw's grave. It was put there by his sister. The stone there now is the third marker. The other two were chipped away by the visitors who come by hundreds. The words read:

SAMUEL BASS

Born July 21st, 1851
Died July 21st, 1878

A brave man reposes in death here. Why was he not true?

Other bands of road agents continued to waylay the
Deadwood stages. Two of the more noted peace officers
who fought against them were Boone May and Scott
Davis. Both of them had encounters with the Wall-
Blackburn gang, which had its hangout at Crook City,
and at different times both were wounded. At a rocky
spot in a gulch known as Robbers' Roost a stage was held
up upon which were riding three soldiers sent as a guard.
They took to their heels. Scott Davis was on board. He
fought till his rifle jammed. The holdups left him lying in
the road with a bullet in his hip. As soon as he had recovered, Davis set out to run these men down. He located
them at Alkali Springs. The outlaws resisted. Davis
wounded Wall, turned him over to the authorities, and
pursued Blackburn. He arrested the man, and the two
outlaws were sent to prison.

Not long after this the Cañon Springs robbery occurred.
It was one of a dozen, but is remembered because of the
fierceness of the fight to save the treasure. A lad named
Hill was on the box beside the driver. They pulled up at
the station and he jumped down to unhitch the horses.
He was shot in the back, turned, and was hit again in the
arm. A bullet struck a passenger in the forehead. Scott
Davis took shelter back of a barn and returned the fire of
the road agents. He wounded one of them. Young Gail [1]
Hill, very badly hurt though he was, blazed away at them
and killed another. Fortunately Boone May and a posse
arrived soon after this, though not in time to save the
treasure. 'Big-Nose' George was leader of this robber outfit.

[1] The name is given by some as Lee Hill.

Jesse Brown and A. M. Willard, joint authors of a valuable source book called *The Black Hills Trails*, point out that at one time the outlaws were so bad that a stage carrying a large gold shipment from Deadwood to Sidney, Nebraska, accepted no passengers and was under the protection of eight guards. Jesse Brown himself was one of them. Among the others were Scott Davis, Boone May, and Gail Hill. Needless to say that with this picked guard the stage was not molested.

George Parrotte, alias Big-Nose George, was driven across the line into Wyoming after a good many robberies. He worked along the Union Pacific tracks, and after trying to wreck a train was followed into the Elk Mountain country by the special agent Vincents and Bob Widdowfield, deputy sheriff of Carbon County. Near the head of Rattlesnake Creek the bandits ambushed and killed them both. This was on August 19, 1878. Two years later Parrotte was arrested at Miles City, Montana, brought back to Rawlins, Wyoming, and convicted of this crime by a jury. He was sentenced to be hanged, but the citizens of Carbon County seem to have been in a hurry. Two weeks before the date of his legal execution Big-Nose George assaulted and injured his jailer in an attempt to escape. He was dragged from the jail and hanged at once. 'Dutch' Charley, his partner in the Vincents and Widdowfield killings, had already been taken from a train at Carbon after his arrest and hanged by neighbors of Widdowfield.

Road agents were operating extensively in the wild Wyoming country of which Buffalo, in Johnson County, was the trading center. The mountains and gulches were full of pockets known only to the outlaws, and game was so plentiful that subsistence was easy. At this time Buffalo, a small cow town, was two hundred and fifty miles to the nearest railroad point at Rock Creek, Wyoming. The Wells-Fargo stage carried treasure from this station to Custer, Montana, a distance of more than four hundred miles. Big-Nose George had operated here, and after his demise other desperadoes carried on the robberies.

'Teton' Jackson was one of the most active of the outlaws. His specialty was rustling horses. Jackson had run a pack train for General Crook in the Sioux wars, but his instinct for theft was too great. He stole some government mules, was arrested, and in escaping killed two soldiers. Within a short time he 'rubbed out' two deputy United States marshals from Idaho and Utah respectively. A reward of three thousand dollars was offered by the Utah authorities for his head, dead or alive.

At this time Teton was about forty-five, a heavy-set man over six feet in height, with a stubby beard and flaming red hair. Little black eyes gleamed from a ruddy face. He was a man of tremendous strength. The Teton fastnesses back of Jackson Hole were his hideout. He knew them like a book, and here he was king. Thieves brought their horses to him to be hidden and rebranded. Desperadoes and murderers fled to his bailiwick for safety. Scores of bad men at one time or another acknowledged him as chief. Openly he boasted that the law could not touch him, and for years he made his claim good.

Frank M. Canton, sheriff of Johnson County for four years, serving as a deputy United States marshal at the time, outfitted a pack train and set out to capture Teton. After a long trip he and his two assistants found Jackson in the cabin of a settler named Lucas at Paint Rock Creek Cañon. The officers flung open the door and walked in upon a group of men playing cards. Some of them had put aside their weapons, thinking there were no sheriffs or marshals within fifty miles of them. The others dared not reach for their sixshooters. For Canton and his men had the outlaws covered.

'What do you want?' Jackson snapped.

'You,' retorted Canton. 'We're taking you back with us.'

In the house were half a dozen rustlers, as hard, tough characters as could be found in the territory. Teton knew they would fight if he gave the word. 'No,' he snarled. 'Not a foot of the way.'

'Yes,' differed the marshal.

Three guns were trained on the leader of the outlaw group. One point stuck out like a sore thumb, too plain for Jackson to miss. His friends might wipe out the officers, but not until after he was dead. He threw up his hands.

'All right. All right. But you're making a mistake, Canton.'

The marshal answered promptly. 'Not as bad a one as you will be making if you let your friends try to rescue you.'

Jackson was convicted and sent to the penitentiary. He escaped, was at liberty for some time, and was recaptured. Attempting to escape a second time, he was killed by a guard.

Among the noted early-day sheriffs of Wyoming was John Owens. He was one of Quantrell's guerrillas, and after the Civil War entered the federal service as a scout and was stationed at Fort Laramie, Wyoming. He had a varied career after leaving government employ. He ran saloons and roadhouses, was marshal of several frontier towns, and served as sheriff of Weston County, Wyoming, for a number of terms. One hears of him at Fort Laramie, at Cheyenne, at Sidney, at Lusk, and at Newcastle.

Owens was a slender man, soft-spoken, unobtrusive of manner. His eyes were dark brown, as steady as searchlights. He talked very little, was very well dressed and punctiliously polite to women. In his courteous deference to them he suggested a generation that was vanishing.

The first marshal of Lusk was Charles Trumbull, a good officer until he took to drinking. Word came to him of a bunch of horses stolen in the Indian Territory and heading for Wyoming. Charles Miley, alias Red Bill, dropped into town and while drunk admitted that he was one of the rustlers. Trumbull arrested Miley and dragged him around, ropes binding his wrists until they bled. Realizing that Trumbull was intoxicated, John Owens stepped in front of him with a shotgun and ordered the marshal to go home and sleep it off. He himself took Red Bill to jail. As Trumbull was releasing the man next day he asked Miley if he held any hard feelings. The accused rustler showed his lacerated wrists. 'Do you suppose I'm a friend of a man who would do that to me?' he asked. Trumbull killed him, and was later sent to the penitentiary.

John Owens succeeded as marshal. Shortly after this

Dan Bogan of Texas appeared in Lusk under the name of Bill McCoy. Bogan had been indicted in May, 1881, as accessory to the killing of 'Doll' Smith at Hamilton. Kemp, who had done the actual killing, was convicted, sentenced to be hanged, and made a desperate attempt to escape a few days before the time set for his execution. He jumped from a second-story window, sprained an ankle, and failed to reach a horse waiting for him. A higher court granted an appeal and saved his neck. At the next trial the sentence was twenty-five years in the penitentiary. Bogan was a hardy ruffian, and he too made a bid for freedom, more successfully than his confederate. As the jury was filing in to report, he snatched a gun from a guard and began firing. During the confusion he flung himself from a window, jumped a horse, and got away.

Soon after this Bogan was heard of in the Texas Panhandle. At Tascosa he ruffled it with the other gunmen who infested the town. He worked as a cowpuncher, gambled, and 'rode the chuck line' when he was short of food. Trouble went with him wherever he was. Accompanied by two companions, he rode through a dance hall firing through the ceiling. The wild panic amused him. When he returned to the front door to repeat the performance he found the proprietor of the place standing there rifle in hand.

'You can't pass except over my dead body,' the man told him.

'That's easy,' the desperado cried, and shot him down, then spurred his horse across the body.

This murder was too flagrant. Bogan started up the trail for Wyoming, where his record was not then publi-

cized. It is known that he spent some time in Jackson
Hole and the gorges back of it with Teton and his gang.
Probably he was active in horse-stealing, which was the
leading industry of the place in those days. The printed
charge was made that this was a family characteristic.

The Lusk *Herald*, date of July 29, 1887, ran a news story
to the effect that Bogan had a brother who was killed by a
sheriff while resisting arrest for horse-stealing, and that a
third brother was in the Texas penitentiary for the same
offense.

Frontier editors were often fearless in performing civic
duties. J. K. Calkins of the *Herald* had several times
pointed out that Bogan, or McCoy, as he called himself in
Wyoming, was a bad citizen who was wanted in Texas for
murder. The Texan took this resentfully. With a companion named Ballou he went into the saloon of Larkin
and Harper Cleveland, a place which the editor occasionally frequented,[1] his mind made up for trouble. He drew
a gun and began to wave it.

'If that editor has any friends here, let them speak out,'
he shouted. 'I've been insulted and I aim to make smoke.'

From behind the bar one of the Clevelands took a
sawed-off shotgun and trained it on the desperado. 'Count
me in,' he said quietly.

Constable Charles S. Gunn was present and ordered
McCoy to leave. Gunn too was a Texan, and before coming North had been a ranger there. He was a man of about
thirty-two, tall, well built, and popular. Not far from

[1] In the early days frontier towns had no place where men could gather except
in saloons. Cattle were bought and sold there, and appointments to transact
business in them were common. They were the clubhouses of the community,
regardless of whether a man did or did not drink.

Lusk he had a ranch where he spent part of his time. The constable was highly respected. He had no bad habits. It is still remembered that he was very fond of children.

McCoy cooled down, but a few days later he had a run-in with another saloonkeeper named Waters. Again Gunn interfered, and this time warned the Texan to amend his ways. The bad man went into Waters' place next day. Gunn followed. McCoy turned on him, and said, 'Charley, are you heeled?' Without waiting for an answer he fired. Gunn fell forward, shot in the abdomen. Slowly he raised his weapon and tried to rise. McCoy put a sixshooter to his temple and killed him. The murderer ran out, waving his revolver. He held back those present while he released a horse from the hitch rack and mounted.

Calvin Morse, a member of the Denver University Club until his death, related the rest of the story to me there.

'McCoy burst out of the saloon, swung himself on Jack Andrews' horse, and started to gallop away. John Owens came swiftly out of a building, a double-barreled shotgun in his hands. He fired one shot, evidently to warn McCoy to stop. Slugs from the second barrel knocked McCoy from the horse. He had been hit in the shoulder, so that he pulled the horse up sharply and the animal slipped on the snow. The revolver, flung from the outlaw's hand, lay two or three feet from him. Owens's brain functioned quickly. His shotgun was now empty, but he gambled on McCoy forgetting that in the excitement. He walked forward, keeping the man covered with the unloaded weapon. Not an instant did he hesitate as he moved toward the killer.

'"Stick 'em up," he ordered. "Don't move."

'In a split second McCoy could have reached his weapon. He made a motion toward it, then gave up. Owens reached the revolver, picked it up, and tossed away the gun.'

McCoy was tried for murder, and given the death sentence. While in the cage at Cheyenne he took the steel shank from his boot and made a saw of it. He cut his way out and released two other prisoners. It was known that he reached Jackson Hole. Probably he changed his name again. Twenty years later Calvin Morse read of his death, the newspaper story having a New Mexico date line. He had been bucked from a horse and had broken his neck.

After Owens arrested McCoy, the companion of the outlaw, named Ballou, made threats about what he would do in revenge. Owens called him out of a saloon where he was dealing a stud-poker game.

'There has been enough killing, Ballou — or else there hasn't. I don't like your talk. If you are in town two hours from now I'll shoot you on sight.'

'Well, I'll go if you say so, Johnny,' Ballou told him.

'I say so,' replied Owens.

Ballou left on the first stage.

From oldtimers in Wyoming I have heard scores of stories about John Owens. At one time he owned a 'hog ranch' [1] near Fort Laramie. Some hard characters came into the place and Owens heard a snatch of low-voiced talk. They had mentioned that the paymaster was coming up on the stage to pay the soldiers. After they had ridden away Owens became troubled about this. He guessed that they meant to hold up the stage somewhere between Chugwater and Laramie, very likely at Eagle's Nest.

[1] This does not mean exactly what it says. A 'hog ranch' was a dance hall.

Owens saddled and cut across country. At Bear Springs he waited for the arrival of the Concord. When it rolled up in a cloud of dust he tied his mount to the near wheeler and climbed up on the boot beside the driver, a Winchester across his knees. George Lathrop, the driver, was uneasy but prepared to see the adventure through. He chewed tobacco methodically.

As one danger point after another was passed he suggested, 'Maybe you're wrong, Johnny, don't you reckon?'

Owens said, 'Maybe.' He never wasted words.

At Eagle's Nest a road agent shouted the order, 'Hands up.'

Owens did not lift the rifle from his knees. 'Boys, you'd better ride on home,' he suggested.

The amazing sequel was that they took his advice. To see him on the boot, prepared to scatter death among them, was a little more than they could stomach. Of course they would get Johnny. But how many of them would Johnny get?

That Owens was a hard man there can be no doubt. He had to be to 'ride herd' on the tough characters who infested Wyoming in the early days. At Cambria he is said to have killed a man. He shot two cattle-thieves at Newcastle. Logan Blizzard was a victim of his straight shooting. Another was 'Doc' Cornet.

Cornet was a gambler in Lusk during the early days. Later he moved to Newcastle while Owens was sheriff there. For some reason he fell out with the officer. He walked into a saloon and 'threw down' on Owens with a cocked single-action .45. It was a mistake to explain his intentions. They were fairly obvious.

'I'm going to kill you, John,' he said

Owens talked, to gain time. 'I wouldn't do that, Doc. Let's fix this up.'

'No. Right now.'

'Do you sure enough mean it?'

'I certainly do.'

The sheriff's weapon flashed to light. A bullet crashed into Cornet's forehead before he had time to fire.

More than one noted gunman has told me he never drew a weapon except to fire at once, unless he was making an arrest. The time for talk is before the guns are out.

Russell Thorpe operated the stage line and Cal Morse was the agent at Lusk. The first time Thorpe ever went into Owens's dance hall there was some shooting and likely to be more. Owens was not present, but he arrived in the midst of the trouble. The stage manager said later that the place became almost at once as quiet as a church.

Logan Blizzard dropped in at a blacksmith's shop to have his horse shod and afterward held up the smith. He was arrested at Sundance and convicted. As Owens was taking him to the penitentiary Blizzard, handcuffed though he was, jumped from a train going forty miles an hour. The sheriff stopped at the next station, got a saddle horse and supplies, and picked up the trail. This escape was a personal affront to his reputation, and though the weather was bitter and a fierce storm was blowing he rode all night. In the early morning he reached a small ranch-house and waited in the barn for somebody to come and feed the stock.

A boy came out of the house rubbing sleep from his eyes. He was surprised to find an armed man waiting in the barn, but he answered questions readily enough. Yes, there was a stranger in the house. He was not now wearing handcuffs. The man had helped himself to their .30-30 rifle.

Blizzard strolled from the house, rifle in hand. The sheriff killed him. Owens explained later that this would not have been necessary if he had not tripped over a box frozen in the ground. Owens fired as he went down, and the bullet struck the outlaw in the heart.

There was some criticism of Owens for his readiness to kill. It is only fair to say, however, that some of the best citizens of Wyoming have told me he was always entirely justified.

Owens took part in one of the last Indian uprisings. A band left the agency at Pine Ridge on a raid. The sheriff of Converse County, Wyoming, asked Owens to join a posse to head the war party back to the reservation. Foster Rogers was herding sheep on Lightning Creek and saw the war party pass. There were seventeen wagons loaded with loot, one hundred and forty ponies, twenty-four dogs. Squaws were driving the wagons, and the bucks, armed with rifles, were on horseback. As they passed, two of the latter rode across to Rogers and demanded tobacco. While they were still with him the battle began. The two bucks rode back to the wagons. Rogers lay down in the greasewood and made himself small. This was none of his party.

Sheriff Miller had made contact with the Indians. He had with him his deputy Falkenburg and Owens, with ten others hastily gathered. Three times Miller ordered the raiders to surrender.

Among the Indians were Chief He Crow, High Dog,

James White Elk, Charge Wolf, and Jesse Little War-Bonnet. Their leader was Eagle Feather, known while at Carlisle as Charley Smith. Eagle Feather stooped from his horse, scooped dirt in his hand, and tossed it in the air as a signal for fight.

Deputy Falkenburg was killed almost instantly and Miller was fatally wounded. For a few minutes there was a constant roar of Winchester and Savage rifles. Several Indians were killed. Eagle Feather went down, shot in both legs. The Indians retreated. Their war chief refused help in getting to a horse. To let the others get away he stayed and covered the rearguard. He lay back of a wagon and fired between the spokes of a wheel.

After the smoke of battle had cleared away the wounded of both sides were taken care of by members of the posse. While Owens was looking after a squaw who had been hurt he felt a hand at his thigh. Eagle Feather, wounded to death, was trying to draw out the white man's revolver to kill him. Though suffering greatly, Eagle Feather died a stoic.

Gentle in manner, John Owens could be very violent in action. At one time he kept a saloon at Crawford, Nebraska, near Fort Robinson. A regiment of wild colored soldiers was stationed at the fort, and when in town they sometimes patronized the gambling-house of Owens. Somebody woke John out of sleep to tell him that there was a riot in his place. He snatched up his single-action Colt's .45 and ran into the back of the saloon. The town marshal was backed against the wall, his hands up. The room was filled with soldiers and they had taken charge. Owens snatched a double-barreled shotgun from back of the bar. When hostilities had concluded the tale of casualties included most of the soldiers. Several were in the hospital for a week, but none were seriously wounded.

Today Owens would not be considered exactly an exemplary citizen. He ran a gambling-house. As a law officer he was often harsh and autocratic. He disregarded the rights of bad men. It must be held in mind that he belonged to the frontier. His ethics were conditioned by the society in which he lived. A man might run a gambling-hall and still be respectable. He might be a killer without being a criminal. When John Owens fought, it was against those who were destructive of society.

So it was with Frank Canton and Scott Davis and Boone May and Gail Hill. They were as hard and tough as the outlaws they quelled. To survive they had to be. But they fought on the side of law and order. They risked their lives to make safe for women and children a country overridden by bandits and ruffians.

VII

Abilene, Wild and Woolly

THREE factors wiped out the Great American Desert which had for generations held back the forward-lapping tide of civilization. One of them was the great buffalo slaughter that drove the Indians to reservations by destroying their food, clothing, and shelter. A second was the wide demand for free land. The third was the Texas cattle drives.

At the end of the Civil War the men of Texas returned from the Confederate armies to find their state bursting with cattle for which there was no market. South of them lay the Gulf and poverty-stricken Mexico, eastward prostrate Louisiana, to the west plains infested by Kiowas and Comanches, untenanted by whites. There remained only the North. Above the border stretched the Indian Territory, and beyond that hundreds of miles of unknown wilderness. If the drover reached settlements at last, it would be to find himself in enemy country, that North which he had spent four years in fighting.

But to the Texas ranches stories had come down of the

great westward trek across the Missouri. There was a
shortage of cattle in this new land. The finger of destiny
nudged in that direction.

Lank 'brushpoppers' combed the thickets for longhorns
and dragged them from the chaparral. The smell of burnt
flesh and the bawling of cattle filled the air as the red-hot
iron of the road brand pressed home. Herds were made up
and started on the long, unknown trail. They encountered
drought and blizzards. Stampedes wore down the drovers.
Rivers bank-high with flood waters had to be crossed.
Bands of marauders turned back the herds. The settlers
in the new lands were afraid of Texas ticks infecting their
own stock. None the less, some of the drovers got through,
sold their herds, and came back with a pocketful of money.
Others found it difficult to make contact with buyers.

While Texas was experimenting with different routes and
shipping-points, an outsider solved the problem for them.
He was Joseph G. McCoy, a trader in stock from Spring-
field, Illinois. A man of vision, he saw that what the
drovers needed was a shipping-point where buyers would
meet them at the end of the long trek. From those who
had followed it he knew that the Chisholm Trail was the
best route north. The most available point for shipment
was Abilene, a little village of log cabins and dugouts on
the new Kansas Pacific Railroad. McCoy backed his faith
with his money. He brought pine lumber from Hannibal,
Missouri, and built loading-chutes, pens, and corrals. In
the early spring he sent a reliable man down the trail to
spread the word to herd bosses that they would find at
Abilene a market waiting for them. The longhorns were
stringing up the trail, each herd marked by a great cloud of

dust, and the word went back from one to another that buyers and commission men were gathered at this new town, the name of which most of them had never heard.

Within a few months Abilene was transformed from a wide point in the road to the roaring metropolis of the cattle trade. Frame houses with false fronts went up like mushrooms. The hammers and saws of the carpenters sounded day and night. Merchants poured in to supply the needs of the cowboys. The Drovers' Cottage, presided over by Mrs. Gore, became the congested headquarters of sellers and buyers. Many trail men are alive today who remember her good food and the kindness with which she nursed the sick and wounded.

Dozens of saloons and gambling-halls were opened. From Kansas City, New Orleans, and St. Louis arrived supple-fingered faro dealers and poker-players, desperadoes who had worn out their welcome at home, and women of ill repute, all of them parasites to feed upon the wages of the cowhands who were surging into the town hungry for excitement after months of hardship and abstinence on the trail.

Texas Street had come into being, the dusty end of a long trail destined to be a Road of Empire. For the gaunt and rangy longhorn, the successor of the buffalo, made it possible for settlers to subdue the Great American Desert, as our old geographies called the territory now occupied by a dozen states. The young riders whooped into town a dirty and unkempt crew. Most of these were fine young men, from good, religious families, and the effect of a barber and a bath, plus some new clothes from Karatofsky's dry-goods emporium, was to remind them that they were no longer wild asses of the desert. Others wanted to 'see the elephant' and to take a whirl at the faro table. The weaker and the more willful found themselves allured by temptation on all sides. The Bull's Head saloon of Ben Thompson and Phil Coe was a fascinating spot, as were dozens of other resorts. The dance halls, known as Hell's Half-Acre, also attracted the lads. For many weeks they had not seen a girl, and often they were not proof against bright eyes and friendly smiles.

During the summer months Abilene was probably the busiest spot in the world for its size. Hundreds of thousands of cattle changed hands and rolled away in Kansas Pacific cars to a market. The cowboys almost never walked. They stuck to the saddle, except when in places of amusement or when loading stock. Dust rose from the street in clouds. Even in the small hours of night the noise did not die down. One could hear the shouts of men, the crack of muleskinners' whips, the clatter of horns and hocks, the 'Hi-yippy-yi!' of the cowboy, the bawling of cattle, the bark of pistols. Drovers, commission men, thugs, cowboys, speculators, workmen, and sporting characters swarmed up and down the streets.

Abilene was wide open. Cowpunchers were given the keys of the town and told to cut loose their wolves. All day and night could be heard in the gambling-houses the rattle of chips. Roulette, faro, monte, chuck-a-luck — all the tables were busy. For the trail-riders, in their hickory shirts, run-down-at-the-heel boots, and striped trousers, had money to burn before they started on the long trek home.

Lawlessness increased so fast that the town decided to

have a civic organization. For it is a deep-seated instinct of
the Anglo-Saxon to believe in law. T. C. Henry, later the
'wheat king of Kansas,' was elected mayor. He appointed
a marshal. An ordinance was passed forbidding the wearing of pistols on the streets. To put teeth into the law the
town fathers built a jail. It was to be a symbol of the new
order.

The first person put in the jail was the colored cook of
a trail herd. The wild riders of the outfit galloped down
Texas Street in a cloud of dust, firing into the air as they
rode. They broke open the door of the jail, rescued the
cook, and took him triumphantly back to camp. One
marshal was ducked in a horse trough. His successor
found himself locked up in his own calaboose. The printed
posters calling attention to the ordinance against carrying
arms were riddled with bullets.

Half a dozen marshals held the position within the
space of a month. Two guaranteed law officers were im-
ported from St. Louis. They arrived on one train, sur-
veyed the carnival of disorder, and departed on the next,
glad to escape with their lives.

One Thomas J. Smith had made application for the
job, but Mayor Henry had rejected him. He was too quiet
and soft-spoken to control these reckless Southerners, the
mayor decided. Yet there had been something about the
man's manner that impressed Henry. He stood just under
six feet, broad of shoulder, erect, lean, with smooth mus-
cles that moved as quick as those of a cat. His eyes were
gray-blue, very clear and very steady.

After Smith had gone back to Kit Carson, Colorado,
where he was marshal, stories about the man drifted to

Henry. At Bear River, Wyoming, he had shown amazing courage in standing up to a self-styled vigilance committee which had arrested one of the boys working for the construction company with which Smith was connected. As a result of this he had been chosen peace officer at one after another of the end-of-the-line towns which sprang up as the railroad advanced. These towns were always wild and untamed. Cut off by hundreds of desert miles from civilization, the road gangs were turbulent and violent. The vultures who had gathered to fleece them of their earnings — gamblers and thieves and brothel-keepers — had no respect whatever for law.

Billy Breakenridge, later of Tombstone fame, met Smith while he was the law in one of these mushroom towns. He wrote in his book *Helldorado*:

> Kit Carson was a typical western frontier town, principally gambling-saloons and dance halls. Cowboys, buffalo-hunters, teamsters, railroad men, and soldiers were there to make it lively.
>
> The town marshal, named Tom Smith, was the bravest man I ever had the pleasure of meeting. He was...a powerful, athletic man, very quick and active, always neatly dressed, and very quiet and gentlemanly. He looked like a successful business or professional man. He rarely carried a gun, but depended on his strength and agility in arresting and disarming the men he went after. He did not know what fear was. He was not a two-gun man with a lot of notches on his pistol, but he would shoot if compelled. When the men got too boisterous, he would go among them, and if they did not do as he told them he would arrest and lock them up, knock them down if necessary and disarm them. They all respected him, for he played no favorites.

It was the custom, Breakenridge explained, to elect as marshal in these frontier towns someone known as a dead shot, with a reputation as a man-killer. Officers of this type shot down offenders without trying to make an arrest. 'Smith had different ideas,' writes Breakenridge. 'He told me one time, "Anyone can bring in a dead man, but to my way of thinking a good officer is one that brings them in alive."'

At his wits' end, Mayor Henry sent for Smith. Abilene had got completely out of hand. He explained the situation to Smith and suggested that the candidate look the town over before he undertook to 'ride herd' on it. Smith drifted down Texas Street and into the Lone Star Saloon. From there he wandered to the Alamo and to the Old Fruit. He took in the busy stockyards and Hell's Half-Acre. An interested observer, he saw a bunch of cowboys shoot the lights out of a saloon because they thought the proprietor was short-changing them. He witnessed vice and crime. Criminals and desperadoes whom he had known in other towns were much in evidence. Abilene had become a mecca for thieves, swindlers, gunmen, professional gamblers, and courtesans.

Having made the tour, Smith returned to the office of the mayor. Henry asked him if he still thought he would like to be marshal. Tom said that he would.

'Do you think you can put an end to this lawlessness?' the mayor wanted to know.

Smith said he believed he could control it.

'How?' Henry snapped.

'Pistols and liquor aren't a good combination. I would take away the weapons from the cowboys while they are in town and from the gamblers too.'

'We have an ordinance already. Nobody pays any attention to it.'

'Why not enforce it?'

'How can you do that?' Henry said impatiently. 'There are a thousand of them and one of you.'

'I would take the pistols away one at a time,' Tom mentioned.

'How can you take a gun from a drunken, hell-roaring cowboy who would as soon shoot as not?'

'I think I can,' the applicant said quietly.

Henry swore him into office and sent him on his way, reluctantly. For he could see that Smith was a brave, resolute man and he believed (so he wrote years later) that he was letting the man go to his death.

The new officer sauntered down Texas Street. Evening was approaching, and night always quickened the life of the trail-end towns. The false fronts of most of the buildings announced that they were saloons and gambling-halls. Into them trooped scores of young men wearing high-heeled boots and big hats. When the herd was bedded down for the night and guards detailed, the cowhands [1] not on duty slapped a saddle on their mounts and went to town. In frontier towns the saloon was the clubhouse. There was nowhere else to go for entertainment. Those drifting in and out might be only homesick boys, or they might be hard, tough hombres. Plenty of the latter type came up the trail, desperadoes and bullies and killers, among them the Clements and their relative John Wesley

---

[1] The terms 'cowhand' and 'brushpopper' were used to designate riders for a ranch. The name cowboy came in later, when so many lads were used on the trail.

Hardin, the most notorious 'bad man' Texas had produced. Later, the Texas killer wrote that he had seen
many wild towns but Abilene beat them all. The magnet
of easy money was a sure lure for scoundrels. There were
crooked games, and quarrels were frequent. Since everybody was a law to himself and all carried pistols,[1] most
difficulties ended in smoking guns.

News of the appointment of another marshal preceded
Tom Smith down the street. A dozen men were anxious
to try him out. Big Hank, a trail-rider who had for
months bullied the outfit for which he worked, was the
first to challenge the new officer. He advanced trucu-
lently.

'So you're the guy that's going to run this town, are
you?' he demanded.

Smith showed his star and admitted quietly that he was
the newly appointed marshal. 'There's an ordinance
against carrying pistols,' he added. 'I'll have to ask you
for yours, sir.'

Big Hank broke into violent language. Stripped of
rhetoric, the purport of his remarks was that no man alive
could take his six-gun from him. The marshal held out his
left hand for the weapon. He had moved in close.

'Not on yore tintype,' the trail-rider boasted, and
backed away to get room for the draw.

Tom's fist moved forward, swiftly, to the point of the
cowboy's chin. For some time Big Hank took no interest
in the subsequent proceedings. When he did, he found
himself being chivied out of town with peremptory orders
not to return.

[1] In early days revolvers were always called pistols in the West.

J. H. (DOC) HOLLIDAY
IN THE EARLY EIGHTIES

TOM SMITH
Marshal of Abilene
1870

JOHN KING FISHER
Deputy Sheriff, Uvalde County, Texas

JOHN SELMAN
1878

The story of Big Hank's discomfiture spread like a prairie fire.

The town was amazed, but there was an undercurrent of opinion that perhaps the man from Kit Carson might have had luck. It was not reasonable to expect an unarmed man to take a weapon away from a drunken ruffian primed to kill. It could happen once, from the sheer surprise of it. But if the marshal tried it again he would be planted in Boot Hill with his toes turned up to the daisies.

Wyoming Frank shared this view. He considered himself a bad man from Bitter Creek, and no shorthorn marshal was going to read the riot act to him. He was in camp when the story reached him. Promptly he declared intention to find out about this. He roped a bronco, saddled, and rode to town. Several companions accompanied him to see the fun. They had a few drinks and then went out to find the marshal. He was not at first to be found, and Wyoming Frank announced triumphantly that he had left town to avoid meeting him.

But presently Smith appeared. He was strolling down the middle of the street, apparently at peace with the world. The cowboy gave a whoop of joy and bore down on him. He straddled forward, a big two-gun man ready for action at the drop of the hat. The fingers of his right hand hovered close to the butt of one of the sixshooters.

'I hear you want my gun, fellow?' he called.

The marshal came close to him before he answered. 'Yes, sir, if you please,' he said, open hand extended.

'You don't get it,' Wyoming Frank stormed. 'I'll pour lead into any galoot who tries to take it.'

'That would be a fool business,' Tom replied. 'There's

an ordinance about firearms. We all have to obey the law.'

He had crowded in close to the cowboy, so close that the bad man had no space to draw the weapon. The bully backed away to get room, but the officer pressed on him. Wyoming Frank retreated into a saloon, watching for a chance to draw without having his wrist seized. Smith followed toe to toe. The eyes of twenty men focused on the two. In another moment the cowboy would kill the marshal. So most of those present thought.

Backed to the bar, Wyoming Frank poured out threats and invective. He was working himself up for a killing. Once more the marshal's right arm shot out, again to the jaw. The big man, staggered, was flung back against the bar. A left and another straight right finished the job. The man with the gun half-drawn crumpled up and went down.

Tom Smith made one mild comment. 'I told him he had better let me have his gun.'

The saloonkeeper came forward and handed a revolver to the officer. 'I won't need this while you are marshal here,' he said.

All of those present trooped forward to give up their weapons. The cool courage of the new marshal won instant support for him. They would have to give way anyhow, or else kill him, and even the toughest of the Texans did not want to shoot down a man like this.

Smith called on the merchants and the saloonkeepers and arranged that in their places of business they should have a check rack where trail men and gamblers could leave their pistols as long as they were in town. The good people of Abilene rejoiced that law had come to them in the person of this young man. Tom Smith did not drink or gamble. Mayor Henry said that he never heard him use an oath or tell a questionable story. Yet he did not hold puritanic views about the conduct of others. All he asked of them was that they obey the rules of the town laid down for them. He was a friendly man, given to smiles, and there was a quiet Irish wit in him. He was very fond of children and won their confidence easily.

The trouble with law maintenance in Abilene was that the place had such a shifting population, one generation succeeding another so swiftly that the marshal had to impress himself on newcomers over and over. He had a sense of psychological values not learned from books. At roundups he had found that cattle do not attack a man on horseback. Astride his horse Silverheels he covered his domain. When he rode down Texas Street slowly, erect in the saddle, he commanded more respect than if he had been on foot. Moreover, he could see more of what was taking place and could get to the scene of a disturbance more quickly.

He was shot at a good many times without being hit, so often, in fact, that the superstitious thought he bore a charmed life. Time and again he went into brothels and gambling-dens to stop trouble or to drag out a man he wanted. Though the fellow was sometimes surrounded by his companions, Smith never failed to bring his man out with him. While he was marshal law and order was maintained in Abilene. He became the hero even of the men he was forced to discipline.

After six months' rule he was killed, not by a cowboy

or a gambler but by two 'hoe men'[1] living a few miles from Abilene. Andrew McConnell had slain a neighbor called Jack Shea over some trivial dispute on his land near Chapman Creek. Tom Smith went out to help a man named McDonald arrest the murderer. A partner of McConnell, one Miles, was in the cabin with him. Disregarding threats, Smith walked into the house and told the killer that he was under arrest. McConnell shot him. After McDonald had escaped Miles helped the other man kill the marshal.

In a Kansas City newspaper J. B. Edwards paid tribute to the memory of the marshal many years later.

> Poor Tom Smith, one of the bravest men ever on the border or in the West! Modest, quiet, commanding the respect of both good and bad alike, successfully keeping our city, overrun as it was with Mexicans, gamblers, and cowboys, as well as lewd women, quiet and orderly, never using his weapons of death the whole season, he laid down his life at the age of about thirty-two while doing his duty as an officer of the law.

In the town of Abilene there is today a slab of granite with a bronze plate upon which is carved the appreciation of the town.

THOMAS J. SMITH
Marshal of Abilene, 1870

Died a Martyr to Duty, Nov. 2, 1870

A Fearless Hero of Frontier Days, Who in
Cowboy Chaos, Established the
Supremacy of Law

---

[1] A hoe man was a farmer. It was a term of contempt used by the cowboys for those who tilled the soil with their hands. The hoe man had his revenge. He fenced the land and pushed the trail drover farther and farther west until it was no longer possible to bring herds north except by rail.

Tom Smith died to maintain the law on the frontier, just as did Ed Masterson at Dodge, William Tilghman at Cromwell, Oklahoma, Fred White at Tombstone, and Sheriff Hazen in the hills of Wyoming. All of them knew the risk they took, and they accepted it as a matter of course.

Mayor Henry knew it would be impossible to find another man like Tom Smith. He looked the field over, and his eye fell on one far inferior to Smith in character but with a more resounding reputation. The man was James Butler Hickok, usually known as Wild Bill. He was a notorious killer, though many of the legendary tales of his exploits circulated by unreliable writers were untrue. Nobody could have looked the heroic part more adequately than Hickok. He was extremely handsome, and he carried himself with the nonchalant grace of a Greek god. His appearance impressed all who saw him, so that it was easy to believe the tales told of him. General Custer wrote of him:

> In person he was about six feet one in height, straight as the straightest of the warriors whose implacable foe he was; broad shoulders, well-formed chest and limbs, and a face strikingly handsome; a sharp, clear blue eye...a finely shaped nose, inclined to be aquiline.... On foot or on horseback, he was one of the most perfect types of manhood I ever saw. Of his courage there could be no question. His deportment was... entirely free from all bluster or bravado.

Since Custer was inclined to be flamboyant himself and also wore his hair long, it might be well to cite the testimony of an old newspaper man, Henry M. Stanley, later renowned for his African explorations. He backs up all that General Custer wrote, with the exception of the statement that he did not like to talk of himself. Stanley quotes a conversation he had with the scout:

> 'Mr. Hickok, how many white men have you killed to your certain knowledge?' After a little deliberation, he replied, 'I suppose I have killed considerably over a hundred.' — 'What made you kill all these men? Did you kill them without cause or provocation?' — 'No, by heaven! I never killed one man without good cause.'

This claim is interesting, because it gives a clew to Hickok's character. Owing to his renown, his career was known to those who then lived in the West. There is no record of killings by Wild Bill that reaches anything near a hundred. He is almost the only bad man of the frontier whose reputation started from tall tales he told about his own brave deeds. The story that made Wild Bill the most romantic hero of the West for fifty years was written by Colonel George W. Nichols and appeared in *Harper's*, issue of February, 1867. The article is done in dime-novel style, and it consists largely of alleged direct quotations from the scout. He boasts from the first page to the last. He says: 'It was at the Wilme Creek fight. I had fired more than fifty cartridges, and I think fetched my man every time.' As to that statement, comment is superfluous.

But the prize piece of fiction is his account of the McCanles affair at the Rock Creek Ranch. It has been repeated a hundred times in print, usually with the comment that this was the most desperate hand-to-hand combat ever fought by one man against ten. It was instead a cold-blooded murder.

'You see, this McCanles was the captain of a gang of

desperadoes, horse thieves, murderers, regular cut-throats, who were the terror of everybody on the border,' Hickok is quoted as saying. He goes on to tell in much detail how ten of the gang attacked him in his cabin — and he killed ten of them. 'There were eleven buckshot in me,' he concluded. 'I carry some of them now. I was cut in thirteen places, all of them bad enough to have let the life out of a man. But that blessed old Doctor Mills pulled me safe through it, after a bed siege of many a long week.'

All this tissue of falsehood was exploded in the *Nebraska History Magazine,* issue of April–June, 1927. George W. Hansen, an old pioneer, dug up the court records which had been lying at Beatrice, Nebraska, for sixty years in an old envelope yellowed by age.

David C. McCanles was not a border ruffian and a desperado, as claimed by Hickok, but the most prominent and public-spirited settler in the neighborhood. He organized the first school in the country. Prior to that time he had been four times sheriff of his county in North Carolina. One of the reasons why he left that state was because he was a loyal Unionist and foresaw the coming of secession. His brother James (also alleged to have been a member of the 'gang') after the tragedy moved to Florence, Colorado, organized a bank there, and was twice elected to represent his district in the State Senate. The McCanles family was of good pioneer stock. In 1927 more than seventy descendants of Dave McCanles were living.

The facts of the fight at the Rock Creek Ranch are beyond dispute. Dave McCanles took his ten-year-old son with him to the ranch to find out if a deferred payment for the ranch (which he had sold to the Overland Stage

Company) had been brought him from the company by Wellman, the keeper of the station. Two neighboring farmers went with him, but turned off at the barn and did not accompany him to the house. None of them were armed. McCanles was a determined fellow. He suspected that Wellman was holding back the money from him. There were some hot words. Hickok seized a rifle and shot McCanles. The other two farmers came running from the barn. They too were killed by Hickok, Wellman, and Brink, the stock-tender. During the slaughter Monroe McCanles, the ten-year-old boy, ran away and hid, thus saving his life. The killing took place July 12, 1861. On July 15 the sheriff of Gage County arrested the three murderers and drove them to Beatrice, thirty miles away, in a heavy lumber wagon. Not one of them showed a scratch.

The county had no jail and no money. The Civil War absorbed the attention of everybody. McCanles had arrived recently from North Carolina and was not known widely. The Hickok story was that the victim was a rebel sympathizer and had been stealing horses for the Confederates. The justice decided to drop the whole business without a trial.

The story told by Hickok and his abettors was absurd, though it served him at the time. It asks us to believe that David McCanles, the most prosperous man of the neighborhood and the father of five children, a strong Union sympathizer, was attempting to run off the stage company's horses in broad daylight with the aid of a ten-year-old boy and two unarmed companions. To reach the Confederate forces he would have had to cross the Abolitionist state of Kansas, now heavily occupied by Northern troops.

As to the number of men engaged in this affair at the Rock Creek Ranch, the court records prove the facts conclusively. Hickok and his two companions were charged with the murder of the three slain men. The other seven named in Wild Bill's story as victims of his prowess were creatures of his imagination.

The most significant fact about the fights of Wild Bill is that he was extraordinarily careful in looking after his own skin. Whenever he thought danger was impending he killed. It was a settled principle with him to take no chances. A dead enemy was no longer dangerous.

We have been keeping Mayor Henry waiting too long. He engaged Hickok as marshal to hold down the lawless element. The choice was not a fortunate one. The new marshal believed in a wide-open town. A gambler and a drinking man, his alliances were with the vicious rather than the decent element. Lawlessness and disorder increased during his régime. All he asked of the parasites feeding on Abilene was that they operate in such a way as not to annoy him. At the end of the year his contract as marshal was not renewed.

Hickok killed only two men while he was at Abilene. He had trouble with Phil Coe, the joint owner with Ben Thompson of the Bull's Head gambling-house. It is not clear whether this arose wholly over a woman or in part because Hickok had an interest in the Alamo, a rival place.

A bunch of Texas trail drovers were having a wild night preparatory to the start back home. It started good-naturedly enough. They seized citizens, ripped the clothes from them, hustled them to Karatofsky's, and bought them new suits. Phil Coe was one of them. He took a shot at a dog which snarled at him. Hickok walked out of the Alamo and demanded what the trouble was. Coe answered not too graciously. In the duel which followed Coe was killed. 'Mike' Williams, assistant marshal, came running around the corner to the scene. Hickok whirled on him and killed Williams. He did not wait to find out whether the runner was friend or foe. One cannot think of Tom Smith shooting down his own deputy because he dared not take time to discover he was an ally. In battle Hickok's reactions were lightning-quick, but one finds back of them at times a hint of panic. There was no need whatever to destroy McCanles and his friends or to rub out Williams. Wild Bill was a more dangerous man than most because he thought of his own safety only and had not the poised courage to restrain himself from the hurry of violence.

Hickok had acquired all the self-protective devices of the killer who has achieved a reputation. There were 'bad men,' such as Clay Allison and Ben Thompson, who were too reckless to take precautions. There were others, men like William Tilghman and Tom Smith and Colonel Sanders of the Montana vigilantes, who walked the straight line of duty and paid little attention to their own safety. But most notorious gunmen took as few chances as possible. There is no record that Wild Bill ever played cards except with his back to a wall, save on the one occasion when he was murdered. At night he slept with a revolver at hand and crumpled newspapers all over the floor to prevent anybody from stealing upon him noiselessly. When he turned the corner of a street he always made a wide curve instead of going round at a sharp angle. The price of life for Hickok and his kind was eternal vigilance.

The trail drovers could overcome blizzards, stampedes, swollen rivers, and Indian attacks in their long trek up the Chisholm Trail. But they could not defeat the fences of the hoe men. Year by year, as the covered wagons pushed across Kansas in greater numbers, more land was taken up for homesteading. The cattle trail moved westward, to reach other shipping towns. Ellsworth, Hays, and Dodge took the traffic away from Abilene. Saloons and gambling-halls moved to the new towns. The bad men and the rowdies flitted to richer pastures. Abilene became a nice, quiet church town which had no need of fast-shooting marshals to keep the peace. Its day of hectic glory was past.

VIII

A Plague o' Both Your Houses

A COMBINATION of factors made Texas in the seventies the most lawless spot on earth. West Texas was frontier country, and the Apaches and Comanches were raiding it ruthlessly. The Civil War had unsettled the lives of men, and Reconstruction days were building up a bitterness that found expression in outrages hard to understand now. Outlaws from all over the South and the border states poured into Texas. Some infested the towns and others skulked in the brush, from which they rode out on nefarious night errands. The King-Fisher and Sam Bass gangs of bandits were only two of many. Bad men were looked up to and admired. Such notorious killers as John Wesley Hardin and Ben Thompson had hundreds of devoted adherents.

In the chaparral a man with a horse and a rope could start a brand for himself by the simple process of the free use of a running-iron. Gunmen were employed by ranchers to protect and increase their herds. Life was cheap and one held his own or took what belonged to another by stealth or strength.

There were a dozen family feuds raging, the start of most of which had been quarrels over cattle. Notable among these were the Horrell-Higgins and the Taylor-Sutton vendettas. In judging the participants one should consider the times and the circumstances. A false sense of honor, family pride and loyalty, the call to clan unity, were as much involved as passion, revenge, and hatred. It was a wild country. Most of those engaged in the Taylor-Sutton feud, for instance, would under ordinary conditions have been good citizens supporting law and order.

The Suttons and the Taylors were the most important cattle-owners in De Witt County. Their stock ran in part the same range. A difference of opinion concerning ownership led to trouble. Both the Taylors and the Suttons were large families, and they had intermarried with a good many families in the neighborhood equally numerous. In the course of time all these relations became drawn into the trouble that developed. Before order was at last restored conditions were such that neutrals, looked on with suspicion by both factions, were almost forced to take sides. De Witt became a county divided against itself. Men went about their daily work carrying weapons. Armed bands roamed the county. Captain McNelly of the Texas Rangers, probably the most feared officer in the history of that organization, reported to his chief that he met Joe Tumlinson at the head of seventy-five men and that the feud leader told him the only way to have peace was to kill off all the Taylor party. Tumlinson was a deputy of Jack Helms, one-time sheriff and assistant United States marshal. Both he and his nominal superior were adherents of the Sutton group.

Two young men rode in to Clinton, De Witt County, to a dance held in the courtroom of Judge Henry Clay Pleasants. They were Buck Taylor and Dick Chisholm. While they were hitching their horses shots rang out. Both of them lay in the dust. They had ridden to their last dance. John Wesley Hardin, the worst killer in Texas history and an ally of the Taylors, rubbed out Jack Helms in an impromptu pistol duel. The body of a cowboy was found on the range after his riderless horse appeared at the ranch. A cattleman was shot while walking from his house to the barn.

Scrap Taylor and two of his companions were arrested for rustling and taken by the sheriff to Clinton. Before morning all three of them had been hanged. A mob had stormed the jail. So the factional struggle went on from bad to worse. All peaceful citizens feared a local private war more disastrous than the one lately fought between the North and the South.

Both sides rallied for a battle to decide the issue. They came together at Clinton. The Suttons were deployed in and about the courthouse and the Taylors moved up from the river to attack. Stores had been hurriedly closed and women and children herded into houses.

Into the open space between the two forces walked a man, in his hands a shotgun. The man was Judge Pleasants, the hero of the Taylor-Sutton feud. He stood there, facing first one party and then the other, and delivered a one-man ultimatum.

'There will be no fighting here,' he announced in a clear, ringing voice. 'I mean to see that peace comes to this county. Go home, and stop this mad business.'

Both sides were taken by surprise. Judge Pleasants was a man of character and of influence. He had been trying to rally the citizens of the county to neutrality, and its officers to enforce the law against the feudists. He was looked on with suspicion by the firebrands of both sides, but these wild fighting men knew bravery when they saw it. After all he was the law, and the leaders did not want to put themselves in the wrong. While they hesitated, a few of the leading women of the town walked across the courthouse square and joined the judge. That ended the battle of Clinton before it started. The clans slipped out of town by different roads.

In spite of the efforts of Judge Pleasants the feud ran on for years. Scores were assassinated. There were spies in both camps, and every unguarded word was dangerous. No man, however innocent of offense he might be, felt safe from an unexpected bullet.

The Suttons decided to migrate, and made arrangements to leave secretly. Bill Sutton, his wife, and Gabriel Slaughter drove to Indianola to take the steamer there. As they walked to their cabins William Taylor and a companion followed them. Guns roared, and Sutton and Slaughter fell dead.

Six months later Will Taylor was tried for murder. It was said freely that he would never live to hear the verdict. The rangers stood between him and the vengeance of his enemies. He was given ten years, appealed the conviction, and later had it reversed by the courts. While Taylor was in prison awaiting his trial at Indianola there were very heavy rains and cloudbursts. Fearing that his prisoners would be washed away, the jailor moved them from the building. During his temporary freedom Taylor distinguished himself by saving the lives, at the risk of losing his own, of several women and children caught in the rushing waters.

Not long after this Jim Taylor and two of his allies were trapped in a cottonfield and shot down. Someone had warned Judge Pleasants of what was going to take place. He hurried to the scene, but arrived too late. Those of the Sutton party who had done the killing were still there, and the fearless judge denounced the act bluntly to the guilty men according to the story of his son, told in C. L. Douglas's *Famous Texas Feuds.*

The feud ran on, though no Taylor or Sutton was left to lead the gunmen. By this time there were more than thirty indictments for murder on the records, none of which were being acted upon by the authorities.

At last the lawless element went too far. Doctor Philip Brazell, a neutral non-combatant, lay very ill at his farmhouse. A leading physician of the district, he had taken care of the sick and wounded of both sides during the seven-year feud. After nightfall a party of men came to the house and dragged him from his bed in the presence of his wife. The doctor and his three sons were taken into the woods. The two younger boys managed to escape. Their father and older brother were shot to death. No motive for this crime can be given other than the fear that the doctor, about to die, might reveal to the authorities something he had learned while attending some of the feudists.

Judge Pleasants had tried to end the long years of terror by appeals to good citizens and local peace officers. He knew now that way could not succeed. Witnesses were afraid to testify. A number of them had been murdered to prevent their appearance in court. He wrote to the Governor and asked that a company of Texas Rangers be sent to De Witt County.

Lieutenant Lee Hall, an intrepid and dashing officer, was in charge of the detachment. He consulted with Judge Pleasants. They gathered what evidence they could against the Brazell murderers. It was agreed that Hall should arrest the guilty ones and the judge should see that justice was done in the courts. A grand jury was called and indictments found against seven men.

One of them was Joe Sitterlie. He was about to be married, and a dance was given at the home of the bride to celebrate the event. Hall decided to be an uninvited guest, and he took with him twenty-five fighting men armed with Winchesters and revolvers. It was a bitterly cold night. When the rangers arrived the young couple had been married and the dance was in full swing. Hall surrounded the house and moved forward alone to the porch.

He was met by William Meador, one of the seven wanted for the Brazell killings. Meador was marshal of Cuero and Sitterlie was a deputy sheriff.

'What you doing here?' the marshal demanded.

'I came to arrest you and six others,' Hall answered.

'How many men have you?'

The ranger told him.

'You can't do it. There are more than fifty of us.'

Hall pushed past him into the house. At sight of him there was a tumult of shouts and threats. He waited till it had died down.

'My boys surround the house,' he said. 'I want the following men.' And he read the list.

'By God, no!' a voice cried. 'We'll fight it out.'

'Suits us,' Hall cried. 'We'll get the women and children
out of here and go to it.' The angry dancers had pushed
him back toward the door. He cried to his men: 'They're
moving out the women and kids. It's to be a fight, boys.
Get ready to blaze away when I give the word.'

'We don't want to kill you all,' Meador cried.

'You won't,' Hall answered; then, abruptly, 'Give me
that gun,' he ordered.

The sharp, implacable challenge, backed by the ranger's
cold, steady gaze, was too much for the marshal. He
passed over his revolver. Hall called in two of his men to
collect weapons. All the wedding guests were disarmed.

The bride made a personal plea to the lieutenant. 'This
is my wedding night, and I'll only be married once. Let
the dance go on, please.'

Hall agreed. Some of the troopers did the squares with
pretty partners while the others patrolled outside. When
morning came the rangers took their prisoners to Clinton,
but not until Hall had warned those he left behind that if
any attempt to rescue the prisoners was made his men had
orders to kill them first.

The prisoners were arraigned before Judge Pleasants.
Some of the best lawyers in Texas were brought in by the
prisoners to argue that bail should be allowed. The Sutton forces were confident that the judge would free the
men pending trial. Many threats were made that if
Pleasants remanded them to jail he would not live a week.
The *habeas corpus* hearings took several days. Both the

Taylor and the Sutton factions attended the proceedings in force.

The morning came when the judge was to make his decision. It was noticed that a score of rangers were scattered through the courtroom at strategic points.

Judge Pleasants rose, a strong, resolute man who knew well that he might be reading his own death sentence. As he did so, six rangers walked down the aisle, Winchester rifles in their hands. Three of them stood on each side of the judge, slender, brown-faced men as hard as iron-wood, and confronted a roomful of embittered feudsmen. N. A. Jennings, the ranger who stood next the judge on his right, describes the scene in his book, *A Texas Ranger*. Like the others, he threw a cartridge into the breech and cocked the weapon in the sight of all. Except for Hall's audacious capture of the indicted men the night before, no such convincing demonstration of law had ever before been seen in De Witt County.

The judge let his gaze travel slowly down the lines of hostile clansmen before he spoke. When he did so every word was cold, incisive, and implacable. He told them that De Witt County was a disgrace to the State of Texas, that over it had roamed bands of armed men, committing terrible outrages and killing whom they pleased. 'There are men in this room, not prisoners at the bar but free on-lookers, who are murderers, bushwhackers, and assassins,' he went on, again letting his eyes sweep the benches deliberately. 'Without reviewing the long record of lawlessness, I shall tell you now that in Clinton and De Witt County those evil days are past.... The foreman of our grand jury has been threatened for bringing the rangers

here. That responsibility is mine, and mine alone....
These men at the bar are committed to jail. Bail is denied
them. Moreover, since the jail here is not strong enough
the prisoners will be taken by Lieutenant Hall to Galveston
for safekeeping.'

Jennings comments that he would never forget how the
gray-haired old judge's eyes flashed and his voice rang out
as he pronounced his decision in a room packed with hatred
and tense emotion.

Judge Pleasants had received anonymous letters to the
effect that the men had been chosen to kill him if he did
not release the prisoners. Most of the good people of the
county were of the opinion that the threats would be
carried out very soon. The judge walked the streets of
Clinton with an outward serenity that gave no sign of a
fear that he was moving in the shadow of death. It is
pleasant to recall that he lived for many years, an honored
and respected citizen.

The case against one of the defendants was at last
dropped. Two were acquitted, three convicted. Meador
died before his trial. In the end those convicted escaped
legal punishment on account of court technicalities.

But Doctor Webb, in his book *The Texas Rangers*, tells
an anecdote current for years. The arrested feudists
were kept in jail so long that one of them ate peaches
from a tree that sprouted from a seed dropped out of
the window by him after eating the fruit brought by his
wife.

Whether this story is true or not, it is sure that the
arrested men were in prison a long time. During their in-
carceration the fires of passion died down. Men no longer

walked in fear of their lives, for law had come to De Witt County.

In looking over the records of those who have made explosive history on the frontier, especially in the Southwest, one notes again and again the large number of cases where quiet, God-fearing parents have raised numerous sons who chose a way of life entirely alien to that of their fathers. The Taylors, the Horrells, the Youngers, and the Daltons were all examples of this. Caught in the borderland lawlessness that followed the Civil War, the sons of these families, naturally high-spirited and adventurous, imbued with the clan spirit, slipped into paths that made them destructive rather than constructive forces in their communities. Not all of them were outlaws. Many were strongly individual, with outstanding qualities that might have been of great value. The pity is that they were not disciplined to self-control.

Sam Horrell and John Higgins ran cattle. They were friendly neighbors, and their sons were brought up together. Some of the Horrell boys were rather wild and fond of going on sprees. But that was something their good father hoped added years would cure. If the times had not been so badly out of joint the lads might have settled down. But it was in the days when Texans were still being ruled by carpetbag government from Washington. The disfranchised natives resented this bitterly.

A squad of state police under Captain Williams rode to Lampasas to restore order. They walked into the Jerry Scott Saloon, where a group of the Horrell faction were drinking, and inside of three minutes Captain Williams and three of his troopers were dead. The fourth, a negro, was spurring out of town in terror. Mart Horrell was seriously wounded. His brothers carried him to the Huling House for treatment.

Jerry Scott and Mart Horrell were arrested and taken to Georgetown. The other Horrells raised a rescue party and stormed the jail. Though the citizens helped the officers to resist, the door was battered down and the cattlemen released their friends.

A Horrell migration seemed wise. There were six brothers, and they had a legion of relatives, some of whom were also related to the Taylors and to John Wesley Hardin, the famous killer. Openly and defiantly they gathered their cattle and crossed the line into New Mexico, serving notice that they did not expect to be interrupted. Nobody interfered, and the herd and wagons, accompanied by Turners, Dixons, Bowens, and other kin and adherents, moved up the Pecos Valley to the Ruidosa.

The nearest town was Lincoln. At a Mexican *baile* the Texans had trouble with the natives. In the fight that ensued Ben Horrell was killed, as were also former Sheriff Gillam, Constable Martinez, and others. A great many were shot down in the feud which ensued, including Ben Turner, a devoted friend of the Horrells.

The Horrells did not like New Mexico, and it did not like them. Again they gathered their horses and their cows, loaded the wagons, and started the long trek back to Texas. The Lone Star State was safely back in the Democratic column by this time, and the returned travelers offered to stand trial for the Williams killing. A Lampasas jury acquitted them, and the future might have been peaceful except for their own turbulence and a sure instinct they had for finding trouble.

A feud started between them and their old boy companion, Pink Higgins, who was entitled to call himself, but seldom did, John Pinckney Calhoun Higgins. Pink had driven trail herds to Kansas and had built up a strong background of friends. He was a quiet, cool man, skillful with firearms, and an adept at the job of self-preservation.

The Horrells had gone into the butcher business. They had a shop in Lampasas and a slaughter pen outside. Merritt, the youngest of the four brothers, had a difficulty with Pink as to the ownership of some stock the former was driving. They served notice on each other that when they met again there would be war. The scene of that meeting was at the old Jerry Scott Saloon, in the same room where Captain Williams and his troopers had been killed some years earlier. According to the story told by James B. Gillett in his book, *Six Years With the Texas Rangers*, Merritt Horrell was not armed when Higgins walked in the back door. Another account says he had a rifle lying on his knees as he sat at a table playing cards. In any case, Pink walked out of the saloon leaving young Horrell dead on the floor.

Pink Higgins was an unusual character. He was as strongly individual as the Horrells, but he had schooled himself to efficient self-restraint. Though a completely honest man and no trouble-hunter, he was as dangerous to his enemies as any cowman in Texas. During his life he killed others many times, never for pleasure, apparently with no subsequent regrets. A friendly biographer mentions that at one time or another he was under indictment for having killed fourteen men. In fairness, it ought to be said that he was never convicted of any of these homicides.

As soon as Mart and Tom Horrell heard of the shooting of their brother they slapped saddles on their mounts and headed for town. According to the story Tom told immediately afterward to the sheriff, they were waylaid by their enemies before they reached Lampasas and were both wounded.

Sam Horrell was a quiet farmer who did not go in for plain or fancy killings. Like his father, he preferred to follow paths of peace. Shortly after the feud broke out he gathered his belongings and moved with his family to West Texas.

It was in March, 1877, that Merritt was killed. Three months later the two factions had a pitched battle at Lampasas. The principals on one side were Mart, Bill, and Tom Horrell, three of their cousins, and several friends. Opposed to them were Pink Higgins, the Mitchells, a brother-in-law named Terry, and other adherents. The combatants found what cover they could, but several were killed. It developed into a long sniping battle. Captain John C. Sparks of the rangers chanced to be in town with two or three of his men. He managed to reach the leaders of both sides and arranged a truce. The terms of this were that each side was to retire from Lampasas, taking its dead and wounded with it.

Major Jones ordered Sergeant N. O. Reynolds to Lampasas with a few rangers. Instructions were given him to arrest the Horrell band and bring them to town. The sheriff warned Reynolds bluntly that it was a suicide

assignment. Nobody, he said, could capture the Horrell
outfit without a desperate fight. With them they had
eight or ten of the boldest 'warriors' in the country.

'It's my job,' the sergeant said. 'I reckon they will
listen to reason.'

Rain was falling when he and his few men left town, and
the sky was heavy when a lowering dawn broke next morning. The sergeant crept up to the silent house, the rest of
the posse at his heels. Fortunately no dog barked to betray
their approach. The ranch-house might be empty. It
might be full of men ready to let fly a volley at them.
From the chimney no smoke was rising.

Reynolds tried the latch and very softly pushed the
door open. Very cautiously he edged into the room, every
movement sounding like a pistol shot. He half-expected a
blast of gunfire to meet him. His men tiptoed in after him.
There was one large room, and many men lay sleeping in
bunks and beds.

Reynolds poked one of the Horrells with the barrel of
his rifle. 'Wake up, Mart,' he said.

Horrell sat up, rubbing sleep from his eyes. His companions awoke, each to find himself covered by a Winchester at cock.

'Who are you?' Tom Horrell asked.

'We're rangers,' Reynolds told him, 'and we have come
to take you back to town.'

The outlaws were twice as many as the rangers. Horrell
counted heads.

'No!' he exploded. 'I'd rather die fighting than be
turned over to a mob led by Pink Higgins.'

'You won't be turned over to a mob,' Reynolds promised. 'The rangers don't do business that way. When we take a prisoner we keep him.'

'So you say. We've got no guarantee of it.'

'Only our record,' the sergeant agreed. 'But I'll give you a guarantee of one thing. If any of you drags out a gun there will be a dozen dead men in this room inside of two minutes.'

Tom Horrell was a game man himself, and as his steady eyes searched those of the ranger he felt sure he had met one whose word he could trust. Moreover, Reynolds meant to fight, and though he might be defeated it would be at heavy cost.

'All right,' he said. 'We'll take you up on that. All we ask is a fair hearing in court. This fuss isn't one of our seeking. Pink Higgins and his gang forced it.'

Reynolds took his prisoners to town, fourteen of them. The news of the capture spread like a prairie blaze. Everybody in the county wanted to have a look at the man who had rounded up as desperate a band as ever lived in Texas. The sergeant was given a commission for his daring exploit.

Major Jones of the rangers came into the picture here. He brought Company C to town and arrested the leaders of the Higgins faction. His proposal was to declare a truce to the feud. He suggested it to the Horrells and they laughed at him.

'You don't reckon Pink Higgins would let a piece of paper stop him, do you?' Tom derided. 'Why, that bird is a killer from way back.' And he recited a list of alleged homicides committed by Higgins, including the shooting of two negroes friendly to the Horrells.

'He has the reputation of being a man who keeps his word,' Major Jones insisted.

In the end he induced the Horrells to write and sign a letter to Higgins, Mitchell, and Wrenn, the leaders of the other faction, in which they proposed 'a peaceful, honorable, and happy adjustment of our difficulties which shall leave both ourselves and you all our self-respect and sense of unimpaired honor.' The letter concluded with a promise, in the event that the armistice was accepted, 'to bury the bitter past forever, and join with you as good citizens in undoing the evil which has resulted from our quarrel.'

Perhaps the leaders of both parties to the feud recalled boyhood days when they had eaten at each other's tables, slept under the same tarp at cow-hunts, and even fought against the raids of Comanches together. At any rate, Higgins met the offer halfway and signed a treaty to terminate enmities and avoid revenges for past offenses.

Unfortunately, men of violence cannot always blot out their pasts. A desire to change one's way of life is not enough. The Horrell-Higgins feud died down. But Tom and Mart Horrell moved on to more trouble. A storekeeper at Meridian was robbed and while defending his property killed. There was some evidence implicating the two brothers. The reputations they had built up for lawlessness was an argument more potent than the evidence. A mob collected, stormed the prison, and shot the last of the turbulent Horrells to death.

Higgins moved to the Panhandle, perhaps because he had built up too much enmity in Lampasas County. He married and raised a family. Apparently he was an

exemplary husband and father. Two of his sons became
highly respected judges in Texas; his daughters married
well and brought up families of their own. Yet it would
be too much to say that Pink Higgins returned to peaceful pursuits when he went to the Panhandle. He became
a detective for the big Spur Ranch. His business was to
stop cattle-rustling, and he did it effectively and ruthlessly.
A big outfit, harassed by cattle-thieves on every side, did
not inquire too closely into the method by which its protection men stopped brand-blotting and other forms of
stealing. Higgins was accused of rubbing out rustlers in
the same way that Canton and Elliott and Tom Horn and
Fin Clanton were alleged to have done it in other parts of
the country. In early days there was always much lawlessness connected with the raising of stock. To catch and
convict bands of thieves was almost impossible. Cowmen
felt that unless they were willing to be driven out of business they had to take short cuts to punish the outlaws.
Men like Pink Higgins were convenient instruments to use
in getting results.

A one-time manager of the Spur Ranch, C. A. Jones,
wrote a story for the *Atlantic Monthly* some years ago
about Pink Higgins. He called it 'The Good Bad Man.'

In it he gives an account of how Higgins felt forced to
put an end to William Standifer, another stock detective
employed by the Spur Ranch. Enmity had risen between
the two men, and according to the tale of Higgins his
fellow-employee had made up his mind to 'get' Pink. The
latter tried in every way possible to avoid a battle, but
came to the conclusion at last (so he told the story to
Jones) that he had to fight or be assassinated.

One morning he met Standifer. Both of them were on horseback, riding in the same direction but on trails that would eventually meet. Higgins watched his enemy like a hawk. He felt sure that before the other stock detective opened hostilities he would dismount and use his horse as a shield.

When Higgins saw the man's foot lift from the stirrup he was out of the saddle like a flash, at the same time slipping the rifle from its scabbard. Standifer got in the first shot and wounded the horse of Higgins. Pink dropped to one knee and waited.

"Standifer was shooting, but he was jumping around like a Comanche, and his shots were going wild,' Higgins related afterward. 'I waited for him to stop jumping. When at last he did, I let him have it. I knew I had got him when the dust flew from his sleeve and he started to buckle. He dropped the gun into the crook of his arm and started to walk off. . . . He fell face forward, his feet flopped up, and he didn't speak. . . . I got on my horse and rode to a telephone and told the sheriff at Claremont I thought I had killed Standifer. He said if I wasn't sure I had better go back and finish him.'

As casually as that oldtimers regarded a homicide when one of the victims was a 'bad man.' Probably if Higgins had been the victim the comment of the sheriff would have been the same.

The contradictions in the character of such a man as John Pinckney Calhoun Higgins can be explained only by keeping in mind the conditions under which he lived. He was held to be a hard man, merciless to transgressors, but honest and upright, judged by his own code. To his friends he was kind and generous. And to his family he was a man who gave affection tempered with firmness. Perhaps the summing up of Jones is as fair an appraisal as one can reach — a good bad man.

IX

'Stick 'Em Up'

DURING the generation following the Civil War a profitable way of life financially was train robbery with bank 'stickups' as a side line. The occupation had two drawbacks. Those who did well at it could not keep their easily acquired wealth from slipping swiftly through their fingers. The second disadvantage was more serious. Night riders who took up the business did not live long. Nine out of ten of them came to sudden violent ends.

The first eminent practitioners of the 'Hands up!' fraternity were Jesse James and his gang. In spite of efforts to make a Robin Hood out of him, this bandit leader was a cold-blooded killer who had learned under Quantrell utter ruthlessness. His associates the Youngers held more closely to the code of the frontier, to the clan spirit which taught a man to 'go through' for his comrades.

After a dozen daring and successful bank and train robberies the James-Younger outlaws made the mistake of leaving their own terrain to rob a bank in Minnesota,

five hundred miles from the district they knew, with the
thickly settled state of Iowa between the scene of the
holdup and home. The adventure would probably have
come to grief in any case, but the cashier of the bank,
J. L. Haywood, gave his life to make failure certain.

There were eight of the robbers. The two James brothers
and Bob Younger went into the bank to get the money.
Jim Younger and Pitts guarded a bridge across which
they had to retreat. Chadwell, Miller, and Cole Younger
stayed with the horses and watched the street.

Though they had twice before this killed bank cashiers
during holdups — at Liberty and at Gallatin, both in
Missouri — the raiders expected no trouble at Northfield.
But when Frank James ordered Haywood to open the safe
the cashier faced him boldly and refused.

'We'll kill you if you don't,' Jesse warned.

'I know that, but I won't help you if I die for it,' the
obstinate man flung back.[1]

He was shot down instantly. The teller bolted for a side
door, was hit in the shoulder, but made his escape.

In the building opposite the bank a Doctor Wheeler had
his office. He was a hunter, and from a rack he picked up
a gun loaded for big game. Through the office window he
began firing. His first shot dropped Bill Chadwell from
the saddle. He sent a bullet tearing into Pitts, and when
the bandits in the bank came out wounded Bob Younger.

Word spread like a prairie fire that there was a bank
holdup. Men snatched up their rifles — for this was close
to a game country where most of these pioneers hunted
— and from doors and street corners peppered at the out-

[1] The assistant cashier testified to the words at the coroner's inquest.

laws. With the exception of the James brothers all the rest of the gang were hit. The robbers clattered out of town, leaving their dead behind them. Far out on the prairie they pulled up to tie to their saddles the sagging bodies of those who were worst hurt.

The fugitives reached Mankato, greatly hampered in their flight by the desperate condition of Bob Younger. Jesse James made a callous proposal to Cole Younger bluntly.

'Bob is going to die anyhow,' he said. 'We'll be caught if we stay with him. Let's finish the job they started in town. He'll be out of his misery then.'

Cole looked at him, chill anger in his eyes. 'Go ahead and save yourself if you like. Jim and I are sticking with Bob.'

The bandits separated. Frank and Jesse James rode away. Clem Miller elected to stay with the Youngers. Perhaps he was afraid that his wounds might hamper him and Jesse would rid himself of the encumbrance. After half a dozen close calls Frank and Jesse reached Missouri.

The pursuit centered on the rear guard of the robbers. The Youngers and Miller hid in a swampy wood to spend the night. When morning broke they realized they were surrounded.

All day the battle lasted, four hundred against four. Miller exposed himself to get a better shot. A bullet crashed into his head. Jim and Cole were both hit again. Bob was in very bad condition. Cole talked the situation over with Jim. They tied a white handkerchief to the barrel of a rifle and surrendered.

They were tried and given life in the Minnesota Penitentiary. When I was a college boy selling books at Still-water I visited the prison and saw them. Cole was libra-rian. He was soft-voiced and gentle of manner. Only the steadiness of the steel-barred eyes gave hint of the manner of man he was.

After twenty-five years Cole and Jim were pardoned. Bob had died in prison. He never fully recovered from his wounds. Outside the walls of the prison Jim found no place for him. He shot himself. Cole had been converted to religion. He lived the rest of his life quietly. Occasion-ally he preached, his own misspent life the text.

Long before this time Jesse James had been treacher-ously killed by one of his band, Bob Ford, who in turn was shot down at Creede, Colorado, by 'Red' O'Kelley without warning. Charley Ford committed suicide. Only Frank James was left to be stared at by weak-minded admirers.

Of the Collins-Bass gang, Heffridge, Collins, Berry, Bass, and Barnes went out to the sound of roaring guns in the hands of law officers. The others slipped away into obscurity. The proportionate mortality in the Dalton-Doolin gang was even greater. With the settling up of the country and the coming of the rural telephone, chances for escape were constantly diminishing. Oklahoma and the Indian Territory were still wild, rough country, but the deputy United States marshals knew the Cherokee Strip almost as well as the bandits. Such officers as Bill Tilgh-man, Heck Thomas, Chris Madsen, and Bud Ledbetter were first-class trailers, expert shots, and game to the core. They were the leaders of a group who stamped out the bad man and made law respected in the borderland.

The Daltons were cousins to the Youngers, and in spite of their wild lawlessness were far removed from the Jesse James type of outlaw. None of them were killers from choice, except as this was forced on them from their manner of life. Daring and reckless frontiersmen, when guns came out they fought in the open to kill to ensure their own safety, but in all their long record there is no evidence of cold-blooded murder or treachery.

Louis and Adeline Dalton had fifteen children. They were a stalwart outdoor breed. The daughters married neighboring farmers. Some of the sons took up land, married, and lived close to the soil, good citizens all the days of their lives. But five of the boys had the love of adventure stirring unquenchably in their blood. The legends which had gathered around their notorious cousins and the still better-known James brothers were part of the family heritage. As youngsters they had seen Jesse James on their place. After his death the favorite horse of the outlaw chief came into the possession of the boys.

Like their neighbors, the Daltons ran cattle. All the lads were cowboys. They rode the range with other hardy cowhands, all good riders and excellent shots. Working on the Bar-X-Bar and the neighboring Turkey Track Ranch were Bill Powers, George Newcomb, Charley Bryant, Dick Broadwell, Charley Pierce, and Bill Doolin, all of them later associated with the Dalton and Doolin gangs. Four out of the five wild Daltons, and all the cowboys named above, went out of life violently and suddenly, shot to death by officers or citizens supporting the law. If they learned anything at all from the experience of others, they must have known that they would come with unexpected swiftness to the end of the crooked trails they were following, that for them there could be no future for which to plan.

It must be remembered that in the Indian Territory at this time there was no law except that which was enforced by the deputy United States marshals operating from Fort Smith, Arkansas, under the direction of federal officers in conjunction with Judge Isaac C. Parker's court. Never before or since has there been such a judicial set-up as this one. The marshals were hard, grim men, and many of them died in the performance of their duty. The judge was firm and harsh. Before him at one time or another stood twenty-eight thousand criminals dragged there to receive justice. During the twenty-five years of his incumbency one hundred and sixty-eight men were sentenced to the gallows, of whom eighty-eight were actually hanged. In such an environment as surrounded those in the Cherokee Strip, though there were many bad men the good citizens far outnumbered them. The parents of thousands of youths watched them anxiously as they grew up, for they knew there came an hour when spirited lads stood at the forking of the trails, one branch leading to an upright and constructive life, the other to crooked paths that could have no safe ending. Each of the Daltons came in turn to that place of dividing roads. Some took the plodding way of hard work and respectability. Grat, Bob, Emmett, and Bill Dalton followed the other trail.

There was an older brother, Frank, in whose blood the call to adventure also sang. But Frank lined up on the side of the law. He was one of the deputy United States marshals who went out from Fort Smith to run down the

whiskey-smugglers and the other criminals who infested
the Indian Territory. In a desperate battle, during which
several outlaws were killed, Frank Dalton came to his
death. Grattan was chosen to fill his brother's place, and
shortly afterward Bob joined the force. Young Emmett
also served as guard.

But Grattan and his younger brothers lacked the disciplined self-control of Frank. They went wild, first in
California and later on their home terrain. Having left
the government service, it was not long until they were
outside the law. Bob and Emmett Dalton, with George
Newcomb and Charley Bryant, robbed a Santa Fe train
at Whorton in the Strip. They made a haul of fourteen
thousand dollars and a safe getaway. Newcomb, Pierce,
Broadwell, and Powers were with the Daltons when they
held up an M.K. & T. train near Wagoner. The take this
time was nineteen thousand dollars, not counting non-
negotiable paper. Then came the Red Rock robbery.

One of the gang had already 'handed in his checks,' as
the border phrase went. Charley Bryant had been captured by Ed Short, one of the old fighting marshals of the
border. The outlaw was put on a train by the officer, who
was careless enough to let his handcuffed prisoner get his
fingers on a revolver. The two men stood in a baggage car
and blazed away at each other. Both were killed.

It was on a pleasant July evening in 1892 when the
Dalton gang stopped the 'Katy' train near Adair, Oklahoma. Some hint of the attack had reached the authorities
and a posse was on board the train. There was a sharp
battle, in which three of the guards were badly wounded.
The bandits robbed the express car and departed into the

night. It was not the custom of the Daltons to rob the passengers.

There is vanity in train and bank holdups. A bandit gets the hero complex. The Daltons decided to outdo the James-Younger gang by robbing two banks at the same time. They picked the Condon and the First National Banks at Coffeeville, Kansas. There were five of the band present, Broadwell, Powers, and Grat, Bob, and Emmett Dalton. A negro with supplies waited in the Cherokee Strip for the return of the robbers after their exploit. He waited, but they never came. At last word reached him that four of the lusty riders were dead, the fifth dying from twenty wounds, many of them made by buckshot.

The bank 'stickups' went wrong from the first. Before a gun was fired the adventure was doomed. Somehow the word spread that the Daltons were robbing the Condon. Coffeeville was on the edge of a hunting country. The citizens found their guns, and when the Oklahoma men came out with their loot the battle began. Bob and Emmett reached the hitching rack where the horses had been left. They waited for their accomplices to come. At last Broadwell, Powers, and Grat Dalton appeared. From all directions bullets poured upon the robbers, and they returned the fire.

The town marshal, Charles T. Connelly, went down, dead. Bob and Grat Dalton were down. Powers, Broadwell, and Emmett had been wounded. All three of them reached their saddles, but Powers was killed before his second foot had touched the stirrup. Broadwell wheeled and spurred away. Just outside of town he dropped from the saddle lifeless. Emmett rode back through the lane of

fire to pick up his brother Bob. A shotgun in the hands of
Carey Seaman, a barber, sent eighteen buckshot into the
back of Emmett as he stooped for the leader of the band.
He slid to the ground.

Four citizens were dead, four bandits. Several others
were wounded. Amazingly Emmett Dalton recovered.
He went to the penitentiary, was paroled, and finished his
life as a Los Angeles business man.

The rest of the band took no warning. Under Bill Doolin they reorganized. Tilghman captured Doolin. He
escaped, to go on more forays. As I have written, he came
to a sudden violent end, as did Newcomb, Pierce, and Bill
Dalton.

The bad man never learns from the experience of others.
The Dalton and the Doolin gangs were hardly out of the
way before other desperate men were organizing to try
their luck at the same hazardous game, this time in the
rough country of Wyoming. They were called the Hole-in-
the-Wall gang, this bunch of former cowboys who preyed
not only on Wyoming but on a great stretch of country
that included bits of Montana, Nevada, Utah, Idaho,
Colorado, New Mexico, and Oklahoma.

Leaders of this group were 'Kid' Curry, whose real
name was Harvey Logan, and 'Butch' Cassidy, also
known as George Parker. Two other Logan brothers,
John and Loney, and a cousin named Bob Lee were members of the outfit, as was also Harry Longabaugh, a big,
bow-legged fellow who was often dubbed 'the Sundance
Kid.' O. C. Hanks, Tom O'Day, Ben Kilpatrick, Will
Carver, and Elza Lay rode with 'the Wild Bunch' on their
raids, though it was seldom that the whole party was to-

gether at any one time. 'Flat-Nosed' George Curry (no
relative of the Logans) was a prominent member of the
party.

This part of the Northwest was always a wild district.
Ten years before Butch Cassidy arrived on the scene,
the Montana Stock Association, of which Granville
Stuart was president, in alliance with the Wyoming
cattlemen, held a drive of rustlers which lasted for two
or three months and resulted in the death of seventy of
the thieves, according to the evidence of some of those
engaged in it. This had been an effective lesson, but the
rustlers were back at their old ways again. Cassidy was
convicted and sent to the penitentiary at Laramie,
Wyoming. He was well liked, and at that time had no
reputation as a bad man. His friends induced Governor
Richards to pardon him. Shortly after this the bank and
train robberies began.

The headquarters of the gang was at Lost Cañon, sixty
miles from Thermopolis, though they shifted their habitat
frequently. Sometimes they were at Robbers' Roost,
sometimes in Brown's Park. Utah saw a good deal of them.
Occasionally some of them drifted into Idaho.

They robbed a bank at Belle Fourche, South Dakota,
and another at Montpelier, Idaho. In June, 1899, the
Wild Bunch robbed the eastbound Union Pacific express
at Wilcox, Idaho. The trail was picked up quickly, and
they were pursued as far as Casper, Wyoming, by Sheriff
Hazen of Converse County. The escaping men turned
suddenly on the posse, and in the exchange of shots the
sheriff was killed, the outlaws 'holing up' in the mountains.

The 'Black Jack' Ketcham gang was operating in New Mexico, and its membership was more or less interchangable with that of the Hole-in-the-Wall group. With Elza Lay and Ben and George Kilpatrick, Butch Cassidy and the Ketchams held up a train at Folsom, New Mexico, in the course of which the conductor killed George Kilpatrick and wounded Black Jack. The sheriff of Huerfano County, Colorado, was hot on the trail of the fleeing robbers. A bullet finished the life of Will Ketcham. Lay's arm was shot off, and he and Black Jack were captured, but not before they had mortally wounded the sheriff, Jeff Farr. Black Jack was tried and hanged. Lay was given twenty years in the penitentiary at Santa Fe.

In August, 1900, Harvey Logan and Ben Kilpatrick held up a Union Pacific train at Tipton, Wyoming, after which they retired for a time to Fort Worth, Texas, where Cassidy and Longabaugh were taking a holiday. It was not too long a rest, for on September 19 of the same year they stopped and robbed the First National Bank at Winnemucca, Nevada. In making a getaway the fugitives divided forces. A posse caught up with one group as far away from the scene as Texas and Will Carver was killed. A year or two prior to this time Carver had shot down a law officer named George Scarborough, who had put an end to John Selman, who had assassinated John Wesley Hardin, who had a record by his own admission of having killed more than thirty men. The homicide chain could be carried back much farther without a break.

Not long after this Harvey Logan (Kid Curry), Ben Kilpatrick, and O. C. Hanks 'stuck up' a Great Northern train at Wagner, Montana. Pinkerton men took the trail.

Ben Kilpatrick was arrested at St. Louis, November 5, 1901, and Kid Curry at Knoxville, Tennessee, after a desperate resistance in the course of which he wounded two officers. Curry was given a short sentence of one hundred and thirty-five years in all, but he overpowered a guard and escaped without serving any of it.

The Wild Bunch was getting near the end of its trail. Charles Siringo, 'Doc' Shores, and a dozen other officers and sheriffs were watching for them any time they made an appearance. Siringo claims in his book that he followed these law-breakers twenty-five thousand miles. A reward of $6500 was offered by the Pinkertons after the Wagner holdup. The circular explained that a man had boarded the blind baggage as the train was leaving Malta, Montana, and that he had crawled over the engine tender and covered the two of the crew who were in the cab, forcing them to stop the engine at the point they wished.

The territory of the different 'bandit' belts throughout the western part of the United States was pretty well defined. One stretched across Texas to Arizona. Another zigzagged through the Rockies in Colorado to the district about the famous Robbers' Roost. A third crossed Wyoming in the sparsely settled country adjacent to the Hole-in-the-Wall district. Here for many years skulked a nomadic population of rustlers, stage-robbers, and fugitives from justice. Among the foothills southeast of the Big Horn Mountains, with the nearest railroad a hundred miles distant, where the gulches and mountain pockets offered natural hiding-places, law officers had small chance to pick up the trail soon enough after the train-robbers had struck.

The Union Pacific Railroad organized a band of rangers to protect its line. Every train carried with it armed guards. Tim Keliher, chief of the Wyoming branch of the Union Pacific secret service, was put in charge of this. He picked as deputies Jeff Carr, a well-known law-enforcer of Wyoming, Pat Lawson and Tom Meggeson, noted trailers, and Joe La Fors, the deputy United States marshal who brought to justice the notorious Tom Horn. Headquarters were at Cheyenne. A baggage car was specially fitted up for the rangers and an engine put at their service. At one end of the car the horses were tied, at the other canteens, tin stoves, cots, and supplies of food were kept ready for the call. Inside of ten minutes the rangers' car could be on the way to the scene of any holdup.

Wyoming did not look so good to Butch Cassidy and his friends after that. They shifted to Colorado for their next raid. At Parachute a train was held up, but little booty was secured. Doc Shores, a hawk-eyed oldtimer, took up the chase. He trapped the robbers in a gulch near Rifle, Colorado. Kid Curry, badly wounded, was heard to call to his companions, 'Good-bye, boys. Don't wait for me.' A moment later he sent a bullet from a .45 revolver into his brain.

One after another the Hole-in-the-Wall bad men were arrested or 'rubbed out.' George Kilpatrick had been shot to death near Folsom, New Mexico, and his brother Ben was serving a long sentence at the Columbus Penitentiary. (It may be mentioned that after his release Ben returned to his evil ways and lost his life at Sanderson, Texas, March 13, 1912, while attempting to hold up a train.)

Two minor members of the gang, named Madden and Bass, were breaking rocks for their share in a Great Northern Railroad robbery. At Laramie Bob Lee was behind bars and at Santa Fe Elza Lay. Flat-Nosed George Curry had come to the end of the trail at Thompson Springs, Utah, and O. C. Hanks at San Antonio, Texas, both shot while resisting arrest. While resting at his old home in Dobson, Missouri, Loney Logan had been trapped and destroyed trying to fight his way out. His brother John had 'gone west' years before this. A turbulent fellow, John had an arm filled with slugs as he 'hurrahed' a town, and it was later amputated. The wound was hardly healed before he ordered a ranchman named Winters to leave his homestead. The nester declined, was threatened, and saved his life temporarily by shooting John before the latter did as much by him. Kid Curry took care of the Winters' account later.

Only Butch Cassidy and Harry Longabaugh were left. Both of them could see the writing on the wall. No matter how they dodged and backtracked there was no safety for them now in the West. They slipped down to New Orleans and took boat for the Argentine. For years little was heard of them, though rumors came up of their troubles with the authorities there. At last Arthur Chapman verified a story that they had been killed. In 1909 they held up a mine payroll near Quechisla in southern Bolivia. With the pursuit closing in on them, they flitted from place to place hurriedly. In the course of their flight they stole a mule to help them escape.

At San Vicente they stopped to rest at a drinking-place. At last they had made a clean getaway, they thought. By sheer chance a stranger in the place recognized the mule. A Bolivian captain walked into the *tendejon* to make inquiries. One of the fugitives killed him. The troops, now under the command of a sergeant, besieged the place.

The desperadoes had left their rifles in the room they had taken across the patio. After emptying their revolvers it was clear that they had to get the rifles to save themselves. Longabaugh tried to cross the square and fell, desperately wounded. Cassidy dragged him back to cover. Two cartridges were left in the dead captain's revolver. The outlaws decided not to let the soldiers capture them. When the attackers broke in five minutes later they found both the gringos dead.

Roughly speaking, the old-time Western outlaws ran true to type. Most of them had been cowboys before they started to follow crooked trails. When they rode the range there was no outward difference between them and their fellow-punchers, unless it was in the restlessness which always kept them moving and in the recklessness that made them undependable. But within them was an impatience at the steady grind of work, an urgent impulse to take short cuts to easy money. So far they were all alike, but within the type individuals differed. In the terrible Plummer gang Steve Marshland was unique. He would rob, but he would not kill. Other road agents have shared this characteristic. It is said that Butch Cassidy never killed a man until the last day of his life.

In this respect he differed from his co-leader Kid Curry, who left behind him the record of a trail of homicides. At Knoxville, Tennessee, he quarreled with a saloonkeeper and killed him. In revenge for his brother John's death he cut down the nester Winters with a bullet sent from the brush as the homesteader was brushing his teeth. The most famous of his victims was Pike Landusky, trapper, freighter, cowboy, Indian fighter, and saloonkeeper, from whom a town in northern Montana derives its name.

Landusky would have been out of place in any setting except that of the frontier West. He was a long, rangy man, broad-shouldered and strong, and never in his life did he sidestep a fight. A born leader, he had a large following among those with whom he lived. Generous to a fault, he was ready at any time to share all he had with a friend. But he could be a bitter enemy, one so blunt and impulsive that trouble followed him all his life. His chief weakness was a temper so little under control that he was likely on small provocation to fly into furious rages.

For more than twenty years he was an outstanding figure in his part of Montana. For a time he was employed by the Diamond R freight outfit, but later went on his own as a trapper. Dan R. Conway tells a characteristic story of him. In partnership with John Wirt he had acquired a fine lot of furs, which they cached on the Musselshell while they went to town for supplies. In their absence a party of Sioux Indians found the furs and at once appropriated them for personal use. The trappers returned, to find themselves prisoners, but captives who declined to give up their arms. The braves gave them some buffalo meat, which Landusky cooked in a fry-pan for himself and partner. He was boiling with rage but realized the folly of giving way to it.

One of the warriors reached over Landusky's shoulder and snatched up the meat. Pike went berserk. He slammed the pan against the face of the brave, spattering him with hot grease, then drove the barrel of his rifle into the stomach of the Indian and doubled him up. Tearing off the man's breech-cloth, he whipped him over the head with it, an unforgivable offense to the Sioux. Wirt cocked his gun and waited. His opinion was that both he and his partner would be dead inside of five minutes.

The Sioux chief rushed across to Wirt and ordered him to make Landusky stop at once. 'The hearts of my men are bad and they will kill you both,' he warned.

Fortunately one of the braves called out that Landusky was crazy. There could be no other explanation of a rage so wild which must result in death for himself. The other Indians agreed, and the tribes never injured a madman. This was ingrained in them as a part of their religion. The war party caught up their horses and departed. They were on their way to the Crow country to steal riding-stock. On their return they stopped to present Landusky and Wirt with sixteen horses, to pay for the stores they had destroyed.

There was enmity between Landusky and Kid Curry. How it started is not known, but there is a story that Pike was appointed a deputy sheriff to take Curry to Fort Benton for trial prior to his conviction for rustling and that Pike grew angry and abused his prisoner. Curry was a sullen fellow, and he nursed his desire for revenge.

He rode to Landusky and tied his horse at the rack in front of the place of 'Jew Jake,' who was himself a hard character. In a gunfight with the marshal at Great Falls Jake had lost a leg, and he now carried a rifle as a crutch.

Pike stood in front of the bar, an elbow leaning on it,

when Kid Curry pushed through the swing door into the gambling-house. Curry walked to his foe, lashed at his face with a doubled fist, and before Landusky could recover slammed down on his head with the barrel of a revolver. Already shaken and jarred, Pike tried to close with the outlaw. Curry fought him off, beating his opponent to the floor with more crashing blows. Still on the ground, Pike reached for a handkerchief to wipe the blood out of his eyes. The kid pumped a bullet through his heart, claiming afterward that he thought Landusky was about to draw a pistol.

Kid Curry's eyes lifted from the lax body of the man he had just killed and let them sweep the room. 'Anybody want to take this up?' he demanded.

Jew Jake hobbled forward on his rifle-crutch. 'Everybody satisfied, I reckon,' he said amiably.

That was stretching the truth. A good many were not pleased at what Harvey Logan, alias Kid Curry, had done, though they admitted that Pike Landusky's violent explosive temper had brought him close to death a dozen times. Pike had his faults and his virtues. Both were of an outstanding kind. Reckless and undisciplined though he had been, a host of friends regretted his murder.

More than a decade after the Hole-in-the-Wall gang had been exterminated, a road agent of an entirely new kind appeared in Wyoming. He played a lone hand and robbed the coaches from the inside while the train was still traveling across country. After he had mulcted the passengers of two trains of their cash a guard was sent to protect them. The robberies occurred west of Laramie on the Union Pacific. A reward of $6500 was offered for his capture.

The bandit was a country boy brought up near Greeley, Colorado, named William L. Carlisle. Evidently he robbed for the sake of the excitement and the notoriety as much as for the money.

After the second holdup he wrote a letter to the Denver *Post* which shows his vanity and love of the limelight. It ran as follows:

> I am sending you the watch chain that I took from a passenger on my last holdup. I'll return the watch on my next. I'll hold up the Union Pacific west of Laramie just to convince the police that they have not got the right party. Please return the chain to its owner with my compliments.
>
> I remain, sincerely,
>
> THE WHITE MASKED BANDIT

On April 21, 1916, a passenger boarded the Denver–Salt Lake Limited at Laramie. He was a man of about twenty-eight years of age, six feet two in height, and weighed one hundred and ninety-eight pounds. Nobody paid any attention to him. He was just another cowboy on the move, evidently a garrulous chap, for he talked with the guard, the brakeman, and the conductor. Half an hour after the train had left Laramie he prodded the guard in the back with a revolver.

'All right,' he said. 'Time for the holdup. I'll take your gun first.'

The startled guard could make no resistance. In fact, under the urge of the revolver he walked down the aisle in front of the outlaw and held his hat for the passengers to make their contributions in it. Carlisle and his unwilling assistant passed into a second car and continued the levy on travelers' assets. Before the next station was

reached the bandit made the conductor stop the train.
He descended from it and vanished into the night, after
handing to the guard the watch he had promised to return.

The country was full of posses searching for the daring
bandit. A member of one of them came upon Carlisle
hiding in a boulder field. To the surprise of the officer, the
robber flung his revolvers to the ground.

'I'm not a killer,' he called to his hunter. 'If I have to
shed blood to get away I would rather surrender.'

Carlisle spent many years in the penitentiary. When
he was released not very long ago he bought a cigar stand
in a Wyoming town and sold magazines and tobacco to the
public. Long since he had lost his craving for grandstanding.

During the 1920's there was a recrudescence of bank
'stickups,' owing to the discovery that the automobile
made swift escape possible. When the James-Younger
gang held up the gate receipts at the Kansas City Fair
before a thousand witnesses they had to depend upon fast
horses to get away. But by the time the Hole-in-the-Wall
gang was operating the rural telephone made bank and
train holdups highly hazardous. The automobile brought
a new factor into the problem of putting an end to such
raids. All over the West there was a temporary outbreak of
bank robberies. It became possible to strike unexpectedly,
deflect from the main thoroughfares, and dodge from one
country road to another until the hideout was reached.

One of the most spectacular of these raids was the one
upon the First National Bank at Lamar, Colorado. Just
before noon, on May 23, 1928, a blue sedan drove up to
the bank, and from it descended four men, not masked.

They left the engine of the car running and walked into the building. The leader, a tall, brown-faced man, snapped out an order to the staff and to the customers present.

'Stick 'em up!'

Eight or nine pairs of arms stretched ceilingward. The president of the bank, A. N. Parrish, an old man of seventy-seven, was frontier stock and had always said that if an attempt was made to rob his bank he would resist. He jumped for a revolver and fired at the nearest bandit, the bullet hitting the man in the jaw. A moment later Parrish went down, drilled through and through. Several slugs had struck him, and he was dead before his body slumped to the floor. His son snatched up another gun, to come to the aid of his father. He too was instantly killed.

The voice of one of the outlaws cut into the panic. 'Lie down on the floor, every last one of you,' it ordered.

From the vault was taken more than two hundred thousand dollars in gold, notes, and securities. Within three minutes of the sound of the first shot the robbers moved back to the blue sedan, taking with them as a protection against attack Cashier Kesinger and Teller Lundgren. The car raced into the country, and because it was crowded one of the bank officials was pushed out.

Sheriff Alderman of Lamar was already in pursuit in a fast car. He overhauled the robbers, who presently stopped their sedan. One of them got out and fired with a rifle from behind Kesinger. As Alderman had only his six-guns with him he had to give up the chase for the moment.

A dozen posses took the field in automobiles. Planes flew above the road ribbons. Guards picketed the exits of towns. The bandits made a clean getaway. No positive clews of their line of travel could be picked up except the tragic ones of dead bodies. Kesinger was found in an old shack near Liberal, Kansas. He had been shot through the back.

At Dighton, Kansas, on the night of the robbery two men came to the door of Doctor W. W. Wineinger and asked him to come into the country to attend a young man who had been hurt by a tractor. They proposed to take him in their car and bring him back, but Wineinger said he preferred to go in his own. One of the men rode beside him. The doctor suggested that since the weather was muggy the right-hand window might be opened. His companion put a finger against the pane and pushed it out. That one fingerprint cost four men their lives and probably saved four others from the gallows.

The body of Doctor Wineinger was found a week later in a deep gully. His car had been pushed into it after him. The automobile had been gone over with a greased rag to wipe out fingerprints. The one mark on the windowglass was the only one left. An expert dusted, developed, and photographed it.

Meanwhile many arrests were made. Some showed perfect alibis. The evidence pointed to four suspects. Brought to Lamar, they were identified by the witnesses. Feeling against them ran high, and there seemed to be little doubt of a conviction.

The fingerprint had been sent to Washington. Months passed, and one day the discovery was made that this print was identical with another made in 1916 at the Oklahoma Penitentiary of Convict 6591. The convict was William Harrison Fleagle, commonly nicknamed Jake. Chief of

Police Hugh Harper went to Garden City, Kansas, to get his man. Jake had been warned and had fled, but Harper picked up his brother, Ralph Emerson Fleagle.

It was found that the Fleagles had surprisingly large bank accounts. The two brothers and some companions lived intermittently on what they called a horse ranch, but they did little business in horses. Confronted with this and other evidence, after a long grilling Ralph Fleagle talked. One of the bandits, the same man whose jaw had been shattered by the old banker's bullet, was Howard L. Royston, and he was living in California. After Wineinger had given first aid and been murdered Royston was hurried to an undercover doctor at St. Paul, Minnesota. An apartment had been rented and George J. Abshier, the fourth robber, looked after him until he was well. Royston and Abshier were arrested and brought to Colorado. The case against the former suspects was dropped. Fleagle, Abshier, and Royston were convicted and hanged. Detectives followed Jake Fleagle and caught up with him on a train at Branson, Missouri, and when he reached for his pistol shot him to death.

There was nothing romantic about the Fleagles, Dillinger, or 'Pretty Boy' Floyd. They were gangsters of the most cold-blooded types, just as Capone and his associates were. Like the bandits of a generation ago, they had their little day and ceased to be. If there is one point that stands out like a bandaged thumb, it is that in the end the law will catch up with all of them. The aphorism that crime does not pay is trite but true.

X

Nate Champion Finishes
His Diary

THE cattleman was king in the outdoor West for more than a decade. After the Indian he was the first to use the semi-arid plains. The earliest settler, his stock roamed the open range for a score of miles. The influence he exerted wrote the laws of a dozen states and territories, except for the towns and cities with which he had no concern. He worked out a social system, long since vanished, that fitted his environment as a glove does a hand.

And then, almost overnight it must have seemed to him, he was no longer king on horseback. He found his empire slipping from him. The laws he had written could not be enforced. Nature herself conspired with the granger's urge for land and the rustler's cupidity to snatch dominion from him.

The *opéra bouffe* Johnson County Cattle War was a futile attempt on the part of the cattleman to set the clock back. On April 6, 1892, a Union Pacific special train left Denver headed for the nearest railroad point to the

Powder River country in Wyoming. It consisted of a chair car, a caboose, three stock cars loaded with horses, one for baggage, and a flat on which had been put several wagons. About fifty passengers were on board. Twenty-four of them were Texas gunmen. One was a surgeon, one a correspondent of the *Chicago Herald*, and the rest Wyoming cattlemen or ranch employees. All were heavily armed. The object of the expedition was to exterminate sixty or seventy rustlers who had been operating in Johnson, Natrona, and Converse Counties. W. G. Angus, sheriff of Johnson County, and the three commissioners, all of whom were considered by the cattlemen to be allies of the thieves, were to be wiped out with them.

To understand how a scheme of such audacity could be undertaken, it is necessary to get a picture of the situation. After the buffalo had been destroyed and the Indian tribes as a consequence confined to reservations, millions of Texas longhorns were driven north to meet the demand for cattle on the range. Except in the Northwest the carrying capacity of the ranges was already overstocked by 1880. But the grass was still good, and this year and the next were profitable for owners. As late as 1883 twenty big cattle outfits, capitalized at more than twelve million dollars, were started in Wyoming. A good many of these were financed in Great Britain. There was a tremendous boom in cattle, and it was easy to find money for a new land and cattle company.

The business of ranching had become fashionable. One cannot read the books written at that time on the subject without seeing what fantastic delusions were entertained. The range could feed all the cattle of the world for all

time. There were millions to be made raising stock. The
high plains were a poor man's country. With industry
he could get rich in a short time. Baron Richthofen and
Sir Charles Dilke, who probably missed being Premier of
England only because of the non-conformist conscience,
were responsible for two of them. General Brisbin wrote a
third, *The Beef Bonanza.*

In Colorado, New Mexico, Arizona, Texas, Wyoming,
South Dakota, and Montana great ranches were got under
way. Experienced cattlemen who ought to have known
better were swept away by the madness and bought till
their ranges were greatly overstocked. Prices still rose,
though feed deteriorated. English younger sons poured
into Wyoming, Montana, and Colorado. Many of these
were employed as managers, though they had no experience
to justify such a choice. Some of the holdings were im-
mense. The Prairie Land and Cattle Company, organized
in 1881, had three ranches totaling nearly eight thousand
square miles.

Other large ranches in Wyoming were on Powder River,
Crazy Woman Creek, Tongue River, and in the Big Horns.
Most of these were owned by individual Englishmen or by
British companies. Morton and Richard Frewen had the
'76 Ranch, Horace Plunkett the E K. United States
Senators Francis E. Warren and J. M. Carey also had
large holdings, as did other native cattlemen. Wyoming
was at that time a game paradise. Its ranges were filled
with elk, bear, and mountain sheep. The valleys were
covered with antelope. There were so many hill pockets
and gulches that the country was a fine rendezvous for
outlaws. In early days the nearest railroad point to

Johnson County was at Rock Creek, Wyoming, two hundred and fifty miles south of Buffalo. The Wells-Fargo stages had to carry gold four hundred and fifty miles, and there were many robberies. With the advent of the big cattle companies rustlers supplanted the road agents who had been holding up stages.

The character of the cattle country in the high plains changed with extraordinary swiftness. Speaking of Montana, Granville Stuart points out that in 1880 the territory was a wilderness inhabited only by game. There were thousands of buffalo and no cattle worth counting. Three years later the buffalo and game had gone and there were over half a million head of cattle on the range. Before the decade had ended the pour of cattle had grown so great that all stockmen were getting worried about the overcrowding.

The overstocking continued year after year until the feed of the range was permanently injured. Though signs of coming trouble were plenty, more cattle were brought up the trail in 1884 than in any year during the past decade. All the famous drivers were prodding herds northward.

The evils that accompanied absentee ownership could not be ignored. The average cowboy was very loyal to his outfit. He was willing to rough through blizzards, risk his life to stop stampedes, and swim racing rivers for a boss who paid him only twenty-five dollars a month, since he knew his employer personally and had slept under a tarp with him. But he felt no such sense of devotion to stockholders in Edinburgh or London who were represented by a manager not fitted for the job, a young fellow more likely to spend his time at the Cheyenne Club than in the saddle facing the bitter winds of winter. Probably he had a few cows of his own, for he hoped some day to be a cattleman in his own right, and if not too scrupulous he would use his running-iron to burn on a stray calf his own mark of ownership rather than that of the company. There were scores of small cowmen on the boundaries of every big outfit, and it was noticed that the herds of some of them grew remarkably.

The grangers who came in to homestead land for farming and the honest small stockman found the big outfits overbearing and tyrannical. Many of them made common cause with the rustlers in self-defense. They elected county officers opposed to the great companies. The thieves grew bolder, since juries of their friends would no longer convict them. The nesters were very poor. They killed cattle to feed their families and sometimes slaughtered animals of the big companies wantonly. The Anglo-American Cattle Company lost over thirty head on Hat Creek in a stretch of less than two miles, all of them found with bullet holes in them.

The market crashed in 1885 and hundreds of stockmen were wiped out. The large ranches could no longer earn dividends, and some of the managers sold the cows and heifers to keep up a pretence of prosperity by making a showing to the directors. To cap the climax, the winter of 1886–1887 was the worst experienced for many years. The whole West was swept by repeated blizzards, heavy snows, and prolonged extreme cold. Stock crowded into corrals and bellowed pitifully for food. The rancher could do nothing for them. They died by thousands. When at last the spring suns showed, less than one-half of the cattle were alive.

There had always been heavy winter losses, but nothing like this before. A radical readjustment of ranch management had to be made. Stock that had been bred up at much expense were too valuable to be exposed to winter blizzards without food or shelter. Valleys must be watered and pasturage protected. This involved fencing. Free grass belonged to the adventurous past, like the longhorn.

It had long been apparent to the cattleman that he could not continue in business side by side with calf-thieves. From the first he had fought back in the rough-and-ready way made necessary in his opinion by the lack of any law that would function. Through their associations cowmen banded together. They warned suspected rustlers. But hardy cowboys living in out-of-the-way gulches laughed at warnings. Some were shot, some hanged. In *Prose and Poetry of the Live Stock Industry*, printed in 1905 under the authority of the National Live Stock Historical Association, one reads that thirteen rustlers were hanged from one railroad bridge in an early day clean-up extending through four states and territories in the north. That good citizen, John Clay, defends such severity as necessary. His book, *My Life on the Range*, puts the defense of the cattleman in a nutshell. What would any man do, he asks, if a burglar broke into his house repeatedly and stole property, regardless of remonstrance, and the courts laughed at demands for punishment? He would do what the ranchman did, if he had a spark of manhood in him.

In his *Forty Years on the Frontier*, Granville Stuart writes that the Montana cattlemen were peaceful and law-

abiding. When honest settlers came into the country in
their covered wagons the ranchers helped them get a start
on the creeks and fed their families if they were hungry.
The rustlers were not so welcome. The tallies at the close
of the 1883 roundup showed a large loss from rustling.
The thieves had friends among the small ranchers, were
well organized, and had hideouts for stolen stock in the
hills back of the Missouri and Yellowstone Rivers.

A Montana Stock-Growers' Association had been
formed, and several hundred members met at Miles City
in 1884. There was much discussion of the rustling problem. The courts had completely failed the stockmen.
Some of the more radical members of the association
favored raising a small army and mopping up the thieves.
According to Stuart, Theodore Roosevelt, a member of
the association, strongly approved of this summary punishment. Stuart himself spoke against it, on the ground
that the rustlers were well forted, excellently armed, and
knew the country in which they operated as a teacher
does her spelling-book. The convention was opposed to
drastic action against the thieves, but some of the members met at a ranch and decided to do some vigilance
work of their own.

They trapped two rustlers driving stolen horses up
Eagle Creek, and after a running battle shot one and
hanged the other. A half-breed was found with two
broncos in his possession that did not belong to him. He
was hanged from a cottonwood. Two men named Owen
and 'Rattlesnake Jake' Fallon drifted into the country
with horses of various brands. Undoubtedly they had
stolen the stock, though this could not be easily proved.

Owen and Fallon went to Lewistown for a Fourth of July celebration, drank and gambled a lot, and made themselves obnoxious. The signs were clear that they were working themselves up for trouble. Some of the citizens armed, after the two visitors began shooting around recklessly.

Owen caught sight of Joe Doney in front of a store and ran toward him gun in hand. Doney drew a revolver and shot him twice. Meanwhile Fallon was riding up the street exchanging shots with men standing in the doors of buildings. He was hit in the ribs. Looking back, he saw that Owen was down and could not get away. He turned his horse and rode back through a lane of fire to his companion. The outlaws made their last stand together. They emptied their guns, reloaded them, and kept shooting as long as they could lift a hand. An examination made after their death showed that there were nine wounds in the body of one and eleven in the other, almost any one of which would have been fatal.

As the clean-up proceeded, the ranchers reached a cabin in a wooded bottom near which eleven rustlers were camped. One of them was Jake Stringer, described by Stuart as a fine-looking young fellow, well educated, of charming personality. He had piercing gray eyes, good teeth, and an engaging smile. 'Stringer Jack,' as he was called, was the leader of the rustlers. In the desperate battle that followed all the thieves were killed except five. Four of these were later caught and hanged.

The big outfits in Wyoming did not submit to the depredations of the rustler without fighting back. They were under great disadvantages. Few men were kept

riding in the winter, and the temptation to prey on unguarded herds was one many nesters did not resist. The
companies had stock detectives in the field who mingled
with the thieves and learned of their operations. Unable
to obtain convictions in the courts, the cattle companies
hired men to drygulch the brand-blotters. Though they
did not admit this publicly, in private they justified their
course. They could point to the record. In Johnson
County alone, out of one hundred and eighty indictments
for cattle-stealing during four years, there had been only
one conviction, and in that case the jury by a quibble had
reduced the crime to petty larceny.

One of the leaders of the party opposed to the big
ranches was Nathan D. Champion, a strong, bold man
known to be a first-rate shot and game to the core. In
his book *Malcolm Campbell, Sheriff*, Robert B. David tells
a story illustrating Champion's audacity. Bob Tisdale
was working his stock on the south fork of the Powder
River when Champion and his men, heavily armed, joined
the roundup and branded the calves openly. There was
nothing Tisdale could do about it.

In October, 1891, Nate Champion and another man
were attacked in their cabin at daybreak while still asleep.
Champion seized his revolver. Half a dozen shots were
exchanged at a distance of a few feet. The attackers bolted
from the room, leaving two rifles at the door. They were in
such a hurry to go that they lost their overcoats and did
not stop to get the bedding at the camp ground where
they spent the night. Some of this was identified as belonging to a stock inspector named Joe Elliott. He was
arrested and released on a five-thousand-dollar bond.

A few months prior to this time Tom Waggoner, who had a horse ranch near Newcastle, Wyoming, was arrested by three men who said they were United States marshals. Very likely he knew the fate in store for him. He was working at the stable when taken, and he asked if he might go to the house to get his coat and say good-bye to his wife and children. This was refused. One of the men offered him his coat. Waggoner was handcuffed and put on a horse. His body was later found hanging to a tree several miles from his ranch. Since he was a handsome, likable young fellow with many friends, his death stirred a bitter resentment against the large companies.

In November O. E. Jones, commonly known as 'Ranger,' went to Buffalo, Wyoming, to buy lumber for flooring. He was building a house, expecting to get married soon. Ranger was a jolly young man, thrifty, not given to drink or other forms of dissipation. While driving home in a buckboard he was shot down from ambush. About the same time John A. Tisdale, also on his way home from Buffalo, with Christmas presents for his children and provisions for the winter, was assassinated from cover. Both these murders were charged to the cattlemen of the big ranches. Frank M. Canton, an inspector for the stock association, who had been sheriff of Johnson County from '82 to '86, was accused of these killings, arrested, and released under a thirty-thousand-dollar bond put up by cattlemen at Cheyenne. He makes the claim, in his book, *Frontier Trails*, that he proved by several witnesses that he was ill in bed at the time of these crimes.

All this violence had brought about a very bitter feeling. The lives of some of the managers had been threatened, and some of them moved their families into southern Wyoming, a section more settled and less turbulent. In the spring of 1892 rustling was particularly active. The big outfits felt they had to give up or fight. They decided on a campaign so ruthless that it would daunt cattle-thieves by serving as a permanent warning.

Tom Smith,[1] a famous deputy sheriff of Texas, was sent down into the Lone Star State to gather a band of 'warriors' for the invasion. The men he chose were well-known gunmen, most of whom had been deputy United States marshals in the frontier borderland of the Pecos, the Panhandle, and the Indian Territory. They were hard customers who had fought mostly on the side of the law against bands of outlaws and thieves. It must have been made plain to them that they were being taken to Wyoming to shoot and hang suspected rustlers without benefit of jury.

The cattlemen and their assistants were pledged to secrecy, but fifty men cannot keep a secret any better than two women. In its issue of April 7, 1892, the Denver *Sun* had a news item about the 'mysterious train' which had left the city the previous day. 'The cattlemen in Buffalo, Sheridan, Bonanza, and Riverton, Wyoming, and in Red Lodge, Billings, and Fort Smith, Montana, have formed an organization with the intention of exterminating the rustlers.... The U.P. Officials here when asked about the train denied any knowledge of its having left the city.' The Cheyenne *Leader* reported next day that the train was in Cheyenne en route to the Powder River country. The

---

[1] Not the same Tom Smith who was marshal of Abilene, but the one who appears in this book under the title of 'Tom Smith of Texas.'

Denver *Republican*, on which paper I was later a reporter and editorial writer, carried on the same day an interview with a prominent official of the Wyoming Board of Livestock Commissioners, who said that the small army had left for the region in which the rustlers had been most actively operating, with the full intention of taking such drastic action as would put a stop to the lawlessness.

The cattlemen involved considered the expedition one of law enforcement, an unpleasant public duty they could no longer shirk. The personnel of the party was remarkable. Major Frank Wolcott, a Kentuckian who had served as an officer on the Union side in the Civil War, had been chosen leader. He was a cocky little man, sharp, decisive, and belligerent, one known to be absolutely fearless. The surgeon with the company was Charles Brigham Penrose, a brother of Senator Penrose of Pennsylvania. Many of the stockmen enrolled were well educated, some from Eastern colleges. A young ranchman in Northern Colorado named Harry Wallace, the son of a wealthy English family, insisted on enlisting for the adventure. Six stock inspectors, bitterly hated by the other faction in Johnson County, were among the avengers, including Canton and Elliott. A noted officer of the Black Hills country, Scott Davis, one who had shot or dragged in to justice many a bandit, was among those present. Three foremen for large cattle outfits, Laberteaux of the Blair Ranch, Parker of the Murphy Cattle Company, and Ford of the T A Ranch, had joined 'for the duration of the war.' Also there were the twenty-four Texan gun-fighters, about several of whom interesting stories of the wild days could be written.

The party disembarked at Casper and started across

country. It was a hard trip. The roads were heavy with mud. Wagons bogged down and were pulled out by ropes attached to saddle horns. As they plowed forward mile after mile the roadbed became almost impassable. The temperature fell, and snow began to fall. There was a bitter wind. All night the weary company pushed forward. About dawn they straggled into the Tisdale Powder River Ranch. After breakfast they rolled up in their blankets for a few hours' sleep.

While most of them were still sleeping the foreman of the Western Union Beef Company, Mike Shonsey, arrived with the news that he had slept at the K C Ranch, fifteen miles distant, in Nate Champion's cabin, and that Nick Rae, Ed Starr, and others of the rustlers had also spent the night there.

This was good news, for it showed the enemy was unaware of their presence. Wolcott moved his men during the night and surrounded the K C Ranch. A windswept snow numbed them as they huddled on their mounts. They waited till daybreak. Orders were given not to fire without orders, since there might be innocent travelers spending the night in the cabin.

The story that had appeared in the Denver *Sun* was confirmed by what followed. At the very hour when Wolcott's men were waiting for those in the cabin to appear, a body of vigilantes from Billings trapped a bunch of accused rustlers near Jackson Hole,[1] and in the fight that followed

[1] Owen Wister, in his famous story *The Virginian*, pays his respects to Jackson Hole. He is telling how Trampas vanished after murdering Shorty.

'Somewhere at the eastern base of the Tetons did those hoofprints disappear into a mountain sanctuary where many crooked paths have led. He that took another man's possessions, or he that took another man's life, could always run here if the law or popular justice were hot at his heels. Steep ranges and forests

eight men were killed and several wounded. Clearly there had been an agreement between the cattlemen of Wyoming and Montana to make a simultaneous attack on the thieves.

At daybreak smoke began to rise from the chimney of the K C ranch-house. A man came out with a bucket in his hand and walked down to the river for water. He passed the barn, turned the corner, and was at once ordered to throw up his hands. What took place here could not be seen from the house.

'Who are you?' demanded Wolcott.

The man with the bucket was getting along in years. He said his name was Bill Jones and that he was a trapper. He had a pal named Bill Walker in the house. They had started to camp at the waterhole on the previous night and Nate Champion had strolled down and invited them to sleep in the house, since a storm was coming up.

His story appeared to be true, but he was kept prisoner. After a time his partner, Walker, a much younger man, came down the path to the barn, a pair of Winchesters trained on him every foot of the way. He too was taken into custody. Both men said that the only two men in the cabin now were Rae and Champion.

walled him in from the world on all four sides, almost without a break; and every entrance lay through intricate solitudes. Snake River came into the place through cañons and mournful pines and marshes, to the north, and went out at the south between formidable chasms. . . . Down in the bottom was a spread of level land, broad and beautiful, with the blue and silver Tetons rising from its chain of lakes to the west, and other heights presiding over its other sides. And up and down and in and out of this hollow square of mountains, where waters plentifully flowed, and game and natural pasture abounded, there skulked a nomadic and distrustful population. This in due time built cabins, took wives, begot children, and came to speak of itself as "The honest settlers of Jackson Hole." It is a commodious title, and doubtless today more accurate than it was once.'

Nick Rae came out of the cabin and stood gazing round to see where the trappers were. Several rifles roared. He fell, but began crawling to the cabin on his hands and knees. Bullets hit all around him. Champion jumped from the doorway and carried his companion back into the house, shooting with his revolver as he did so. He barricaded the door and prepared to stand off the attackers.

From the flashes of the guns Champion could tell that the cabin was surrounded. A high bluff ran on the south side of the river, and in the brush along this ridge Tom Smith and half a dozen of his men lay down and covered the rear. Others were stationed in gullies along both flanks, while the main body were at the barn and in the cottonwood trees along the river.

Nate Champion saw at once that he could do nothing for his friend. The man was riddled with bullets and the span of his life could be counted in hours. The doomed man moved from window to window, firing only when one of the attackers exposed himself. Two of them he wounded, though not seriously.

A heavy fusillade was poured at the house, but with no harm to the defender as far as Wolcott could see. He passed word to his men to stop wasting their ammunition. Meanwhile a neighboring ranchman heard the shooting, crept forward in the brush to investigate, and slapped a saddle on a horse to carry word of what was taking place.

There seems to have been a strange slackness on the part of the attackers. While they were in conference deciding what next to do, a boy driving a wagon came down the slope from the south toward the river. With him, on horseback, was a man named Jack Flagg, his father, a rancher who was on the black list of the cattlemen. As he cantered down the hill toward the bridge, closing in the space between him and the boy, a bookmaker would have given odds of fifty to one against his getting through alive. The wagon was on the bridge before Scott Davis caught sight of Flagg and his son.

'Don't shoot,' Flagg shouted. 'I'm with you.'

He crouched low in the saddle and dashed across the bridge.

'It's Jack Flagg,' a voice shouted.

The rifles crashed, but the horse fairly flew up the road to the north. The boy was ahead of him lashing the team forward. As soon as he was out of range the lad pulled up, cut the fastest horse loose, and swung to its back. Flagg had stopped to help him. A moment later both of them were racing for safety. It took some time for the attackers to reach their horses, and the two escaped to carry news of the invasion to Buffalo.[1]

The siege of the house dragged on for hours. Champion not only kept his enemies at bay but found time to write a remarkable story of the battle.

April 9 — 6 A.M.

Me and Nick was getting breakfast when the attack began. Two men were with us, Bill Jones and another man. The old man went out after water about daylight. Did not come back. His friend went out to see what was the matter and he didn't come back. Nick started out and I told him to look out, that I thought there was someone at the stable that would not let them come back. . . .

---

[1] An oldtimer from Johnson County, L. Davidson, a newspaper man who wrote ringing editorials in the Buffalo *Echo* at the time of the invasion, mentioned recently in a letter to me that Jack Flagg is now living near Jackson, Wyoming.

Nick is shot but not dead yet. He is awful sick. I must go and wait on him. It is now about two hours since the first shots....

Nick is still alive. They are still shooting and are all around the house. Boys, there is bullets coming in like hail....

Them fellows is in such shape I can't get at them. They are shooting from the stable and river and back of the house....

Nick is dead. He died about nine o'clock. I see a smoke down at the stable. I don't think they intend to let me get away this time....

It is now about noon. There is someone at the stable yet. They are throwing a rope out of the door and drawing it back. I guess that is to draw me out. I wish that duck would get out farther so I can get a shot at him....

Boys, I don't know what they have done with them two fellows that staid here last night....

Boys, I feel pretty lonesome right now. I wish there was someone else here with me so we could watch all sides at once. They may fool around till I get in one good shot before they leave....

It's about three o'clock now. There is a man in a buckboard and one on horseback just passed. They fired at them as they went by. I don't know if they killed them or not. I seen a lot of men come out on horses on the other side of the river and take after them....

I shot at a man in the stable just now. Don't know if I got him or not. I must go and look out again. I see 12 or 15 men. One looks like —— (name erased later by the attackers). I don't know whether it is or not. It don't look as if there was much of a chance of my getting away. I hope they don't catch them fellows that run over the bridge toward Smith's....

They are shooting at the house now. If I had a pair of glasses I would know some of those men. They are coming back and I got to look out....

Well, they have just got through shelling the house again like hell. I hear them splitting wood. I guess they are going to fire the house tonight. I think I'll make a break tonight if I live....

Shooting again. I think they will fire the house this time. It's not night....

The house is all fired. Good-bye, boys, if I never see you again.

NATHAN D. CHAMPION

The besieged man pushed the diary into his bootleg, flung open the door, and made his bolt for life. He ran south, partially concealed by the thick smoke. Those on the bluff caught glimpses of him as he ran. He was making for a gash which cut through the rimrock. Tom Smith's Texans cut him down after he had fired one defiant shot. Half a dozen bullets from the sharpshooters had pierced him.

It is said that Major Wolcott looked down at the dead man and said, 'By God, if I had fifty men like you I could conquer the whole state of Wyoming.'

Upon the bloodstained breast of the dead man was pinned a card upon which was printed, 'Cattle-thieves, beware.'

A cattle-thief Nate Champion may have been, but he had an indomitable courage that did not flinch at death. One against fifty, he stood off his enemies for many hours, and was forced from the cabin only when the place was blazing after a wagon with burning hay had been rolled against it.

The correspondent of the *Chicago Herald*, under date of April 14, paid tribute to his courage. He wrote:

Champion was as brave as a lion. The poor devil came out with his rifle in his hand. He was in his stocking feet and jumped square into the arms of the two best shots in the whole party. He fired but one shot as he ran. The whole gang opened up on him. Their first volley broke his arm and he couldn't use his rifle. He stumbled and fell, riddled with bullets. . . . The men searched his body. On it, soaked with blood and with a bullet hole through it, they found a small notebook in which he had calmly set down the incidents of the fight and the last hours of his life.

By delaying the invaders Champion had made success impossible for the cattlemen. Flagg and his boy had reached Buffalo, and already riders were out rousing the country. Excitement was intense. Ranchmen poured into Buffalo and Douglas. Heavily armed posses were hurriedly organized.

Unaware of how great the excitement was, the Major pushed his troop forward toward Buffalo. Late at night they reached the Hesse Ranch, twenty miles from their destination. After hot coffee and food, they mounted again, just missing a posse under the command of Sheriff Angus which was hurrying to the aid of Champion. At the T A Ranch on Crazy Woman Creek Wolcott halted his forces for a rest. While there, a horseman galloped in with the information that hundreds of rustlers, nesters, and town residents were massing against them.

Wolcott called the leaders of the expedition into conference. They decided to stop at the T A and prepare against attack. The ranch-house was large and roomy. It was well situated for defense, since it was in the center of a saucer the rim of which was cut by many ravines and gullies. Rolling hills surrounded the place. On an elevation near the house Wolcott set his men to work building a fort. Crazy Woman Creek ran past barn and house, so that plenty of water was at hand. During the night trenches were dug at the summit of the hill, and above them a barricade constructed of heavy timbers with loopholes for firing. A dozen of the best sharpshooters in the party occupied this fort. The stable and the ranch-house were also fortified with heavy timbers found on the place.

Sheriff Angus with a huge posse arrived and attacked the ranch. The wild fusillade of those scattered in the brush outside the T A fences did little damage, but each hour brought fresh men to aid the besiegers. Cut off as his party was from its wagon train, Major Wolcott realized that help would have to be sent them from the outside if his men were to be saved. George Dowling volunteered to run the lines of the enemy and get a telegram to Douglas, from which point it could be sent to Governor Barber. Another man, Calhoun, who had been wounded by Champion at the K C, also ran the circle several hours after Dowling. His wounds were troubling him and he wanted to get to a doctor.

Though 'Red' Angus was officially in charge of the attackers, the real leader was Arapahoe Brown. He showed great skill in pushing the assault on the ranch and also in keeping his men from exposing themselves. For moral support he had a Methodist minister, M. A. Rader, a fiery evangelist who later had a church in Denver. More than once I have listened to his slashing sermons exhorting repentance. He was a frontiersman who could ride, shoot, and fight as well as preach the gospel.

Rifle pits were dug by the attackers. They pushed their

lines forward, using baled hay as a protection while they advanced. The captured supply wagons of the invaders furnished both food and ammunition to their foes. As the days passed the forces of Arapahoe Brown crept closer and closer. His men could slip along the creek bed to communicating ditches. A thin, sleety snow was falling most of the time. This was hard on his men, but Brown knew that lack of food must eventually drive the besieged to attempt a sortie or to surrender. Escape would now be extremely difficult, for many of the horses had been shot. Nearly five hundred men were in the trenches surrounding the ranch, all of them armed with Winchesters, old Sharps used for buffalo-hunting, or other rifles. Robert B. David says that by absolute count seventy per cent of the Johnson County army were ranchers, fifteen per cent merchants and workingmen, and the remainder gamblers, rustlers, and loafers.

Arapahoe Brown set his men to work building a movable barricade. The running-gears of two wagons were set side by side some yards apart and fastened by a log framework. A solid front of heavy timbers was erected, with loopholes that could be covered with sliding timbers when not in use. Back of this a large number of men could push forward while sheltered from the fire of those within the ranch-house and its buildings.

The situation of the defendants was by this time desperate. They did not know that Governor Barber had telegraphed to Senators Carey and Warren at Washington asking them to appeal to the President to order troops from Fort McKinney to the relief of the cattlemen. Benjamin Harrison, then President of the United States, sent an order to Colonel Van Horn through General Brooke to rush troops to the aid of the beleaguered.

Wolcott and his men had decided they must make a dash to escape. As day broke, they prepared to make the attempt, though all of them knew that many of them would be shot down by the enemy. While they waited for the signal a bugle blew on the hilltop half a mile away. The troops had arrived.

If that bugle had sounded one hour later only a few of the Wolcott party would have been alive to hear it. As it was, a dozen men were killed and as many more wounded in the rustler cleanup. Eight of those killed were in the Jackson Hole fight, the others in Johnson County. Old-timers have always been amazed that in a battle lasting several days and involving so many men the mortality was so small. The reason of course was that none of the fighting was in the open.

From the arrival of the soldiers the rest is anticlimax. It consisted largely of political sparring. The rescued invaders were taken to Fort McKinney and from there to Cheyenne. All of them were arrested and indicted, but the cases never came to trial. To attempt a conviction of the invaders would have bankrupted Johnson County. Echoes of the trouble continued for years. Dud Champion, a brother of the murdered Nate, met Mike Shonsey near the Horseshoe Bar Ranch about a year later. In the duel which followed Champion was killed.

The effect of the campaign was to diminish the power of both the cattlemen and the rustlers. Some of the big ranches sold out. The others no longer attempted to dominate the country politically but attended more

strictly to the business of raising cows. The honest settlers, not now forced to line up with the thieves to protect
themselves against the high-handed operations of the large
outfits, elected and supported officials who put a stop to
wholesale cattle-rustling.

Wyoming was no longer frontier territory.

XI

Ben Thompson, Gun-Fighter Extraordinary

IN THE opinion of 'Bat' Masterson, himself a famous gunman of the frontier, Ben Thompson was the most dangerous man with a revolver among the scores of desperate fighters who flourished in the West a generation ago. He wrote:

> It is doubtful if in his time there was another man living who equaled him with a pistol in a life-and-death struggle. Thompson in the first place possessed a much higher order of intelligence than the average man-killer of his time. He was absolutely without fear and his nerves were those of the finest steel. He shot at an adversary with the same precision and deliberation that he shot at a target. A past master in the use of the pistol, his aim was as true as his nerves were strong and steady.
>
> Wild Bill Hickok, Wyatt Earp, Billy Tilghman, Charley Bassett, Luke Short, Clay Allison, and Jim Curry were all men who...played their part on the lurid edge of our Western frontier at the same time Ben was playing his, and it is safe to assume that not one of them would have de-

clined the gage of battle had he flung it down. However, I am constrained to say that little doubt exists in my mind that Thompson would have been the winner.

The testimony of Masterson ought to have some weight, both because of his own record as a pistoleer and because of his intimacy with and personal friendliness toward at least five of those whom he names. Earp, Tilghman, Bassett, and Short were his friends, as was Thompson. The others he knew at least casually.

Ben Thompson was born in Canada of English parents, but when he was a small boy the family moved to Austin, Texas, where he attended school and later learned the printer's trade. But the plodding routine of everyday work was not for Ben Thompson and his brother Billy. They lacked the discipline of home training. Their father, a rover, vanished and was never seen again by either of the boys. The mother lacked firmness. Both her sons were born to trouble as surely as sparks fly upward.

Even as a boy Ben fell out with the law. He had peppered another lad with mustard shot to show his accuracy. The wounded youth had taunted him with being a bad marksman, and to prove his point had squatted on all fours at what he thought a safe distance, his back to Thompson. At the trial Ben was found guilty but recommended to mercy. Governor Runnels pardoned him.

He fought against the Comanches, and when the Civil War broke out enlisted with the Confederate forces in the regiment of Colonel John R. Baylor. In spite of his courage he was a bad soldier because he was so wholly undisciplined. Before entering the army he had killed a Frenchman for forcing his attentions on a young girl. Scarcely a

N. H. Rose

BEN THOMPSON

week after reaching camp he quarreled with Sergeant Vance and shot him in a pistol duel. When Lieutenant Haigler rushed forward sword in hand to assist Vance, Thompson also dropped him. Vance had been the attacker, and when Ben escaped from the guardhouse no strenuous effort was made to capture him. He re-enlisted with another command, and got into difficulties almost at once while at San Antonio by running whiskey into camp for his friends.

After a hard campaign Ben was invalided home. As soon as he could walk he obtained a transfer to Colonel 'Rip' Ford's frontier regiment. Stationed at Eagle Pass, the monotony of the life was too much for him. He was in the habit of slipping across the border to Piedras Negras, where he could sit in at the monte tables. Apparently he deserted soon after this, for he bobbed up at Laredo next. On the Mexican side of the line he found himself in a fight with a roomful of natives. He escaped, leaving behind him three dead men.

I give these details because I think they are a sufficient answer to the claim of his friends that he was a man who avoided trouble, and that he never took a life unless forced to do so. Thompson was a professional gambler, a bold and quick-tempered one, and as such he invited the differences of opinion that resulted in bloodshed. He became a killer because he chose that way of life, preferring idleness and excitement to the humdrum work of a pioneer.

Major W. M. Walton, a lawyer of Austin, Texas, who wrote a history of Ben Thompson, describes him as of average height, dark complexion, stout build, eyes blue, hair black, and very quick in his movements. He was soft of speech and gentle of manner, with no suggestion of the ruffian in his appearance. He was notably fearless, frequently defended the weak, and was devoted to his friends and family.

Yet all the evidence suggests that Ben liked to fight, especially when he had been drinking. Danger exhilarated him like wine. Apparently he did not have sense enough to be afraid. He would take the most suicidal chances without a moment's hesitation. None of the other notorious gunmen of the West were quite like him in this respect. A good many of them killed only when the break was in their favor. Others were brave enough, but they walked warily along the perilous path they trod. Clay Allison was perhaps the nearest of kin to him in this respect, but even Clay did not so continuously set himself up as a target for his enemies. Law officers and desperadoes alike were often forced to ignore their foes, to walk about their daily business assuming a sense of safety they did not feel. But Thompson, with characteristic lack of patience, would have none of this cautious watchfulness. It was his way to push open a door and strut into a place with cool bravado, knowing he was surrounded by men ready to try to kill him if they dared. He always carried a chip on his shoulder.

One cannot vision Ben Thompson as a good husband and father, since his character was based not on principle but on the urge of his reckless willfulness. Yet he loved his family, in an indulgent, careless fashion, and was in turn idolized by them. No doubt they generally saw only the best side of him. His friends could be counted by the score, and so great was his hold over them that those at hand were usually ready to help him out of the difficulties into

which he was always plunging. The man had a never-
failing charm.

To understand a man like Thompson is difficult.
Though his acts were impulsively violent, he was subject
to gusts of warm kindliness. No friend ever called on
him without response. Always he lived at war with himself. He realized that his life was a failure and that he had
not the will-power to change it. To Walton he said:

> Sooner or later [he is speaking of frontier days] a gambler
> meets with an untimely death; if not from the pistol, then
> from fatal disease contracted by dissipation and exposure
> consequent on such life. Every time a man sits down at
> a table to gamble he takes his life in his hands. Fatal
> difficulties arise from cause and no cause; men are killed
> in their own quarrels and in those of others. I have a son,
> and I had rather follow him to the grave than see him con-
> tract the habit of gambling. Yet I continue in that way of
> life; but so help me God, I never have and never will assist,
> encourage, or influence any youth or man to engage in this
> hell-earning business, which I will probably follow until I am
> dead.

Every sentence of his one-paragraph sermon had its
genesis in Ben Thompson's own experience. In the wild
borderland where he lived he had seen a dozen young men
shot down on account of hot words that had arisen at a
gaming-table. He watched acquaintances fading away
from tuberculosis brought on by the foul air and confine-
ment of the packed rooms, among others the two notorious
gunmen Luke Short and 'Doc' Holliday. Many times he
turned lads away from his faro layout and advised them
never to come into the place again. Even his mention of
men's losing their lives by being dragged into the difficul-

ties of others found dramatic confirmation at the hour of his own death. King Fisher was in no way involved in the feud with Sims and Foster. He was at the Vaudeville Theater with Ben only to pass an idle hour. The assassins had nothing against him. But he paid the penalty of being trapped in a quarrel which was none of his.

With the downfall of the Southern Confederacy, Thompson slipped across the line and joined the forces of Maximilian, Archduke of Austria, who was trying to maintain himself as Emperor of Mexico against the will of the people. He served with General Mejia, and was at Queretaro when Maximilian made his last stand against Escobedo. Betrayed by Lopez, the Austrian was captured May 14, 1867. Along with Mejia and another general, Maximilian was executed a month later. Thompson had escaped and was safe with the forces of Marshal Bazaine, who was retiring from the country on orders from Napoleon III.

His days of warfare over, Thompson spent the rest of his life as a professional gambler, except during the time when he was marshal of the city of Austin. The trail-end town of Abilene was just rising into its hectic hour of fame. With an army companion, Phil Coe, Ben started the Bull's Head gambling-house and saloon. It became the favorite resort of the Texans who came up the Chisholm Trail with the longhorn herds. Wild Bill Hickok was town marshal. It was his business to control the gamblers and the cowboys. The claim of those opposed to him was that he had an understanding with some of the houses by which tribute was paid him for protection. The Bull's Head was not one of those favored, and its owners were unfriendly to Hickok as he was to them.

Ben left Abilene for Kansas City, to meet his family and bring them to Kansas. While there, he rented a buggy and took his wife and children for a drive. The vehicle tipped over. Ben and his wife had broken limbs, and little Benny's foot was crushed. They spent several months at a Kansas City hotel recovering. During this time the feud between Hickok and Coe had developed into enmity. There was, the story runs, the favor of a woman involved in it.

Phil Coe was a fine specimen of physical manhood. He stood six feet four, was built like a Greek god, and had a remarkably handsome face. There was a frank warmth in his manner that Hickok lacked. Wild Bill too was strikingly handsome, but there was a coldness about him that chilled advances. The lady favored Coe, and the vanity of the other man could not brook the humiliation of rejection. The two men met on the street at night, passed hot words, and fought a duel. Coe was killed. Hickok heard the slap of feet running toward him, whirled, and fired instantly. 'Mike' Williams, a deputy marshal hurrying to support Wild Bill, stumbled and went down. Hickok had fired two shots and killed two men, one of them his friend. When Thompson returned to Abilene many months later Hickok had left for the Black Hills, where he was assassinated some years afterward.

Ellsworth succeeded Abilene as the center of the cattle trade. Ben drifted there, to live by his wits in the gambling-houses. His brother Billy came up the cattle trail a few weeks later. Bill Thompson was a more eye-filling picture than Ben. He was handsomer, larger, and louder. A man given to drink, he was always getting into scrapes

from which his older brother had to extricate him. One of
the worst of these took place a few days after his arrival at
Ellsworth.

The town at that time had about a thousand regular
inhabitants, not counting the large number of cowboys
who brought the cattle up from Texas and spent a few
weeks there. North and South Main Streets were the
principal thoroughfares. They ran parallel, one on each
side of the railroad tracks. The Gores had moved the
Drovers' Cottage from Abilene. There was another hotel
known as the Grand Central. There were of course a score
of saloons and gambling-houses, one of the most prominent
of which was Joe Brennan's. Most of the buildings had
false fronts. There were sidewalks — in places. And of
course hitch racks in front of all the business houses. The
town roared with life. There was much lawlessness, and a
police force of four was employed to patrol the streets.
The personnel of the marshal's assistants changed almost
from week to week. Ed Hogue and Ed Crawford were on
the staff during Thompson's stay. So was John Morco,
known as 'Happy Jack,' who claimed that he had killed a
dozen men in California. The sheriff was Chauncey B.
Whitney, a fine man. He was a Civil War veteran and had
also been with Forsyth at the desperate battle of Beecher's
Island, where fifty scouts dug in and held off for nine days
many hundred Indians.

Among the Texans in Ellsworth were two young men
from Austin, Neil Cain and Cad Pierce. They had come
up the trail, found the place to their liking, and were in no
hurry to get home.

As Thompson has said, quarrels flared up from slight

causes. One day Neil Cain was dealing monte at Brennan's and Cad Pierce was betting. Both the Thompsons were present, Billy drinking as usual. A cattle-buyer, one John Sterling, was among the heavy bettors. He had a difference of opinion with Ben Thompson, and since he was intoxicated slapped the face of the Texan. Ben for once was patient. He advised the man to go sleep off his anger. Instead, Sterling took some more drinks with Happy Jack and returned with the policeman to Brennan's. The two men stood in front, cursed the Texans, and invited them to come out and fight.

That was an invitation the Thompsons never declined. Ben armed himself with a Henry rifle and Billy with a breech-loading shotgun. Before they reached the door the shotgun went off accidentally and sent a charge of buckshot into the ground almost at the feet of Seth Mabry, one of the famous Texas trail drivers. The pot-valiant challengers hunted for cover, and when the brothers reached the street were not in sight. From doors and windows Hogue and Happy Jack and Sterling fired at the two Texans. Ben's rifle cracked twice, close enough to the two officers to send them back to the shelter of the buildings.

Sheriff Whitney heard the firing and came running. 'What's all this about?' he demanded.

Whitney and the two Texans were friendly, and Ben offered to give up the weapons if the sheriff would first disarm the two policemen. At that moment Hogue's head and the end of his sawed-off shotgun appeared at a window. Ben flung a bullet at him. A second later Ben heard the crash of a gun behind him. He turned, and saw Whitney sinking to the sidewalk. Billy was lowering his weapon.

Ben cried, 'You've killed our friend, Billy.'

To this day nobody knows how this happened. The gun may have gone off a second time by accident, or Billy may have been firing at Hogue and stumbled at the edge of the sidewalk. He was more or less intoxicated.

The excitement in the town was intense. Billy's explanation might have been accepted if he had not been such a firebrand. Already he had been arrested twice since coming to Ellsworth for creating a disturbance. Some of the trail drivers rallied to support the brothers, among others Neil Cain and Cad Pierce. Ben took command. He asked Cain to bring a saddled horse that was hitched back of a store. While Billy galloped out of town he and the Texans held the road to prevent pursuit.

Mayor Miller struck a bargain with Ben to give up his rifle if Happy Jack, Sterling, and the others engaged in the fray were also disarmed.

The resentment of the town did not die down even after Ben left. A new policeman, Ed Crawford, shot and killed Cad Pierce. The furious trail drivers rubbed out Crawford a month or two later. Happy Jack strutted around making threats. He was a public nuisance, and in the end a policeman, Charley Brown, put an end to him in self-defense. Billy Thompson was a fugitive for three years, after which he surrendered, was tried, and acquitted. Law on the frontier often came to very erratic conclusions.

It is significant, as showing how the Texans stood together, that one of Ben Thompson's bondsmen after the battle at Ellsworth was Seth Mabry, who just missed being another of the victims of the drunken homicide Billy Thompson.

Ben made several sporadic attempts to reform. He ran for city marshal of Austin on the Democratic ticket and was defeated. After this for several years he toured through Missouri, Louisiana, Colorado, New Mexico, and Nevada, usually stopping at new camps, where professional gamblers found good pickings.

As he grew older Ben Thompson began to drink heavily at times. When in liquor he was very wild and undependable. He would flourish a pistol, and sometimes shoot holes through barroom looking-glasses and lamps. On such occasions the crowd stampeded for safety. Next day he always went to the proprietor and apologetically settled the bill. The police made no attempt to arrest him for such pranks. They looked the other way when he was on a rampage. It was safer to meet public criticism later than to face Ben's guns.

Mark Wilson was the proprietor of a saloon and vaudeville house at Austin known as The Senate. He was a stout, red-haired, ruddy Irishman, brave, generous, but hot of temper. Some difficulty had arisen between him and Ben, who in bravado sent a bullet crashing through an expensive chandelier hanging from the ceiling of the saloon. Wilson gave orders that he was not to visit the saloon or theater. His patronage was not desired.

This warning acted on Ben like a red rag to a bull. He sent word to Wilson that he intended to drop in, have a drink at the bar, and attend the vaudeville performance. On schedule time he pushed through the swing door to the bar and swept the room with his eyes for signs of danger. All appeared peaceful. The bartender, Mathews, continued to polish a glass, his gaze fixed on the intruder. Wilson was not in sight.

Ben turned toward the bar, and as he did so Wilson appeared on a landing leading to the theater, a double-barreled shotgun in his hands. He blazed away, and a load of buckshot crashed into the wall back of Thompson. A half-second later the roar of a Winchester rifle filled the house. Mathews had snatched it from the service bench behind the bar where it had been lying. Both men missed their mark by inches, though they were within a few yards of their intended victim. Thompson's bullet caught Wilson in the neck, and before the man had fallen there were three more bullets in him. Again Mathews fired, the ball ripping through Ben's trousers at the hip. In a panic at his failure, the bartender ducked behind the bar. Ben did not take the trouble to run around the bar to get at his man. He guessed at his position and fired through the woodwork. The bullet struck Mathews in the mouth and tore into his throat. The battle had not lasted four seconds. Wilson was dead and Mathews dying. Thompson surrendered to the police, was tried, and acquitted.

In an essay on gun-fighters Bat Masterson once developed the point that courage and proficiency in the use of arms were only two of three factors necessary for the man-killer. The third was the cool nerve to be deliberate and steady at the moment of emergency. Both Wilson and Mathews had plenty of courage. They were given a handicap of three shots at a distance so close that to miss seemed impossible. No doubt they had been under a great strain while they waited for Thompson to come, for they knew what a swift and deadly shot he was in battle. In their excitement they fired too fast. A fraction of a second to take deliberate aim would have saved them.

The city of Austin must have found mitigating circumstances in this killing, for it elected Thompson chief of police a short time later. The responsibility steadied him. He drank less. His administration was one of law enforcement. During his incumbency there was remarkably little crime in the town.

Prior to his election he had sown the seeds of future trouble at the Vaudeville Theater in San Antonio. The resort was owned by Jack Harris. Joe Foster was one of his faro dealers. W. H. Sims had a financial interest in the place, which had long been a plague spot in the city.

While on one of his drunken sprees Ben Thompson had played faro heavily, lost, and come to the conclusion that the bank was unfair. He refused to pay his losses, and backed out of the gambling-house with drawn revolver. Harris served notice on him to stay away from San Antonio, and in particular never to show his face at the Vaudeville if he wanted to go out alive.

After his election Ben took the train to San Antonio one day with his children. He left them with friends and dropped in at the Vaudeville, probably to show Harris and his employees that he was not afraid of them. He asked the bartender where the shotgun brigade was. Harris had gone home, but a messenger ran there to tell him the news. He came at once, entered by a side door, and secured a shotgun. Word of this reached Thompson, who was just leaving. He turned, looked through a Venetian blind that separated him from the barroom and caught sight of Harris on a landing above.

'What are you doing there with that gun?' the Austin marshal shouted.

'I'm here to kill you,' Harris called back.

Thompson fired through the blind and killed his foe. He passed into the darkness of the night and walked to the Menger Hotel, which stands today on the old plaza not a stone's throw from the Alamo where Crockett and Bowie and Travis died. Next day he surrendered to the police.

In San Antonio and Austin there was tremendous excitement. Harris had been a power in ward politics and the local sentiment was all in his favor. In the trial which followed half a dozen lawyers prosecuted and as many defended. The jury was out all night and brought in a verdict of 'Not Guilty.' When Thompson and his wife reached the capital city they received an ovation. The opinion of those in Austin was that there had been a conspiracy to kill Ben and that he had escaped by good fortune and his own quickness.

While in prison awaiting trial Thompson had resigned his official position. He returned to his old habits. The gambling-houses at Laredo, San Antonio, Galveston, Corpus Christi, New Orleans, and St. Louis saw much of him.

Brother Bill faced a trial in De Witt County for a murder committed years before. As usual, Ben was there to help him. The jury acquitted him. It seems to have been a habit with all juries that tried the Thompsons. Both of them were fast becoming terrors to the communities they infested. Ben shot full of holes an organ belonging to a poor Italian with a monkey. Next morning he hunted up the man and gave him enough to buy a new organ. The Cattlemen's Association held a banquet at Simon's restaurant. With some fancied slight in mind Ben dropped in on the revelers and shot the plates away from in front of them. He 'got away' with the escapade at the time, but old Texans have told me that he signed his own death warrant that night. Men like Mabry and Littlefield and 'Shanghai' Pierce were not going to let a desperado terrorize them for long. But before the stockmen took action Ben came to the end of his trail at the hands of those of his own kind.

King Fisher saunters into the story at this point. He was the gentleman who put a sign on a public thoroughfare: 'This is King Fisher's Road. Take the Other.' That was one of his jaunty ways of defying the law.

Most travelers did take the other road, for Fisher was the head of a band of outlaws who operated in Dimmit and Maverick Counties from a ranch near Nueces on the Pendencia Creek. He was a notorious killer and one of the best-known cattle thieves in Texas. In recent years he had married and become the father of a family. Perhaps on this account he had let it become known that he was a reformed character. At this time he was a deputy sheriff of Uvalde County and was a candidate for the position of sheriff at the next election.

He was a bold scoundrel and had frequent clashes with the Texas Rangers. The famous Captain McNelly had more than once arrested him, only to meet him a few days later out on bail. One of McNelly's rangers, N. A. Jennings, set down on paper a description of this gay and debonair outlaw.

> Fisher was about twenty-five years old [at the time Jennings met him], and the most perfect specimen of a frontier dandy and desperado I ever met. He was tall, beautifully

proportioned, and exceedingly handsome. He wore the
finest clothing procurable, but all of the picturesque,
border, dime-novel kind. His broad-brimmed white Mexican sombrero was profusely ornamented with gold and silver
lace and had a golden snake for a band. His fine buckskin
Mexican short jacket was heavily embroidered with gold.
His shirt was of the finest and thinnest linen and was worn
open at the throat, with a silk handkerchief knotted loosely
about the wide collar. A brilliant crimson silk sash was
wound about his waist, and his legs were hidden by a wonderful pair of *chaparejos* ... to protect the legs while riding
through the brush.... His boots were of the finest high-
heeled variety, such as cowboys love to wear. Hanging
from his cartridge-filled belt were two ivory-handled, silver-
plated sixshooters. His spurs were of silver and ornamented
with little silver bells.[1]

At the time of which I am writing Fisher was about
twenty-eight years of age. He was still the most picturesque character in Texas, though he had trimmed down his
gaudy personal appearance. For some months there had
been a hard feeling between him and Ben Thompson, but
friends had brought about a complete understanding. He
was in Austin, March 10, 1884, had spent the day with
Ben, and was due to leave for Uvalde County by train
that evening. He persuaded Thompson to go with him on
the return journey as far as San Antonio, unfortunately
for both of them, as it turned out.

Ben had been drinking a good deal during the day, and
by the time they reached San Antonio he was ready to
make an evening of it. The two men attended a performance of *East Lynne* at Turner Hall, then went to the
Vaudeville Variety Theater. It was the first time Ben

[1] Quotation taken from Jennings's *A Texas Ranger*.

had been inside it since he had killed Harris. Sims and Foster were managing the place now, and word had come to them that Thompson was in town.

Sims met the pair of notorious killers at the bar and had a drink with them. Ben said he would like to meet Foster and bury the hatchet. They went upstairs and took seats in the back part of the theater. Sims left, to bring Foster. The weight of evidence is that Thompson was abusive to the owners of the theater and that Fisher tried to calm him, though some apparently unprejudiced witnesses denied this as to Thompson. After a time Sims and Foster drew back from their guests, and a volley rang out from a curtained box. Neither Thompson nor Fisher had a chance to draw a gun. The theater policeman Coy ran forward and fired a bullet into Thompson's head. In the excitement Foster tried to draw his revolver. It caught, went off, and shot him in the leg. He died eleven days later.

So was fulfilled Ben Thompson's statement written years earlier, that men of his and King Fisher's kind are killed in their own and others' quarrels. But long before his time wise Hebrew writers had prophesied the same thing. As a man reaps, he must sow. If a man kills with the sword, he must perish by it.

XII

Bat Masterson, Philosophic Gunman

He was a chunk of steel, and anything that struck him in those days always drew fire.' The quotation is from Billy Dixon, one of the great scouts and pioneers of the West, a quiet, simple man who did his full share in the winning of the high plains for civilization. He was speaking of Bat Masterson, who had been one of his comrades in the Adobe Walls fight, the most spectacular battle with Indians in the Southwest.

William Barclay Masterson was born in Iroquois County, Illinois, but he moved out to the frontier while still a boy. Kansas was Indian country then. The Comanches and Kiowas were often on the warpath, for they resented bitterly the destruction of the buffalo, which supplied them with food, clothing, and shelter, making their wandering nomadic life possible. Life on the border was adventurous, and it exactly suited the blue-eyed lad who had come to make his fortune. He was a jack-of-all-trades, in the course of years hunter, scout, owner of a trading-post, free-lance gambler, sheriff, restaurant-keeper, deputy United States marshal, faro dealer, newspaper reporter, and proprietor of a gaming-house.

He became one of the legendary bad men [1] of the West, but the reputation was one he did not enjoy. No killer by choice, he always regretted the circumstances that had built up his reputation. By nature Bat was genial, very loyal to his friends, and not a good hater. He loved a practical joke. In his early years especially he was a gay and friendly companion, not at all likely to take offense at trifles. Almost all his gunplays occurred while he was officially on duty or because he was championing the cause of a friend.

Boys became men at an early age in the old West. Masterson and a partner took a grading contract in 1872 with the Atchison, Topeka and Santa Fe Railroad while the former was not yet eighteen. They did well at it, but the partner decamped with the profits. Bat took whatever work he could find, but after a time naturally drifted into buffalo-hunting. For this suited his temperament. It offered great dangers, a carefree outdoor life, and large profits.

No estimate can be made of the countless millions of buffaloes which roamed the plains. Yet in a very few years the great herds were almost completely wiped out. As many as fifteen hundred hunters were out during the busiest seasons. The slaughter was so great that the boldest hunters crossed into the forbidden territory south

---

[1] The term 'bad man' had two connotations. It might mean exactly what it said. Or it might refer only to his prowess with a gun. Many a good peace officer was known as a bad man; that is, one criminals had better avoid.

of the Arkansas River. The plains Indians were becoming more hostile, since they saw that with the extinction of the bison they would have to starve or be forced to accept reservation limitations. Many hunters lost their lives. Those who continued to cross the deadline worked in larger groups.

Some of the storekeepers at Dodge City who had been dealing in buffalo hides made an arrangement with a group of hunters to build supply stores in the wilderness at Adobe Walls. This they did. Rath and Wright, Myers and Leonard, and James Hanrahan all put up trading establishments. When they needed food or ammunition the hunters brought their wagons in laden with hides and returned to their camps carrying what they had bought. News came in that several men at these isolated camps had been killed. Among them were some skinners working for Emanuel Dubbs, whom I last met twenty years ago at Clarendon, Texas. The group at Adobe Walls felt no alarm for themselves. They were convinced the Kiowas would not attack so large a band. Used to being on the plains far from a settlement, the rough hunters enjoyed themselves here. They danced and fiddled and played jokes on one another. A special reason for rejoicing was that the migrating herds were very numerous in the surrounding district. The season's kill would be a good one.

At Adobe Walls on the morning of June 27, 1874, were twenty-eight men and one woman. William Olds had brought his wife from Dodge to start a restaurant. The night had been hot, and all the doors were open to catch a breeze. The two Sheidler brothers and a Mexican bullwhacker were sleeping out in their wagons, expecting to set out in the morning with several loads of hides to the railroad.

A strange accident that seemed to many providential saved the lives of more than a score of people at the Walls. Several hours after midnight a report like the crack of a gun awakened the two men sleeping in Hanrahan's saloon. The cottonwood ridgepole of the building, carrying the weight of dirt piled on the roof, had given way noisily. Mike Welch aroused some of the others to help them repair the roof. A dozen men worked on the building until dawn began to sift into the sky. It was then too late for them to go to sleep again. Billy Ogg went down to the creek to round up horses, for he and Dixon were starting back to camp. He gave a yell and ran for the houses. Billy Dixon looked toward the timber.

What he saw gave him the shock of his life. Hundreds of Indians were coming out of it, whipping their mounts forward toward the little settlement. In the story of his life, edited by his wife, Olive K. Dixon, he described that charge.

> There was never a more splendidly barbaric sight.... Hundreds of warriors, the flower of the fighting men of the southwestern plains tribes, mounted upon their finest horses, armed with guns and lances, and carrying heavy shields of thick buffalo hide, were coming like the wind. Over all was splashed the rich colors of red, vermilion and ocher, on the bodies of the men, on the bodies of the running horses. Scalps dangled from bridles, gorgeous war-bonnets fluttered their plumes, bright feathers dangled from the tails and manes of the horses, and the bronzed, half-naked bodies of the riders glittered with ornaments of silver and brass.

Behind this headlong charging host stretched the plains, on whose horizon the rising sun was lifting its morning fires. The warriors seemed to emerge from this glowing background.

The Sheidlers and the Mexican bullwhacker were wiped out before they could leave the wagons. Billy Ogg just managed to reach Hanrahan's in time. William Tyler was shot through the lungs, stumbled into one of the stores, and died half an hour later. The rest were for the moment safe, though every pane of glass was shot from the windows during the first five minutes. Swiftly the defenders barricaded doors and windows with sacks of flour and grain. Many of them had been awakened from sleep and fought in bare feet and underclothes all day.

Dixon's guess was that there were about seven hundred Indians, chiefly of the Kiowa, Comanche, and Cheyenne tribes. Quanah Parker, a half-breed whose mother had been taken by the Comanches while on a raid, was the leader of the attackers. He inspired his men with such boldness that at first they actually hammered on the doors of the buildings with their rifle butts. But the buffalo-hunters were at this time without doubt the best rifle shots in the world. They were equipped with the powerful Sharps buffalo gun. Moreover, they were inured to danger and did not panic. The firing was too deadly for the tribesmen. They fell back to a safer distance. Again and again they charged, with heavy loss. From behind the picket and sod walls the marksmen shot them from their saddles as they galloped forward.

Masterson, who had taken refuge in Hanrahan's with Dixon and seven others, says that Quanah Parker had with him a bugler who sounded the charges for the Indians. The man was shot through the back with a fifty-caliber Sharps rifle late in the day.

Nearly all the horses and cattle had been destroyed by the Indians, but one was found and a messenger volunteered to try to go to Dodge for help. A buffalo-hunter, Henry Lease, set out on the hazardous journey. Other men slipped out at night to carry a warning to outlying hide camps.

In the end the tribes gave up the attack and broke up into a number of war parties which raided Texas, New Mexico, and even Colorado, killing more than a hundred victims before the campaign was over. In his book Dixon picks out one man by name who should be remembered especially for his valor during the Adobe Walls fight. The man was Masterson, the youngest of the party.

Four months later Billy Dixon almost lost his life in the Buffalo Wallow fight. He was a scout with General Miles and was sent to carry dispatches to Camp Supply. With him he had another scout, Amos Chapman, and four soldiers. On the second day, at sunrise, they came abruptly upon a large body of Kiowa braves, who swiftly surrounded them. The guns began to smoke at once. Several of the whites were wounded, one of them mortally. The others thought he was dead. Dixon led a dash for a buffalo wallow a hundred yards distant. Amos Chapman sank down, shot in the leg, before he had gone a dozen steps. Billy made two or three attempts to reach him, but was driven back to cover by the heavy fire. At last he succeeded in getting to his comrade and bringing him to the wallow on his back.

The beleaguered men dug up sand and entrenched themselves. All day the battle lasted. A storm came up and flooded the depression in which they lay. Ammunition ran short and one of the troopers, Peter Rath, made a dash to recover the belt of the dead soldier Smith. He succeeded in doing this, and surprised his companions by telling them that Smith was still alive. All of them felt that they were doomed, but they could not leave their friend on the hillside alone, perhaps to be captured and tortured. Dixon and Rath crept through the brush to him and somehow managed to drag the poor fellow back to the buffalo wallow. The pressure of the attack all through the day was very heavy.

The only chance of escape seemed to be for one of them to go for help. Dixon knew the country and would not get lost. On the other hand, he was the best shot. The wounded men in the hollow refused to let him leave them. Rath slipped away in the darkness of the night. The others listened despairingly. Every moment they expected to hear the sound of a shot that would tell them their messenger had been killed. But none came.

Smith died in the night. The others huddled on the wet ground and shivered. At daybreak the Kiowas were not in sight, but all of them felt they were not far away. Dixon decided he must go for help, since it was likely that Rath had not got through the Indian lines. Not more than a mile or two from the wallow he met a command of soldiers guarding a supply train.

Amos Chapman lost his leg. It was amputated at the knee. But for more than fifty years he did very well on one and a half legs. He died in 1925.

BAT MASTERSON

General Miles recommended Medals of Honor for the five survivors. He wrote to Washington:

> The simple recital of their deeds, and the mention of the odds against which they fought, how the wounded defended the dying, and the dying aided the wounded by exposure to fresh wounds after the power of action was gone, these alone present a scene of cool courage, heroism, and self-sacrifice which duty ... prompts us to recognize.

After the Adobe Walls battle Masterson returned to Dodge. He served as marshal and deputy sheriff, and then was elected sheriff, though still too young ever to have voted for president.

Shortly after Bat took office Dave Rudabaugh and his gang robbed a train at Kinsley, Kansas. This was not in Ford County, but Masterson did not let a little thing like that stop him. He organized a posse and started in pursuit. The trail did not lead to Lovell's cow camp, but that was where the posse went. A near blizzard was swirling over the prairie and Bat guessed the bandits would be driven to seek shelter there. His judgment was vindicated. When Rudabaugh and his outlaws came riding in, half-frozen from the cold, Bat was waiting to welcome them. Caught in a trap, they were forced to surrender without firing a shot.

Rudabaugh was a bad character. He later drifted out to Las Vegas, was arrested for some offense, and escaped after killing the jailer. When next heard of he was one of Billy the Kid's gang. Pat Garrett rounded him and the Kid up, after killing two of the gang. The sheriff brought them in to Las Vegas, to take the train. The jailer Rudabaugh had killed was a Mexican, and a mob shouting

Spanish imprecations gathered at the station to lynch him and incidentally Bill Bonney. They reckoned without one long, lank officer who had a different idea. Pat Garrett stood on the platform of the car and told them, in the peculiar cool drawl he used, that he reckoned they could not have his prisoners. If it came to a showdown, he said, he would give the outlaws arms and let them help to fight off the mob. The leaders of the would-be lynchers after an hour of furious threats saw the train move out of the station with the prisoners still on board. Rudabaugh was tried, sentenced to death, and once more broke jail.

Dodge was what newspapers from outside called 'a hell-popping town,' but Masterson held down lawlessness even while permitting a lot of rollicking wildness. The Texans were a tough lot, and the memory of the war still rankled in them. They liked to lord it over the Kansas 'Yankees.' There was a good deal of killing and Boot Hill grew rapidly. Gradually it dawned on the men from the Lone Star State than an undue percentage of these casualties were from down South. Bat arranged an armistice. Guns were checked at stores and saloons instead of being worn openly.

Masterson was no fighting fool. He was not in the habit of going out of his way to look for trouble, and 'If someone brought a fuss and laid it on his lap,' as one oldtimer put it, 'he sure didn't go off half-cocked but always handled it mighty nice.' So when Clay Allison came to Dodge announcing that he wanted to get him a sheriff for breakfast Bat did not feel called upon to rush out with his gun smoking. Allison was a notorious man-killer, a heavy drinker, a boaster, and a brawler. But he was also a fighting cowman with no judgment. With him were a dozen Texans, all more or less drunk and ready for war. Some peace officers would have felt it necessary to vindicate their courage by organizing a posse and meeting the invaders halfway.

But Bat saw no reason for starting a battle that would cause the death of eight or ten men. He knew the ways of the more rowdy trail drivers. They drank, shot off their mouths and their guns, drank some more, and went back to camp to sleep off their jamboree. In the end nobody was harmed. Dodge was a wild town, and it expected occasionally to hear the sound of guns harmlessly celebrating a premature Fourth of July. That was Bat's philosophic point of view. Better a few 'Hi-yippi-yi' yells lifted triumphantly into the night than a lot of dead bodies lying in a row on the sidewalk. So started the legend that Clay Allison came to Dodge and made Bat Masterson hunt his hole.

The comedian Eddie Foy was showing at Springer's Theater. One night Ben Thompson drifted backstage and sat down to watch Foy put on his make-up. He was pretty well jingled and in a mood to be annoying. 'Get yore head outa the way,' he ordered. 'I'm going to shoot out the light.' Foy grew stupidly obstinate and refused to move. Again Thompson warned him to duck his head. The actor sat there, the paint on his face, terrified eyes staring at the gunman. He did not duck. Perhaps he was too petrified. Bat Masterson burst into the room and caught Ben's wrist. He thrust the muzzle of the gun upward. 'Don't be a fool,' he said sharply.

Thompson took it in good part. He knew the sheriff felt friendly to him. 'All right, Bat,' he laughed. 'I was just foolin' with the tenderfoot.'

A few years later Billy Thompson was shot in a gun-fight at Ogallala, Nebraska. He lay wounded at a hotel, and since the feeling was strong against him there was a good deal of talk of lynching as soon as he recovered some-what from his wounds. Ben could not go to the rescue, since Ogallala had banned his presence. Masterson did not like Billy, but he promised Ben to do what he could for his brother. Bat arrived there and worked out a plan. Some of his friends staged a mock battle near a big dance hall. There was such a roar of guns that the attention of every-body centered on that spot. Meanwhile Bat made for the westbound express, carrying the wounded man on his shoulders. He locked Thompson in a sleeper and took him to Buffalo Bill's ranch at North Platte, where the desper-ado stayed until he was recovered sufficiently to start more trouble.

Ed Masterson, a younger brother of Bat, was appointed marshal at Dodge. He lived up to the family reputation. The Dodge City *Times*, date of November 10, 1877, gives an account of one of his adventures. He walked into the Lone Star dance hall just as Bob Shaw was about to punc-ture Texas Dick. Ed mentioned that the law had arrived. Shaw shot him in the breast, the bullet coming out under the right shoulder. Temporarily the marshal's arm was paralyzed. He transferred the revolver to the left hand, shot Shaw in the arm and the leg as he went down, and from the floor continued to take an interest in the proceed-ings. In the course of the fuss Texas Dick received a bul-let in the groin and Frank Buskirk, an innocent but inqui-sitive bystander, another in the arm.

Bob Wright, a prominent business man who was one of

the earliest settlers in the town, reached the scene while smoke still filled the hall. As it cleared away he saw the marshal lying on the floor propped up on an elbow. In one corner of the room he had corralled all the combatants and was holding them prisoner.

Five months later Ed Masterson came to the end of his trail when he attempted to arrest two cowboys, Alfred Walker and Jack Wagner, for some law violation. Without warning they shot him down. Sheriff Masterson walked into the place a minute later. He saw his brother die, then left to find his murderers. In the battle that followed both Wagner and Walker were slain. Bat was uninjured.

A great deal of nonsense has been written exaggerating the lethal record of famous gunmen. One chronicler puts it down in a book that Bat Masterson while peace officer at Dodge added thirty-seven to the graves on Boot Hill. It would not be possible to point to four killings there in which Masterson was involved. While a scout in the army he killed Sergeant King in self-defense. Not counting Indians, the men rubbed out by Bat can be counted on the fingers of one hand. He lived in Denver a score of years, and while there killed nobody.

As has been mentioned, one of Bat Masterson's outstanding characteristics was his blind loyalty to friends, no matter whether they were right or wrong. Time and again he proved this. When in trouble they never hesitated to call on him. So he became involved in their troubles. Twice after leaving Dodge he returned, on both occasions to get others out of difficulties. One visit was on behalf of his brother James, who ran a dance hall in partnership with a man named Peacock. They had a disagreement in regard to discharging their bartender, Al Updegraph, a brother-in-law of Peacock, and in the course of it threats were made. Naturally James wired to Denver, knowing that Bat would hop the first train.

The stay of Bat was short but exciting. On his way up from the station he met Peacock and Updegraph. They did not wait to inquire why he had come. They knew. Firing began at once. Updegraph was wounded and retreated. Peacock left with him. Bat surrendered to the authorities, was fined a few dollars for disturbing the peace, and departed on the afternoon train after arranging a hurried sale of his brother's interest in the dance hall.

The other trip to Dodge was made in answer to a call from Luke Short, a gambler and well-known gunman. Wyatt Earp also dropped in at the same time. This alarmed the officials who were interfering with Luke's business and a swift adjustment was made of the difficulty.

It must be admitted that Masterson's acquaintances and friends were a turbulent lot. The record shows that he was called upon to support and negotiate for them a great many times. They included Ben and Billy Thompson, Doc Holliday, Luke Short, Charley Storms, and the Earp brothers, as will be seen later.

Any number of stories might be told to show how promptly and intelligently Bat enforced the law in Ford County. The Kenedy incident will serve as an illustration.

Young Kenedy was the black sheep of a famous family of Texas cattlemen. He had a quarrel with Mayor James Kelly, and while drunk decided to settle the matter.

Knowing the position of the bed in the room where Kelly slept, he went to the house and fired twice through the flimsy wall. It chanced that Kelly was sick and in a hospital, and that a young actress named Dora Hand was a guest in the house and sleeping in the bed. She was killed instantly.

Sheriff Masterson picked up some clews as to the identity of the assassin and hurriedly gathered a posse to pursue the man. In that posse were William Tilghman, Charles Bassett, and Wyatt Earp. Kenedy refused to surrender and was shot from the saddle. The bullet had struck him in the arm. The sheriff took him back to Dodge and saw that he was held safely in jail.

After Dodge began to wane a good many of its sporting gentry moved to Tombstone. Bat was there only for a short time. This was in 1881. Luke Short was dealing faro in a gambling-house managed by Wyatt Earp, and he had trouble with Charles Storms, another notorious gambler and gunman. Rufflers were likely to make a mistake about Luke Short. He was small and not impressive in appearance. Masterson chanced to be in the Oriental when the quarrel flared. Both men were friends of his, and he managed to get Storms out of the house before guns were drawn. He left Storms in his room and hurried back to explain to Short that the other man was on edge from drink and would be all right in the morning.

While he was explaining this, Storms appeared before them and dragged out a single-action forty-five-caliber Colt's revolver. He was too slow. Luke's bullet crashed into his heart and he was dead before his body hit the sidewalk. Life was cheap in those days, and some wag wrote a bit of doggerel to put on the tombstone, but since there was no stone the epitaph was not used.

> He had sand in his craw,
> But was slow on the draw,
> So we laid him out under the daisies.

A few years later Bat was at Fort Worth, Texas, when Short killed Jim Courtright, another man with a record as a man-killer. There was some talk of lynching from the friends of Courtright, and Masterson arranged with the jailer to let him spend the night in the cell with the prisoner. There he waited till morning, his guns ready for action. The talk came to nothing, for Courtright had clearly been looking for trouble.

After the Earps and Doc Holliday came to Denver, driven out of Arizona, the authorities of that territory made a requisition for the return of the fugitives. Masterson called on Governor Pitkin and induced him to deny the request. It is possible that the governor had private advice which influenced him, to the effect that the Arizona officers really did not want the gunmen back. To bolster up his case, Bat framed an accusation against Holliday for a highway robbery supposed to have been committed at Pueblo, Colorado. He may not have been guilty of such a robbery there, but it is fairly certain that he held up at least one stage in Arizona.

By the time that Bat Masterson came to Denver to live he had discarded his guns. I was a young reporter and met him after he had been here some years. At that time he was a faro dealer at the Central, owned by Chase and Gaylord. For years he was a local celebrity in the city, an authority on the trail end towns and on more up-to-date sporting matters. If you wanted to find out what had become of 'Dutch Henry,' the famous horse-thief, or how many rounds the Sullivan-Kilrain fight went, you had only to consult Masterson.

I had been sent out by the city editor of the *Republican* to report a cricket game between Denver and Omaha teams, and an English friend had induced Bat to attend for an hour. He thought it very tame, and by way of sarcasm inquired whether cricket or croquet was the British national game.

When in a garrulous mood Bat would sometimes discuss the philosophy of the trigger finger acquired as a gunfighter on the frontier. The West had been full of brave men ready to face death with courage if the call came. Some had been Indian fighters and had displayed an unflawed nerve under the most critical conditions. Others had been trail-riders who had plunged into swollen rivers to try to rescue a comrade when the odds had been all against ever getting out again. He had seen firemen risk their lives without an instant's hesitation. Nobody could question the valor of these men. Yet few of them would have lasted long in the rôle of bad man.

It took three qualities for one to survive long as a pistoleer. The first was pluck, and that was possessed by a thousand men in Denver who could never make a record as gunmen. The second was proficiency with a weapon, which included both accuracy and rapidity. Just as important was the third factor — deliberation, the coolness of nerve that would not allow one to be flustered into the agitation of too hurried action.

Bat would cite cases to prove his point. There was Levi Richardson, an old buffalo-hunter whose courage had been tested a hundred times. Moreover, he was a first-class shot with both revolver and rifle. At Dodge he had a quarrel with a young gambler, almost a boy, named Frank Loving. He sent word to the latter that he would be 'looking' for him. Loving did not let this disturb him. He continued to play poker at the Long Branch Saloon, but he chose a seat where he could have his back to the wall. Richardson arrived. There was a scattering of those within range. The old buffalo-hunter threw down on his foe and emptied a .45 Colt's at him. Not one bullet struck its mark. Quite coolly Loving took aim and killed the older man with one clean shot. No question of courage or shooting ability was involved. The difference lay in their temperaments. One was high-strung and impulsive. The other had the steady nerve to take time to make sure his shot would count.

Though Masterson for a good many years made his home in Denver, he wandered away occasionally to more exciting communities. When Creede was booming he operated a restaurant there in partnership with Watrous, who ran for many years a famous all-night eating-house for those who liked good food. Creede was then a young but robust town where everything went. Cy Warman put his opinion into verse.

> It's day all day in the daytime,
> And there is no night in Creede.

Parson Tom Uzzell brought the gospel to Leadville and other mining towns. At Creede he preached in a gambling-house and a liberal collection was raised. Bat thought it was not enough. In the night he crept into Parson Tom's room and stole his trousers. Uzzell was a good deal disturbed and went downstairs in scant attire to report his loss. When he returned with an officer to his room the trousers were there with just twice as much money in the pocket as there had been before the theft. There was never any real malice in Bat's practical jokes.

President Theodore Roosevelt was a great admirer of the oldtime sheriffs such as Garrett, Tilghman, and Masterson. He offered Bat the position of United States marshal for Oklahoma. The former peace officer declined the honor. 'I'm not the man for the job,' he explained. 'Oklahoma is still woolly, and if I were marshal some youngster would want to try me out on account of my reputation. I would be a bait for grown-up kids who have fed on dime novels. I would have to kill or be killed. No sense to that. I have taken my guns off, and I don't ever want to put them on again.'

But he did — once, and for the rest of his life regretted it. Harry Lindsley, district attorney of Denver at the time, vouched for this story.[1] Like others in his line of business, Bat at times did too much drinking. On one occasion he ran foul of the law. Lindsley went into the office of Hamilton Armstrong, chief of police in Denver, and found him worried. Ham was both a good officer and a good man. He was a kindly soul. I remember that he always called us reporters 'Son.' He liked to be friendly.

---

[1] About a year before his death Mr. Lindsley asked me to look over a manuscript he had written on the Masterson-Marshall episode. This was never published. I am using the facts, rewritten, with the permission of his son, Judge Henry S. Lindsley.

But this day he was plowing through his hair with a nervous hand.

'What's up?' Lindsley asked.

'It's Bat Masterson. He's on a rampage and I ought to have him arrested, but he is sore as a boil and won't stand for it without a fight. I hate to give the job to any of my boys because two or three of them are likely to get killed.'

Just then the telephone bell rang. The call was a long-distance one from Cripple Creek.

'Jim Marshall on the line, inquiring about some guy who has skipped out from the Creek,' Armstrong mentioned as an aside to Lindsley.

Marshall was a Cripple Creek officer, a man known to be resolute and fearless. He had a large experience in dealing with tough characters.

'Have Jim hold the line a minute, Chief,' Lindsley said, and then suggested that Armstrong ask Marshall to come down and make the arrest of Masterson.

Marshall was reluctant to do this. In the first place, it was not his business. Also, he and Bat had been in tight places together during the old Kansas days. In one of the county-seat fights — that between the towns of Cimarron and Ingalls — they had been employed by the Ingalls faction to help get the county records from Cimarron and bring them to Ingalls. A dray had been driven to Cimarron to bring back the papers. It stopped outside the courthouse. As deputy sheriffs, Masterson and Marshall were inside the building throwing the records into boxes brought for the purpose. The Cimarron people hastily gathered to prevent the rape of the records. They opened fire on those outside and drove them away, after which they turned their attention to the two men imprisoned on the second floor of the courthouse. All afternoon and evening the battle raged, but the two deputies could not be dislodged. There was a good deal of promiscuous shooting, in the course of which a citizen of the town was killed. For twenty-four hours the two men held the fort against the mob. At the end of that time friends at Dodge arrived and poured oil upon the troubled waters. The deputies were later tried for murder and acquitted.

But Marshall was under obligations to Armstrong, and since somebody had to arrest Bat he thought he had better do the job. He promised to reach Denver early next day.

By an underworld grapevine route Bat learned what was afoot. He wired to Marshall that he would be waiting for him in front of the barber shop back of the Scholtz drugstore at ten o'clock. Bat kept his word. He had his morning shave in the shop, then planted himself in a chair on the sidewalk beside the striped pole. His fingers hovered near the butt of a revolver. From ten o'clock until eleven he sat there, his keen eyes taking in each passer. Jim Marshall was not among them. After an hour of waiting Bat left his post and crossed the street to the saloon in the Tabor Opera House block where he usually had his morning nip. To the barber he mentioned that he would be back presently, to meet the late Mr. Marshall in case he finally arrived. Bat walked up to the bar and gave his order. He lifted his glass to drink.

A familiar voice startled him. 'Sorry I was a little late, Bat.'

The glass of whiskey stayed poised in the air. Bat

realized instantly that he was trapped. Jim Marshall had slipped in a side door and was standing at his right side. He was ready for business, whereas Bat's gun hand was temporarily engaged hoisting one.

Bat showed no disturbance, though he recognized defeat. He looked at the man beside him — a ruddy, hard-eyed man, not quite six feet in height, well dressed, entirely sure of himself.

Quietly Bat put the question that was engaging his attention. 'Does this mean a killing, Jim?'

'Depends on whether you are reasonable, Bat.'

'Meaning just what?'

'Meaning that it is for you to say.'

'What do you mean, reasonable?'

'Denver is too big a town for you to hurrah, Bat. Time for you to move on.'

Swiftly Masterson reviewed the situation. Most men of his reputation would have stalled as long as he could, hoping for a break. But Bat knew from long experience that the cards were stacked against him. If he reached for his pistol he was a dead man. Moreover, he had asked for this. What Marshall said was true. Denver was no longer a frontier town. He had no right to defy the law. Just now Jim Marshall was the law, and it had served notice on him. Bat was chagrined. But he had the sort of mind that had to face facts realistically. Humiliated though he was, he had to accept the terms offered. By his own conduct he had put himself in the wrong. This was not a question of supremacy between him and Jim Marshall. He had maneuvered himself into an impossible situation before the meeting.

Bob Stockton, the saloonkeeper, drew a long breath of relief after Masterson's next words.

'If I leave, how soon do I have to go?' he asked.

'Could you make the four o'clock Burlington, Bat?'

'I reckon so.'

That ended the tensity. Both men knew the matter was settled. When Bat gave his word he kept it. Masterson left town that day. No newspaper gave the reason for his going. Jim Marshall visited each one in turn and saw to it that the incident did not appear in print.

Masterson went to New York and was appointed deputy United States marshal there by President Roosevelt. One of the telegrams of congratulation received by him came from Marshall. Later for many years Bat wrote on sports for a New York newspaper.

He died at his desk, October 25, 1921. Before him on a sheet of paper were the last words he ever wrote:

> There are many in this old world of ours who hold that things break about even for all of us. I have observed, for example, that we all get about the same amount of ice. The rich get it in the summer-time and the poor get it in winter.

With which cynical but philosophic comment Bat passed from a world that had always amused and entertained him, even on the occasions when the game was going against him.

XIII

Tom Smith, Soldier of Fortune

Tom SMITH of Texas was a soldier of fortune, though all the wars he fought in were private ones. He was not spectacular, and he did not get into the headlines as Bill Hickok and Wyatt Earp did, but if there was fighting in his neighborhood he usually had a hand in it. Yet he was no brawler and had none of the marks of the genus 'bad man.' Generally he was on the side of the law, though on one occasion he traveled a thousand miles to help 'rub out' seventy rustlers and their friends, including the mayor of a town, a sheriff, and three county commissioners.

Smith was born in Williamson County, Texas, probably shortly before the outbreak of the Civil War. He grew up as the other boys of the neighborhood did. It was a frontier country, and such schools as there were offered only the elements of reading, writing, and arithmetic. After my father brought his family of boys from England to the Southwest I was in such a school myself for a season. The teaching was simple and inadequate, the discipline peremptory. Frequently we heard and felt the swish of a

hickory stick. 'I'll wear you to a frazzle' was a warning
not to be neglected. As a spelling book we used an abridged
Webster's Dictionary, taking the words in order as they
came. The McGuffey readers were the only interesting
textbooks. In them Tom read stirring verse and prose.
He learned by heart 'The Charge of the Light Brigade'
and 'Lochinvar.'

But most of his practical education he acquired in that
outdoor school of life which keeps open session twelve
months in the year. He learned to hunt, fish, ride a horse,
and throw a rope. He could plow a straight furrow. From
a distance of thirty yards he could within two seconds
throw five bullets into a space no larger than his head.
Life in the open made him strong, vigorous, and self-con-
fident. Those were the days of the trail drives, and like
most of his young associates he had tasted the dust of a
herd for hundreds of miles while prodding laggards to a
market. To wrestle through blizzards, ride out stampedes,
swim swollen rivers, was a part of the day's work.

Texas was in that decade filled with feuds. One of these
involved the Smith, Olive and Crow families. Fortunately
this died down to inactivity before Tom reached feud-
fighting age, though there was still plenty of smoldering
hatred and resentment. Even without the feuds there
was too much of lawlessness in Texas. Hundreds of criminals, wanted for crimes committed in their own states, had
flitted to the brush country hurriedly to escape punishment. The war had created a disregard for human life that
was appalling. Within a hundred miles of Williamson
County there were scores of gangs of outlaws and hundreds
of hard characters who would as soon fight as eat. Among

them were Sam Bass, Joel Collins, Ben Thompson, King
Fisher, the feuding Suttons and Taylors, and John Wesley
Hardin with his stalwart relatives the Clements, Barrick-
mans, Dixons, Bowens, and Cunninghams. Not all of
these named were 'bad men,' but they were all ready to
resent an affront swiftly, and a 'difficulty' on the frontier
meant that guns would probably begin to roar. Some idea
of the number of desperadoes in the state may be guessed
at by the fact that the Texas Rangers had a small book
containing the names of over three thousand men wanted
by them.

Under such conditions it was a compliment to Tom
Smith's gameness that he was chosen marshal of one after
another of the wild little towns to which the outlaws of
the brush country flocked for excitement. Smith was
called from the Fort Bend country to the town of Taylor,
Williamson County, to serve as its peace officer. A strong
man was needed on account of a gang of toughs which frequented a saloon run by one Sanderson, a notoriously bad
character. The place was a plague spot in the town. It
attracted young men as the flame does a moth. From it
evil and vice were disseminated.

Smith dropped in to let the saloonkeeper and his allies
know he was on the map. He explained, in a voice mild
but not apologetic, that he was not anticipating any
trouble and had called to interest them in helping him to
maintain order. Always a bully, Sanderson flew angry and
ordered him out of his place. He was to get out and stay
out. If he ever came into it again it would be at his own
risk.

The level eyes of the marshal went around the room

coolly from one hard face to another and came back to Sanderson. He was leaving now, he said, quite undisturbed, and he would not be back — unless there was trouble here and his duty called him.

In a few days he was back, to inquire into a complaint of a cowboy that he had been drugged and robbed. Sanderson did not wait to ask questions or to give orders. He reached for his gun, but Smith was too swift and too accurate for him. His pistol still smoking, he issued an edict to the startled bar loungers.

'This saloon is closed and won't reopen. Better get out of town, boys.'

Sanderson was buried next day, and the saloon did not reopen. The air was full of threats. They simmered down to an arrest for murder, brought about through the influence of the vicious element. The arrest was made by Jack Olive, sheriff of Williamson County, a traditional enemy of the marshal. But Olive was an honest man, and he had himself once been marshal at Taylor. He said openly that Tom Smith had done a public service in ridding the district of the Sanderson gang.

The sheriff took his prisoner to Georgetown, the county seat, but he did not lock him up in prison. He put him in charge of a deputy, who slept with Smith on the third floor of the courthouse. A day or two later a Mexican was brought in charged with an offense that stirred the people to fury. During the night a mob gathered quietly to storm the jail and lynch the man. The deputy sheriff tried to talk the infuriated crowd out of its purpose.

'Better let me go and get Olive,' Smith said.

A minute later he was running to the house of the

sheriff. They hurried back to the courthouse. Smith proposed that Olive give him a gun and let him help defend the prisoner. The sheriff did so, and the three determined men faced the mob down. Later Olive testified in favor of Smith at the latter's trial, which resulted in an acquittal.

John T. Olive was a man of notably cool nerve. Some years before this time, while constable at Taylor, he had arrested a man named Armstrong and taken him to Georgetown. The brother of the imprisoned man went to the county seat to get him freed. A man of explosive temper, he quarreled with Sheriff Tucker in the hall of the courthouse and drew a revolver. They faced each other, not two yards distant, with drawn weapons. Under such circumstances a wise man who values his life does not fire. The shock of a bullet, even through the heart, is not felt for perhaps a second. During that time a man, though about to die himself, is likely to kill his enemy. J. E. Cooper, then and now editor of the *Williamson County Sun*, called to Armstrong not to be foolish but to give up his gun to the sheriff. The lawyer for the prisoner, an old Confederate colonel, ran out of the clerk's office, took in the situation, and yelped a warning to the ranchman. 'You doggone fool, while I'm working to get you outa one scrape, cain't you keep from getting into another.' The anger of Armstrong subsided. He surrendered his sixshooter, and it was returned to him before he left town with his brother that afternoon.

The Armstrongs stopped at Taylor to have some drinks. It was dusk when they mounted again. Traveling along the road, they met two men walking.

'Isn't that Jack Olive?' one of the brothers demanded, pulling up.

'Yes,' Olive answered.

'Might as well have this out right now,' Armstrong said, and dismounted.

His brother joined him.

'You boys better go home,' Olive warned. 'See me tomorrow and we'll talk this over.'

'No, sir. Right damn now.'

One of the Armstrongs fired and hit the constable in the temple, a glancing wound. In the duel that followed Olive killed both brothers.

Tom Smith later became deputy sheriff of Williamson County. In January, 1884, he sent the notorious killer Ben Thompson notice to keep out of Georgetown if he wanted to continue to live, and Thompson, one of the most deadly of the Western gunmen, obeyed the order of the deputy sheriff without a murmur. The difficulty arose out of one of Thompson's drunken sprees.

The cattlemen of Texas held a convention in Austin in 1884. On the tenth of January they adjourned, but about forty of them remained to have a banquet in the evening. Among these were many of the famous trail drivers, including Shanghai Pierce, John Blocker, Ike Pryor, and Seth Mabry. In the midst of the festivities Ben Thompson appeared, gun in hand, and began to shoot the plates from the table. A stampede of cattle kings followed. Seth Mabry commented later about the episode. 'I always thought Ben Thompson was a brave man,' he complained, 'but instead of jumping us in the big hall when we were a thousand strong he waited until he had a measly forty of us corralled alone.'

So great was the fear of Thompson that he was not even arrested for this. But the editor of the Austin *Statesman* next morning came out bluntly with a sharp criticism of Thompson and the police. Ben sent word that he intended to pay a visit to the office of the *Statesman*. The editor must have passed a bad night, but he had the courage of his convictions. He went as usual down to the office in the morning. When Thompson walked in on him he sat at his desk, his empty hands on top of it.

He looked at the killer steadily from a white face. 'I'm not armed, Mr. Thompson,' he said.

This was an unfair advantage to take of a gunman, though it is quite possible Ben would not have dared shoot the editor of a daily newspaper. Texans were peculiar. They didn't care how many of his own stripe he killed, but they might object forcibly to the wanton wiping out of a reputable prominent citizen. Thompson contented himself with breaking furniture and mixing up all the type in the plant.

Cooper of the *Sun* had also written a stiff editorial against the action of Thompson, and the bad man had sent notice to Georgetown that he would be up there in a day or two to settle the matter. The editor called Tom Smith into consultation, and Tom told him to worry no more, that he would take care of Ben for him.

Tom Smith did not bother with any heroics. He called on a dozen merchants whose places of business were round the town square and suggested they bring their rifles downtown and put them back of their counters. Most of them had been soldiers in the Confederate Army, and the rest had served with the Union forces. They agreed very promptly. Smith then sent a message to Thompson. The telegram read:

CAN PROMISE YOU A WARM WELCOME FROM OUR MOST PROMINENT CITIZENS. IT WILL BE MORE CONVENIENT FOR US IF YOU SHIP A COFFIN HERE WITH INSTRUCTIONS AS TO YOUR BURIAL.

Ben Thompson read the message and changed his mind. He knew that Tom Smith was both fearless and a fine shot, and he did not like the idea of the old soldiers potting at him from the doors of their stores.

No record can be found of Tom Smith's continuous activities. He was like a stormy petrel, often to be found at the seat of trouble, which was never of his brewing. He was a deputy United States marshal in the Indian Territory, a country in which there seemed to be no law except that enforced by the officers who risked their lives to drag outlaws and murderers back to Judge Parker's famous court at Fort Smith. At various places in Texas we find him serving the law.

During the year 1888 a political feud developed in Fort Bend County on the Brazos River. One faction was known as the Jaybirds. It was composed of the old-line Democrats who were trying to wrest the control of the county from the white officeholders who had been elected by the aid of negro votes. Those opposed to the Jaybirds were dubbed Woodpeckers.

Since the negro vote held the balance of power, the Jaybirds attempted to swing this from its allegiance. Feeling ran high, and probably the means used were none too gentle. There were many personal encounters. A

Brazos planter, J. M. Shamblin, tried to organize a Democratic Club among his tenants. He was shot in his own house through a window while holding family prayers. Henry H. Frost, the leader of the Jaybird faction, was wounded as he returned home one evening.

The Woodpeckers won the election. A few days later the rival candidates for county assessor met. Kyle Terry, the Woodpecker, left L. E. Gibson dead on the sidewalk. Volney Gibson, a cousin of the dead man, killed Terry when the two met at Galveston. The feud blazed into a general battle on August 16, 1889. Sheriff Garvey arrested a Jaybird. Volney Gibson barred the way to the courthouse. Tom Smith, a deputy of Garvey, was standing on the courthouse lawn with J. W. Parker and H. S. Mason. They moved forward to support the sheriff. Almost instantly the street filled with armed men. Guns roared from every side. A former sheriff fell dead. Garvey went down, riddled with bullets. Mason dropped to the ground, disabled. Parker slid against the courthouse steps, badly wounded.

Dusk was obscuring the battlefield but Tom Smith, crouched low, maintained the battle alone. From several points across the street bullets spat at him. He held his ground, emptying not only his own weapon but those of his companions at the shifting shadows of the enemy faction.

A negro was killed, a Texas Ranger wounded by a stray bullet. H. H. Frost received a mortal wound. Volney Gibson, though still on his feet, had been shot in the jaw. Both were victims of Smith's cool marksmanship.

The rangers advised Smith to retire to the cover of the

courthouse. He would not leave until the dead and wounded beside him had been removed. The Jaybirds were still sniping at him when he withdrew. There were eight dead and wounded, but Smith had not a scratch to show for the experience, though he was the only combatant on his side during the latter part of the battle.

Governor Ross ordered troops to the scene and quiet was restored. The Woodpeckers recognized that the march of time was against them. Those who held office resigned. Some moved away. Others dropped out of active politics. Tom Smith left for other fields.

Two or three years later he was in Wyoming working for the stock association. There was war on Powder River between the rustlers and the big cattle outfits. Like Dugald Dalgetty in Scott's *A Legend of Montrose*, when Tom Smith chose a side it became for him the right side. He served faithfully those who employed him. Used to dealing with hard and unscrupulous outlaws, he could be ruthless with his foes. The representative of the cattlemen delegated Smith to go to Texas and enlist twenty-five of the most efficient gunmen he could find among the former sheriffs and deputy United States marshals who had helped free Texas and the Indian Territory of the hundreds of ruffians who had swarmed in those borderlands. The men chosen knew the job for which they were selected. It was to be a war to end wars against the rustlers. They were starting out to shoot and hang scores of thieves who could be checked in no other way.

It is easier to understand the reasoning of these gunmen than that of the well-to-do cattlemen who employed them. One cannot read the records of Judge Parker's

court at Fort Smith, Arkansas, without realizing that
in dragging out of the brush hundreds of villainous murderers, all equipped with rifles and revolvers, these hard-rid-
ing officers could have little regard for fine-spun theories of
law. Dozens of them were killed, shot down by the criminals they went to arrest. The survivors were hard and
tough realists. In the warfare between the law and gangs
of cut-throats there could be no softness.

Living as they did far from the mountains and valleys
of Wyoming, they did not realize that many of these rustlers were of an altogether different type than the bad men
of the Southwest. Most of them were not killers. Many
did not belong to the criminal type, though they were
cattle-thieves. To find a calf belonging to a big outfit and
put one's own brand on it did not seem to the nester a
heinous offense, especially when the real owner was high-
handed and had no regard for the rights of the small
rancher.

Yet the cattleman was fighting for his economic life.
The wholesale rustling had to be stopped, or the owners of
the big ranches had to throw up their hands and surrender.
As one of them put it, the time had come to decide whether
Wyoming was to belong to the honest settlers or the
thieves.

The Wyoming invasion was mismanaged from the
start. Two rustlers, Nate Champion and Nick Rae, were
trapped and shot. Twenty-four hours later the cattlemen
and the Texans were besieged by an infuriated mob of
nesters, rustlers, and small-town dwellers, and were only
saved from being wiped out by the intervention of the
troops from an adjacent fort. The scheme to end rustling

by mopping up the guilty had collapsed ignominiously.

Tom Smith and his men, together with the cattlemen in the party, were taken as prisoners to Cheyenne, Wyoming. They were released on bond pending trial. At the appointed time Smith was not among those who filed into the courtroom to learn their fate. He had been killed in the Indian Territory, November 5, 1892, by a negro outlaw whom he was arresting.

THE END

Bibliography

BOOKS

Angel, Myron. *History of Nevada*.

Anonymous. *Hell on the Border*. Hell on the Border Publishing Company.

Anonymous. *Prose and Poetry of the Live-Stock Industry*.

Birney, Hoffman. *Vigilantes*. Penn Publishing Company, Philadelphia.

Bourke, John G. *On the Border with Crook*. Charles Scribner's Sons, New York.

Breakenridge, W. M. *Helldorado*. Houghton Mifflin Company, Boston.

Brisbin, J. S. *The Beef Bonanza*.

Brown, Jesse, and Willard, A. M. *The Black Hill Trails*. Rapid City Journal.

Browne, J. Ross. *Adventures in the Apache Country*.

Canton, Frank M. *Frontier Trails*.

Chapman, Arthur. *The Pony Express*. G. P. Putnam's Sons, New York.

Clay, John. *My Life on the Range*. Chicago. Privately printed.

Cook, James H. *Fifty Years on the Old Frontier*. Yale University Press, New Haven, Connecticut.

Coolidge, Dane. *Fighting Men of the West*. E. P. Dutton and Company, New York.

Dalton, Emmett. *When the Daltons Rode*. Doubleday, Doran and Company, Garden City, New York.

David, Robert B. *Malcolm Campbell, Sheriff*. Wyomingana, Inc., Casper, Wyoming.

Dilke, Sir Charles. *Greater Britain*.

Dimsdale, Thomas J. *The Vigilantes of Montana*.

Dixon, Olive K., editor. *The Life of 'Billy' Dixon.* P. L. Turner Company, Dallas, Texas.

Douglas, C. L. *Famous Texas Feuds.* P. L. Turner Company, Dallas, Texas.

Dubbs, Emanuel, editor. *Pioneer Days in the Southwest.*

Gillett, James B. *Six Years with the Texas Rangers.* Von Boeckmann-Jones Company, Austin, Texas.

Goodwin, C. C. *As I Remember Them.* Salt Lake Commercial Club.

Hardin, John Wesley. *Life of John Wesley Hardin.* Frontier Times, Bandera, Texas.

Henry, Stuart. *Conquering Our Great American Plains.*

Hunter, J. Marvin, editor. *The Trail Drivers of Texas.* Cokesbury Press, Nashville, Tennessee.

Jennings, N. A. *A Texas Ranger.* Reprinted by the Southwest Press, Dallas, Texas.

Kuykendall, W. L. *Frontier Days.* J. M. and H. L. Kuykendall, Publishers.

Langford, Nathaniel P. *Vigilante Days and Ways.*

Lockwood, Frank C. *Pioneer Days in Arizona.* The Macmillan Company, New York.

Lyman, George D. *The Saga of the Comstock Lode.* Charles Scribner's Sons, New York.

McCoy, Joseph G. *Historic Sketches of the Cattle Trails of the Southwest.* Kansas City, Mo., 1874. Privately printed.

Mills, W. W. *Forty Years in El Paso.*

Osgood, E. S. *The Day of the Cattleman.* University of Minnesota Press, Minneapolis.

Perrigo, Lynn. *Central City.* Thesis for the Ph.D. degree at the University of Colorado, Boulder, Colorado. (Unpublished manuscript.)

Richardson, Albert D. *Beyond the Mississippi.* American Publishing Company, Hartford, Conn.

Richtofen, Baron W. B. von. *Cattle Raising on the Plains of North America,* D. Appleton and Company, New York.

Robinson, Will H. *The Story of Arizona.* Berryhill Company, Phoenix, Arizona.

Rynning, Thomas H. *Gun Notches*. Frederick A. Stokes Company, New York.

Siringo, Charles A. *Riata and Spurs*. Houghton Mifflin Company, Boston.

Steinel, Alvin D. *History of Agriculture in Colorado*.

Streeter, Floyd B. *Prairie Trails and Cow Towns*.

Stuart, Granville. *Forty Years on the Frontier*.

Taylor, Bayard. *Colorado: A Summer Trip*. G. P. Putnam's Sons, New York, 1867.

Tilghman, Zoe A. *Outlaw Days*.

Twain, Mark. *Roughing It*.

Walton, W. M. *Life and Adventures of Ben Thompson*.

Webb, Walter Prescott. *The Texas Rangers*. Houghton Mifflin Company, Boston.

White, Owen P. *Them Was the Days*. Minton, Balch and Company, New York.

White, Owen P. *Trigger Fingers*. G. P. Putnam's Sons, New York.

Williston, George F. *Here They Dug the Gold*. Brentano's, Publishers, New York.

Wright, Robert M. *Dodge City, The Cowboy Capital*.

MAGAZINES

Atlantic Monthly, July, 1934. 'The Good Bad Man,' by C. A. Jones.

Harper's Magazine, February, 1867. Article on 'Wild Bill.'

Human Life. Articles by Bat Masterson.

Nebraska History Magazine, April–June, 1927. Exposé of the 'Wild Bill' myth.

NEWSPAPERS

Arizona Republican.
Cheyenne *Leader*.
Denver *Post*.
Denver *Republican*.
Denver *Sun*.

Fallon County (Montana) *Times.*
Lusk *Herald.*
Rocky Mountain News.
Tombstone *Epitaph.*
Tombstone *Nugget.*
Tucson *Star.*

Index

Index

Abilene, 10, 134–53
Acme Saloon, Hardin killed by Selman, 41, 42
Adobe Walls, 238, 241, 243
Agriculture in Colorado, 87
Allison, Clay, 152, 219, 222, 244, 245
Alvord, Burt, 22
Angel, Myron, 98, 100
Angus, W. G., 197, 215
Apache Kid, 10
Apaches, fear of, 8
Apache Station, camp of Cochise, 8
Arizona, 1–25
Arizona Mountains, Apache and White Mountains, 21; Chiricahuas, 12; Huachucas, 21; Dragoons, 21; Santa Catalinas, Gilas, Superstition, 21; Sentinel Mountain, 5
Armour, Judge C. L., 83
Armstrong, 'Ham,' 253–54

Baca, Abran and Enofrio, 35
Ballou, 128
Bannack, 56, 60
Barajo, Antonio, 28, 29
Barber, Gov., 215, 216
Barnes, Will C., 16
Bascom, Lieut. George N., 8, 9
Bass, Sam, 114, 117, 118, 154, 176, 260
Baylor, George W., 35, 36
Beckwourth, Jim, 73
Beidler, J. X., 60, 68
Benson, Ariz., duel between Tracy and Harry Wheeler, 24
Berry, Jim, 114, 117, 118, 176
'Big Hank,' 142
Big Springs, train robbery, 114, 115
Billy the Kid, 243, 244
Bird Cage Theater, 11

Bisbee, holdup, 12
Blair, Capt., 30
Bliss, Lucien W., duel with Stone, 82, 83
Blizzard, Logan, 129–131
Bogan, Dan, alias Bill McCoy, 125, 128
Booth, Edwin, 95
Boothill Cemetery, list of buried, 11, 12
Bourke, Capt. John G., description of Tucson, 2, 3, 7
Bowers, Sandy and Eilley, 107, 108
Brannan, Sam, 47, 48
Brazell, Doctor Philip, murdered by feudists, 158, 159
Breakenridge, William M., 13, 21; quoted, 139
Broderick, Senator, 50; killed by Judge Terry, 52
Brodie, Col. Alexander O., 22
Brown, 'Arapahoe,' 215, 216
Brown, Jesse, 121
Brown, Sam, 'Chief' at Washoe, 96, 99–102
Brown 'Stuttering,' 112, 113
Browne, J. Ross, description of Tucson quoted, 2
Buchanan, Pres., 81
Buckskin Joe, 84
Buffalo, Wyo., 121
Buffalo Station, death of Joel Collins, 117
Bunton, Bill, 59, 64
Burne-Jones, 106
Byers, William N., 74, 76, 78, 79

Calkins, J. K., 126
Campbell, Marshal, 31–33

Canton, Frank M., 122, 123, 133, 170, 207
Cardis, Louis, 28–30
Carey, Senator J. M., 198, 216
Carlisle, William L., 191, 192
Carson City, 107, 110
Carter, Alex., 54, 62, 64
Carver, Will., 181, 183
Casey, James P., 51; hanged by vigilantes, 52
Cassidy, 'Butch,' alias George Parker, 181, 183, 185
Cavanaugh, J. M., 83
Central City, 83, 86
Champion, Nate, 196, 204, 209, 214, 268
Chapman, Amos, 241, 242
Chapman, Arthur, 89, 186
Chase, Ed., 76, 250
Cheyenne, 92
Cheyenne–Deadwood trail, 112
Chisholm Trail, 135, 153
Chivalry and Shovelry, 50
Chivington, Rev. William, opens gambling house with prayer, 76
Clanton, Billy, 2, 11, 12
Clark, Gruber & Co., mint gold, 74
Clark, 'Hualpai,' 10
Clay, John, quoted, 201
Claybourn, Billy, 11
Clements, Manning, 40, 42
Cochise, 1, 8, 9, 10
Cochise County, 21
Coe, Phil, 137, 151, 152, 224, 225
Coffeeville, bank robbery, 180, 181
Coleman, William T., 47, 51
Collins, Joel, 114–17
Collins-Bass gang, 176
Comanches, 36
Comstock Lode millionaires, 107
Concord Stages, 24, 112
Coolidge, Dane, 24
Cooper, J. E., 262, 264
Conklin, 82
Cora, Charles, 50; hanged by vigilantes, 52
Cornet, 'Doc,' 129, 130
Crabtree, Lotta, 11, 95

Crawford, Ed, 226, 228
Crawford, Hank, 57, 58
Creede, 87, 253, 254
Criterion gambling house, 76–78
Crystal Palace gambling house, 11
Cummings, 'Doc,' 34
Custer, General, quoted, 147

Daggett, Rollin M., quoted in dedication; also, 95; poem quoted, 111
Daltons, 163, 177, 178, 181
Daniels, Bill, 12
David, Robert B., 204, 216
Davis, Governor of Texas, 27
Davis, Jack, 114, 115
Davis, Richard Harding, 14
Davis, Scott, 120, 121, 133, 207
Deadwood, 112–14
Dennis, John, alias 'El Dorado Johnny,' killed by Langford Peel, 104
Denver, 70–80
Denver duels, 81, 82
Denver House, 72, 74, 75, 78
Derickson, George W., 110
Desperadoes of Montana hanged by Vigilantes, 62–66
De Witt County, scene of Taylor-Sutton feud, 155, 159, 161
Diablo Cañon, train robbery, 16
Dickens, Charles, 74, 106
Dilda, 13, 14
Dilke, Sir Charles, 198
Dillingham, D. H., 58, 60
Dimsdale, Thomas J., 54
Dixon, Billy, quoted, 236, 239–42
Dixon, Olive K., 239
Dodge City, 10, 153, 238, 244
Doolin, Bill, 177, 181
Douglas, C. L., 158
Dowell, 'Uncle Ben,' 27
Dubbs, Emanuel, 10, 238
Duffield, Milton B., 2, 3, 6
Dumas, Alexandre, 106
Dunlap, Three-Fingered Jack, 22
Duppa, Darrell, 18
'Dutch Charley,' 121

Eagle Feather, 132

Early names of Denver, 72
Earp, Wyatt, 11, 248–50
Edgerton, Chief Justice of Montana, 58
Edwards, J. B., quoted, 146
Elephant Corral, 75
Elliott, Joe, 204, 207
Ellsworth, trail end town, 153, 225
El Paso, 26–43
Execution of Kelly, Sample, Howard, Dowd, and DeLaney, 11, 13

Fairbanks, train hold-up, 22
Falkenburg, 131, 132
Fall, Senator A. B., 41
Fallon, alias 'Rattlesnake Jake,' 202, 203
Fannin, 119
Field, Eugene, 86
Field, Justice Stephen J., 52, 53
Fisher, King, 154, 224, 233–35
Flagg, Jack, 210, 211, 214
Fleagle, Ralph E., 195
Fleagle, William H., 194, 195
Forbes, Charles, 60, 61, 68
Ford, Bob, 176
Ford, Pat, 55, 56
Fort Griffin, 38
Fort Laramie, 89
Foster, Joe, 231, 235
Foy, Eddie, 245
Frost, Henry H., 266

Gallagher, Jack, 58, 61, 66
Garfias, Henry, 2, 19
Garrett, Pat, stands off mob, 243–44, 253
Geronimo, 1
Ghost towns in Colorado, 84, 85
Ghost town residents, 85
Gillett, James B., 31, 34–36, 119
Gold camp names, 45
Goldrick, C. J., 74, 75, 82
Gordon, James, condemned by People's Court, 79, 80
Gore, Mrs., 136, 226
Gray, Adaline, 17
Greeley, Horace, 70–72
Gregory Gulch, 75

Gunn, Charles S., 126, 127

Hale, Johnny, 32; killed by Stoudenmire, 33
Hall, Lieut. Lee, 159–61
Hardin, John Wesley, 38–42, 141, 154, 156, 164, 260
Harris, Jack, 231, 232, 235
Harrison, Charles, 76–78, 82
Harrison, President Benjamin, 216
Hauser, Samuel T., 60, 68
Hays, Col. Jack, 47
Haywood, J. L., killed by James-Younger gang, 174
Hazen, Sheriff, 147, 182
Heath, John, 11–13
Heenan, John C., 106
Heffridge, Bill, 114, 176
'Hell-on-wheels,' 92
Helm, Boone, 59; hanged by Vigilantes, 66
Helms, Jack, 155, 156
Henry, T. C., 138, 140, 141, 145, 147
Hickok, James B., 147–53, 219, 224, 225
Higgins, 'Pink,' 165, 166–68, 171
Hill, Gail, 120, 121
Hogue, Ed, 226, 228
Hole-in-the-Wall Gang, 181–90
Holliday, 'Doc,' 223, 251
Horn, Tom, 17, 170, 185
Horrells, 163, 164
Horrell-Higgins feud, 163–69
Hounds, the, 46
Howard, Judge Charles H., 28–30
Howard, William A., 48, 49
Howie, Neil, 65, 66
Hunter, Bill, 59

Iliff, John W., 87
'Innocent,' password of Montana bandits, 64
Ives, George, 59, 62–64

Jackson Hole, 208, 209, 217
Jackson, 'Teton,' 122, 123
James, Frank, 173–76
James, Jesse, 173–76

James King of William, 50; murdered by Casey, 51
James-Younger gang, 173–76
Jaybirds and Woodpeckers' feud, 265–68
Jefferson Territory, 73
Jefford, T. J., 9
Jennings, N. A., quotation from book, 161, 233
Jerry Scott Saloon, 163, 165
Johnson County Cattle War, 196–218, 267–69
Johnson, William, 31–34
Jones, C. A., story in *Atlantic Monthly* quoted, 170, 171
Jones, Major John B., 29, 166, 168, 169
Jones, 'Ranger,' 205
Julesburg, 10, 87, 88, 92

Kenedy, 248, 249
Kesinger, Cashier, killed by Fleagle gang, 193, 194
Ketcham, 'Black Jack,' 183
Kilpatrick, Ben, 181, 183–85
Kilpatrick, George, 183, 185
Kingsley, Charles, poem quoted, 86
Kit Carson, 138
Kitchen, Pete, 5, 6
Krempkau, 32; killed by Hale, 33

Lamar, Colo., scene of Fleagle bank robbery, 192–94
Landusky, 'Pike,' 188–90
Lane, George, 59, 62, 66
Langford, Nathaniel P., 60, 68
Law and Order Party, 51, 52
Lay, Elza, 181, 183, 186
Leach, 115, 116
Leadville, 86, 87, 252
Leslie, Frank, 11
Lightning Creek Indian fight, 131, 132
Lindsley, Henry S., 253, 254
Lloyd, George, 35
Logan, Harvey, alias 'Kid' Curry, 181, 183–87, 189, 190
Logan, John, 181, 186
Logan, Loney, 181, 186
Longabaugh, Harry, 181, 183, 186, 187

Loving, Frank, 252
Lyman, George D., 100
Lyons, Hayes, 60, 61

Mabry, Seth, 227, 228, 263
Magruder, Lloyd, 66
Mangas Colorados, 1, 8
Manning Brothers, 32, 34, 37, 38
Marshall, Jim, 254–57
Masterson, Bat, 77, 219, 220, 230, 236–57
Masterson, Ed, 147, 246, 247
Mathews, 229, 230
Maximilian, Archduke of Austria, 224
May, Boone, 120, 121, 131
McCanles, David, 148–50
McClintock, Col., 18
McClure, W. P., 81, 82
McCoy, James G., 135
McDonald, Captain Bill, 21, 127
McGrath, Rev. T. H., 109
McNelly, Capt. L. H., 155, 233
Menken, Adah Isaacs, 95; her famous friends, 106
Mexican bandits in California, 46
Middaugh, W. H., 76, 79, 81
Miller, Sheriff, 131, 132
Mills, W. W., 27, 28, 32
Milton, Jeff, 21, 22, 40, 41
Monk, Hank, 96
Morco, 'Happy Jack,' 226–28
Morse, Calvin, 127
Mossman, Captain Burton C., 22, 23, 25
Murphy, Jim, 118

Nagle, Dave, 53
Nebraska History Magazine, exposé of false Hickok record, 149
Nevill, Captain, 36, 37

Olive, John T., 261–63
O'Neill, 'Bucky,' faints at execution, 14, 15–17, 19, 21
Oriental Saloon, Short kills Storms, Leslie kills Claybourn, 11
Outlaw, Bass, killed by Selman, 39
Owen, 202, 203

Owens, John, 124–33

Paddock, Dick, 103
Parker, Judge Isaac C., 178, 268
Parker, Quanah, 240
Parrish, A. N., 193
Parrotte, George, alias 'Big-Nose' George, 120, 121
Peasley, Tom, 105–07
Peel, Langford, 102–06, 110
People's Court, Denver, 86
Perrico, Lynn, 83
'Persimmon Bill,' 113
Pierce, Cad, 226, 228
Placerville ('Hangtown'), 93
Pleasants, Judge Henry Clay, 156, 159–61
Plummer, Henry, 56, 65, 68, 90
Prairie Cattle Company, 87, 198
Prescott *Miner*, list of Indian victims, 5

Rae, Nick, 208, 210–12, 268
Rath, Peter, 242
Reni, Jules, 88
Reynolds, Sergeant, 166–68
Richardson, Albert D., 70
Richardson, Levi, 252
Rocky Mountain News, 73, 78, 82
Roosevelt, Theodore, 202, 233
Rossetti, Dante Gabriel, 106
Rudabaugh, Dave, 243–44
Rynning, Captain Tom, 23, 25

Salt Lakes War, 27–31
Salt River Valley, 8, 17
Sanders, Col., Wilbur F., 58, 60, 63, 68, 152
Sanderson, 260, 261
Scarborough, George, 40, 42, 43, 183
Schutz, Sam, 29
Selman, John, 38–42
Shakespeare, 85
Sherman, General William T., 51
Shonsey, Mike, 208; kills Dud Champion, 217
Shoo Fly Restaurant, 4
Short, Luke, 219, 248, 249, 250
Sims, W. H., 231, 235

Sitterlie, Joe, 159
Slade, Joseph A., 54, 66, 67, 88–91
Slaughter, 'Gabe,' 157
Slaughter, John, 2, 21
Smith, Thomas J., marshal of Abilene, 138, 140, 142–47, 152
Smith, Tom (of Texas), 206, 213, 258–69
Standifer, William, killed by 'Pink' Higgins, 170, 171
Stanley, Henry M., quoted, 147, 148
Stewart, William M., 95, 100, 101
Stinson, Buck, 54, 61, 65
Stone, Dr. J. S., killed in duel, 83
Storms, Charley, 248; killed by Luke Short, 249
Stoudenmire, Dallas, 32–34, 36, 37
Stringer, Jake, 203
Stuart, James, 49
Stuart, Granville, 59, 182, 199, 202, 203
Sutton, Bill, killed by Taylors, 157
Swilling, Jack, 8
Swinburne, Algernon C., 106
'Sydney ducks,' 45

Tabor, H. A. W., 85, 86
Taylor, Bayard, 71
Taylor, Scrap, 156
Taylor-Sutton feud, 155–63, 260
Taylor, Will, 157
Tays, Lieut. John B., 29, 30
Terry, Judge David S., stabs a Vigilante officer, 52; kills Senator Broderick in duel, 52; killed by Dave Nagle, 53, 95
Texas Rangers, 31; captains of ranger companies, 36
Texas Street, Abilene, 136, 141
Thomas, Heck, 176
Thompson, Ben, 136, 152, 154, 219–35, 245, 248, 263–65
Thompson, Bill, 225, 227, 228, 232, 246, 248
Tilghman, William, 147, 152, 176, 181, 253
Tonto Basin, 21
Tracy, killed by Harry Wheeler in duel, 24, 25

Travis, 119
Trumbull, Charles, 124
Tucson description, 2–5, 10
Tunnel Saloon, duel between Gabriel and Phy, 19
Twain, Mark, *Roughing It* quoted, 89–90, 95, 96, 106, 109, 110

Underwood, 'Dad,' 114, 117, 118
Uzzell, 'Parson' Tom, 252, 253

Van Sickle, Henry, kills Sam Brown, 102, 103
Vigilante Notice, 48
Virginia City, Montana, infested by robbers, 54, 60
Virginia City, Nevada, 94, 97, 104–06, 108

'Waco Bill,' 7
Waggoner, Tom, 205
Walton, Major W. M., 221, 223
Ward, Sheriff J., 11, 13
Warman, Cy, 252
Warren, Senator Francis E., 198, 216
Washoe, 93–111
Webb, Dr. Walter P., 162

Wheeler, Dr., shoots up James gang, 174
Wheeler, Captain Harry, 23–25
'Whiskey Row,' 14
White, Owen P., 42
Whitman, Walt, quoted on battlefield by O'Neill, 14
Whitney, Chauncey B., 226–28
Whitsett, Richard Ed., 81
Willard, A. M., 121
Williams, Capt., 163, 165
Williams, James, 60, 68
Williams, 'Mike,' 152, 225
Williston, George F., 76
Wilson, Mark, 229, 230
Wimmer's Bar, 96
Wineinger, Dr. W. W., 194, 195
Wister, Owen, description of Jackson Hole quoted, 208
Wright, Bob, 246, 247
Wynkoop, E. W., 82
'Wyoming Frank,' 143, 144

Younger brothers, 163
Younger, Bob, 174–76
Younger, Cole, 174–76
Younger, Jim, 174–76